THE GUILDHALL HISTORIANS
Their Treasures Revealed

C. Douglas Woodward has lived and worked in the City of London for most of his life. For 25 years he was a member of the City's governing body, the Court of Common Council, becoming its Chief Commoner.

He founded the City Heritage Society in 1973 and remains its President. He was appointed CBE for services to the City of London in 1994.

Previous books include:

Saving the City's Heritage
ISBN: 0948667907
City Heritage Society (2004)

The Goings on in Guildhall
ISBN: 978 1 84748 226 6
Athena Press (2008)

The Vanished Coaching Inns of the City of London
ISBN: 978 1 905286 30 0
Historical Publications Ltd.

A Miraculous Survival
The history of a Unique City within a City
ISBN: 978 1 86077 703 5
Phillimore & Co. Ltd.

C Douglas Woodward

THE GUILDHALL HISTORIANS
Their Treasures Revealed

Olympia Publishers
London

www.olympiapublishers.com
OLYMPIA PAPERBACK EDITION

A CIP catalogue record for this title is
available from the British Library.

ISBN: 978-1-84897-309-1

(Olympia Publishers is part of Ashwell Publishing Ltd)

First Published in 2013

Olympia Publishers
60 Cannon Street
London
EC4N 6NP

Printed in Great Britain

For Ann as always and the President and members
of the Guildhall Historical Association

Acknowledgements

The cover picture is from a painting by Anthony Hemy, depicting City Councilmen and their ladies enjoying a 'summer excursion' on the Thames in 1880.

My thanks to Fiona Savory for turning my scrawl into a typescript and for her facility with the internet.

FOREWORD

By Sir Brian Jenkins GBE

As President of the Guildhall Historical Association (GHA), I am delighted that Douglas Woodward, with the support and encouragement of his Fellow Historians, has written and published this history of the Association. It is a great honour and pleasure to write this short Foreword to this important book.

The history comprises over 200 papers by some 140 authors – three a year since July 1944. For nearly 70 years the authors, almost all of them, have been and are members of the City's Common Council. Each of the papers is different, in background, position, style and interest. But all have shared a deep knowledge and love of the City and been prepared to research, write and read aloud to their fellow Historians a paper related to the City.

The range of topics covered is legion; from the ancient world to this new century, from war to peace and from matters of national importance to events in the lives of individual Londoners. Many record the direct experience of the writer.

This collection, which of course is still growing, represents a unique picture of one of the most diverse and concentrated cities in the world. Until recently the papers have remained largely private to the members of GHA. But we have decided that they are of sufficient interest to warrant publication. Accordingly they are now available on computer to read and download.

It was Douglas Woodward who pioneered this initiative. He also proposed the production of a book to bring some order to the vast range of papers and provide a clear account and history of the GHA. Douglas is a long standing Historian and enjoyed a distinguished career as a Common Councilman culminating in appointment as Chief Commoner in 1993. As many will know, Douglas has a deep interest in history and has written widely on London including a particularly engaging history of "The Vanished Coaching Inns of the City". He founded the City Heritage Society which has done so much to ensure that conservation is kept in mind during the inevitable developments in the City's built estate. Regrettably, out of modesty, he has not included his paper on the work of the Society in his selection but it can be read on the website.

Douglas's book is a superb and definitive history of the GHA – recording and editing a wealth of fascinating information in a highly readable form. It will appeal equally to all seekers after knowledge – historians and students as well as the public at large. I hope you will enjoy the history and agree with me that it makes yet another significant contribution to the records of this remarkable City.

Brian Jenkins

Contents

AN INTRODUCTION

The Guildhall Historical Association is one of the City of London's most exclusive of gatherings and until very recently one of its best-kept secrets. Yet from this reclusive group there has flowed a collection of information – eclectic, sometimes esoteric but always of absorbing interest.

Since its quiet foundation in the war-time days of 1944, the Guildhall Historical Association - the GHA - has privately published more than 200 papers on an astonishingly wide variety of subjects. They unfold aspects of the City of London's unique style of government across the centuries; the relationships, often stormy, between City and the Crown; make known the origins of sheriffs, aldermen and mayors; and tell of such distinctive officials as Remembrancer, Chamberlain and Recorder; and those colourful individuals who attend upon the Lord Mayor: Swordbearer, Common Crier and Serjeant-at-Arms, City Marshal.

There are papers, too, on the City's famous institutions: the Bank of England, Royal Exchange, the Old Bailey, Smithfield and Billingsgate markets, the Stock Exchange and St. Paul's.

In addition to these predominant aspects of City life and history, members of the GHA have researched into all manner of other topics that have taken their fancy and presented papers on the silk industry and the wine trade, the doings of City residents such as Shakespeare and Dickens, the Royal Marines, hospitals and prisons, the City's musical talent – the Waits and Minstrels, swan-upping, even a description of the drinking habits at Greek and Roman banquets.

This hitherto secret cornucopia of historical research is now made available on the internet for historians, students and, indeed to all seekers after knowledge. This book is published as a definitive history of the Guildhall Historical Association and a record of the two hundred or so papers that go to make up its remarkable literary achievements.

The beginnings

The Guildhall Historical Association was founded on the fourth of May 1944, the creation of five of the City Fathers, long-serving and highly respected members of the City of London's governing body, the Court of Common Council. Its purpose would be to collect, publish and preserve material of historic interest connected with the City – particularly aspects of its unique style of government developed over the centuries.

It was perhaps a surprising moment to embark on such an enterprise, the eve of momentous events about to unfold on the Normandy beaches. Yet the very uncertainties felt at this crucial stage of the War may well have encouraged the five Councilmen in their plan to record for posterity happenings great and small, of earlier uncertainties successfully overcome. It is not stretching imagination too far to believe that they regarded their venture as being supportive of the great doings they knew were about to begin in France.

So it was that when the five met again on the sixteenth of June, the date in their minute-book was recorded as D-Day + 10.

So who were these five? The prime mover was the 71-year-old Cuthbert Whitaker who had served as Common Councilman for the Ward of Farringdon Within for the past 39 years. (He was also second member of the family to edit the famous "Whitaker's Almanack"). It was at his bidding (and after considerable discussion among them) that the other four came to the May and June 1944 meetings at Guildhall House in Gresham Street.

They were Major George Vine of Aldersgate Ward; Fletcher Bremner Coates who was the Chief Commoner that year (that is the leader of the Common Council), Bread Street Ward; Major John Lockhart Gow, Bishopsgate; and Frank Brundle, Cripplegate Without, who was chairman of the City's still much needed Civil Defence Committee. The Lord Mayor, Sir Frank Newson-Smith, had already told Whitaker of his great interest in their venture and was appointed the GHA's President, an office he would hold for the next 24 years. The five Councilmen and the Lord Mayor were the GHA's first members and formed the committee that would direct its affairs and invite others to join them – but only on a most selective basis.

Although that summer of 1944 was seeing the past five years of war at last entering their final phase the conflict was far from over with London the main target for German rocket attacks, some 2,500 people being killed by the V1 and V2 missiles.

But already thought was being given to the shape of post-War Britain. Parliament was engaged with legislation that would transform education and town-planning and revolutionise the country's health services. In Guildhall despite Wartime calls on its members around 150 Councilmen and Aldermen were meeting regularly in Common Council where a special committee was giving thought to reconstruction of the bomb-ravaged City.

On 22nd June the Lord Mayor read to the Court of Common Council copies of messages sent by General Montgomery to his troops on the eve of their embarkation for Normandy and again on their landing there. The messages were read to the assembled members who cheered the stirring words. The Lord Mayor also reported the Corporation's intention to confer the Freedom of the City upon the Prime Ministers of Australia and New Zealand during their forthcoming visit to London.

Down the street the Bank of England was celebrating the 250th anniversary of its foundation and had opportunely declared its 500th half-yearly dividend.

The GHA was about to begin its own business.

The first meeting of the GHA

Cuthbert Whitaker and his associates wasted not a moment in getting the GHA under way.

The first meeting was held on 27th July 1944 with a format that has remained the same over the years. The members and their President met for lunch – albeit a modest one in those days – after which one of them would read a paper. Although there were only six of them to begin with the proceedings were carried out with proper formality. It was appropriate that Cuthbert Whitaker should give the inaugural address.

His chosen subject "Committee Allowances" was by no means a grand topic but one surprisingly full of historical disclosures from another era. He recounted the "Summer Excursions" when Councilmen and their ladies enjoyed river trips on a former state barge. These annual outings began in the 1790's and continued into the 1880's. They had breakfast, lunch and tea on board with a band and dancing while the vessel lay moored at some agreeable riverside spot. These entertainments only came to a stop when a puritanically-minded member of the Common Council named Alphaeus Cleophas Morton put down a motion declaring that the spectacle of middle-aged and elderly Aldermen and Common Councilmen dancing with their ladies in daylight, clad in frock coats and silk hats was liable to bring the Corporation into disrepute.

During 1945 and 1946 there were papers on more serious topics: John Lockhart Gow on "The City's Cash" (the historic origins of the City's private purse); Frank Brundle on more recent history of "Air Raid Precautions and Civil Defence"; George Vine on the intriguing "Special Committee" called into being during Victorian times to combat attempts by Ministers and reformers seeking to change or even abolish the City Corporation; Lt. Col. George Cullum Welch, a new member of the GHA and a future Lord Mayor on "The title and office of Chief Commoner"; and President Frank Newson-Smith on that ancient of groups "The Court of Aldermen" and telling of the creation of the City's wards. These papers are preserved with 200 more in the Guildhall archives and are available now for inspection on the internet.

Exclusivity

From the start it was determined that the GHA should be positively exclusive. Membership would be confined to members of the Common Council (a definition soon amended to make it clear that Aldermen were included). But this was not an association to which any councilman or alderman could apply for membership. You had to await an invitation and even when Common Council numbered 150, the GHA membership only slowly increased from five to ten, then twenty and thirty. Anyone nominated for membership had to be approved by the existing members. Clearly membership was to be regarded as a privilege.

There was certainly no question of anyone outside Common Council being introduced. This exclusion extended even to the high officers of the Corporation although Desmond Heap, a notable City Comptroller and Solicitor, did write a paper recording the opening in 1863 of the world's first underground railway linking Paddington and Farringdon Street, but his paper had to be read by GHA member, Keith Calder who it was that got the vote of thanks. Just one officer was allowed into the select circle of the GHA and that was in 1947 when Philip Jones, Deputy Keeper of the Records, was elected as an honorary member – in recognition of the fact that it was to him members so often looked for help in researching their papers. He was soon contributing papers of his own. Subsequent Deputy Keepers and Archivists were enrolled as members.

Much later the GHA lifted the barrier sufficiently to invite Town Clerk, Geoffrey Rowley, not only to write two papers but to have lunch with the Historians and deliver the papers in person. They were very much up the Town Clerk's street – the first on the origins of the Common Council and the second on the abolition of the Greater London Council and its effects on the City.

Conviviality

Meetings of the GHA were invariably convivial affairs with lunch before the reading of a paper. Catering facilities within the

Corporation in 1944 were somewhat basic so after two meetings in-house the Historians took themselves off to that catering mecca the Connaught Rooms just off Kingsway where even in the darkest days of war they managed to provide some degree of civilised dining. The Connaught Rooms remained the GHA's main meeting place for six years with occasional forays into the livery halls of the Apothecaries, Tallow Chandlers, Vintners and Brewers. In 1956 when George Cullum Welch was Lord Mayor the GHA were invited to hold a meeting in the Mansion House, something that would be repeated as other Historians came to be elevated to the mayoralty.

In July 1951 the GHA forsook the Connaught Rooms for a venue that was close by in the City and a far more appropriate meeting place – the Tallow Chandlers' hall in Dowgate Hill where they would stay for the next 20 years. It was at the Tallow Chandlers that President Frank Newson Smith first addressed the assembled members as "Fellow Historians" and that happy salutation has remained the mode of address ever since.

Presidents and Secretaries

In its nearly seventy years' existence the GHA has only had seven Presidents, Frank Newson Smith holding that office for a record number of 24 of those years. The Historians celebrated his 80th birthday in 1959 and in 1965, still President, he reminded them that the GHA had that year come of age. At 89 he felt constrained to pass the job over to Cullum Welch. One of the City's grandest of old men he died three years later much mourned by his fellow Historians.

Cullum Welch's distinguished tenure of office of twelve years only came to an end with his death in 1980. He was succeeded by a veteran Common Councilman, Sir Tom Kingsley-Collett, but health problems forced his resignation after a two-year stint. Alderman Sir Edward Howard who had served as Lord Mayor 1971-1972 was the next President, followed by Councilman Peter Revell-Smith, Alderman Sir John Chalstrey and Alderman Sir Brian Jenkins – all of whom have brought their own particular lustre to the GHA's presidencies.

Similarly the GHA has had only seven Secretaries. Two of them were founding fathers – Fletcher Bremner Coates the first and Frank Brundle the second. There followed Alderman Alan Lamboll who held the office for a record 27 years until his resignation from the Court of Aldermen in 1982. His successor was another alderman, Ralph Hedderwick, and it is no slur on any of those who followed him to say that his famously witty minutes became one of the GHA's star attractions (there are samples below).

Poor Michael Scrivener's term lasted a mere three months, ended by his premature death. Councilman Tony Moss nobly stepped into the breach to be followed by the present incumbent, Alderman David Wootton.

From Ralph Hedderwick's minute-book

<u>The minute he wrote himself on appointment</u>: The Chairman proposed the election of Ralph Hedderwick to fill the vacancy caused by Alan Lamboll's resignation. This proposition was received with an enthusiasm matched only by the total failure of any Historian to nominate anyone else. On election the new Secretary – to his own and everybody else's surprise – found himself at a loss for words.

Another occasion: the gloom on sixteen faces was lightened almost at once when the President asked Historian Cuthbert Skilbeck to read his paper "Swan Marking, Swan Upping". A vote of thanks was ably proposed by Historian Dewhirst who added a remark about swan upmanship or possibly one upmanship of Historian Skilbeck who was sporting a tie bearing the design of a white swan couchant on a background azure and possibly rampant. His motion was warmly applauded and the Historians went their way – one being heard to whistle the Volga Boat Song and another missing his step on the bottom stair was seen to execute a pas de deux from Swan Lake.

Some interesting occasions

While it is undoubtedly a fact that all the GHA papers offered much of interest some were possessed of special features.

Alderman Denis Truscott accompanied his talk on "Aleconners" (at Brewers' Hall of course) with a barrel of Whitbread's Final Selection Extra Strong Ale while Alderman Gilbert Inglefields' paper on "Transatlantic Threads" was celebrated with Boston Harbour tea.

Historian and Deputy Keeper of the Records Philip Jones was the recipient of the GHA's one and only Dinner. On his retirement in March 1970 to mark his 47 years' service to the Corporation, 25 of them as Deputy Keeper of the Records, the Historians honoured him with a dinner. After the civic toast to the Lord Mayor and Corporation came a toast to Jones and finally a toast to the five founder members – no after-dinner speeches that night but the guest of honour was prevailed upon to say a few words and happily had in his pocket his final GHA contribution, a paper on "The Office of Deputy Keeper of the Records".

Deputy Keepers always played an important role in the GHA as the prime repositories of historical information – as valued presenters of papers of their own and, in earlier times, as "ghost writers". President Sir Edward Howard when praising a paper given by Betty Masters in May 1984 referred to what he delicately termed as her "pianissimo ghost-writing" of some Historians' papers.

Ralph Hedderwick had a comment relating to her paper on Smithfield. "One of her listeners on hearing that over one million sheep had passed through Smithfield in 1821 wondered how far the mutton they had just eaten had hoofed it before slaughter".

Celebrations

The GHA has never been short of things to celebrate. So, in 1989, the President was congratulating Historian Brian Wilson, the immediate past Chief Commoner, on his CBE, and Historian John Holland on his promotion at the Honourable Artillery Company to the rank of

Honorary Colonel of the 105th Parachute Regiment of the Territorial Army.

The 800th anniversary of the mayoralty in 1989 was a great occasion for the City, celebrated by the GHA in the Mansion House as its 150th paper and read by Historian Sir Christopher Collett, the Lord Mayor at that time – who else?

In recent times the GHA has invited a few non-members to deliver papers: Bernard Gillis QC to talk about the City's various courts of justice; and Richard Gilbert Scott on the design and building of the splendid Guildhall Art Gallery for which he was the architect. Two professional historians were specially invited – Professor Caroline Barron to talk about the burning of the City's famous "Jubilee Book" in 1387 and Claire Tomalin to reprise her celebrated biography of Samuel Pepys.

But of course it is the "amateur Historians" who continue, three times each year, to find ever-fascinating subjects for the GHA's entertaining luncheon sessions. There seems no danger that the stream of knowledge will ever dry up or that there will be insufficient Historians to deliver it. Membership of the GHA remains just as much a privilege now as it has over the past seven decades.

PART ONE
EARLY HISTORY AND ASPECTS OF GOVERNMENT

The First GHA paper:
"Committee Allowances"

It may seem strange that the very first paper to have been read to members of the GHA – the one chosen, indeed, by its Chairman to inaugurate their venture – should have been on the seemingly humdrum subject of allowances for the entertainment of the City's Councilmen.

But as with all the GHA papers, it was well researched and full of interesting snippets of information. For example, that in 1894, Graham King, Chairman of the all-powerful City Lands Committee (and thus the Chief Commoner) commandeered the Town Clerk's somewhat palatial quarters for use as a new "Guildhall Club" where, at the conclusion of morning Committee meetings, or before the start of afternoon ones, Councilmen were given lunch – an indulgence that has continued to the present day. (It has to be remembered that unlike all other local authorities, the City's Councilmen are unpaid).

In 1894 professional caterers were employed, first from the "Dr Butler's Head" in Masons Avenue and later Birch's of Cornhill (owned by that most famous of City catering firms, Ring and Brymer).

Cuthbert Whitaker, the speaker on that first occasion, could at least claim that Councilmen's modest perks were well earned. While a Royal Commission had urged thorough reform of every municipality in the land, the Corporation of London was the only one left untouched: "The history of the Common Council of London is a body which has watched vigilantly over the interests of its constituents with great earnestness, unremitting caution and scrupulous justice".

*   *   *

Londinium and its aftermath

Not surprisingly, GHA members have ever been attracted to aspects of the City's early and colourful history and the development of its quite special, indeed unique, form of government which, for 1,800 years, was that of London itself, London and the City being one and the same. Some sixty papers consider such aspects, some of which are the first to be reviewed in this history of the GHA.

In September 1947 Whitaker (now Sir Cuthbert) produced as his major contribution an historical digest of eight tightly-written pages which provides an excellent introduction to London's beginnings and early history.

It begins with a dramatic flourish:

"The history of the Crystal Sceptre, which is handed down by each Lord Mayor to his successor in office, is symbolic of its origin, or of the year when it was first taken into use, but it is known to be mainly of Anglo-Saxon workmanship and to have been enlarged after the Norman Conquest. It is borne by the Lord Mayor, as a matter of prescriptive right, at the coronation of the Sovereign of the realm".

England, he writes, was made for invasions from Europe, London being the primaeval geographical bond between England and the lands it faced.

The first invaders, the Romans, were soon firmly established and by AD 61 the historian Tacitus could describe Londinium as "a town of the highest repute and a busy emporium for trade". Recovery after its destruction by Queen Boadicea was rapidly accomplished and, provided with stout protective walls, became the centre of the Roman road system and the seat of Rome's administration of Britain.

Whitaker rightly believed that Londinium did not collapse when the Romans left Britain. The walled city afforded protection not only for its own inhabitants but also for the refugees fleeing Saxon invaders from south and east. (The Saxons being a farming people were far more concerned with the fertile lands of south-east England than with towns and are likely to have left London much to its own devices – until they saw its potential value as a trading port).

London was chosen by a Saxon king as the place for a church dedicated to St Paul early in the 7th century and was described by Bede, like Tacitus before him, as "an emporium of many nations coming by land and sea".

Wrote Whitaker: "There is no doubt that municipal institutions flourished in London under the Romans, and even as fragments of the Roman Wall can still be identified, so can the imprint of their institutions be seen in the modern government of the City".

Alfred and his successors made special provision for the accommodation of merchants from north-western Europe, and later privileges were granted to traders from Italy and the Baltic, the majority of whom made London their chief port of call. The City itself developed a code of law for mercantile cases, which was afterwards absorbed into the law of the land. This led Sir Laurence Gomme, in The Governance of London, 1907, to regard the City as an independent kingdom, making its own laws.

With the Norman invasion there came a king who recognised from the start how valuable London could be to him, not only for its mercantile prowess, but as a bastion against the still far from cowed Saxons surrounding him. About 1070 William granted the citizens of London their first royal Charter:

"William, King, greets William, Bishop, and Gosfrith, Portreeve, and all the burgesses within London, French and English, friendly. And I give you to know that I will that ye be all those laws worthy that ye were in King Edward's day. And I will that every child be his father's heir after his father's day, and I will not suffer that any man, offer you any wrong. God keep you".

New immunities and further privileges were gained by the citizens from the Crown and are embodied in a long succession of royal charters. That granted by Henry I in 1132 is a landmark in the development of municipal independence and recognises the fully *county* status of the City. London was no longer to be regarded as the inexhaustible reservoir from which revenue was drained away by royal officials. The City would collect its own customs and dues and elect its own justices.

Perhaps the greatest advance however came with Prince John who, in the absence of his brother Richard, at the Crusades, acknowledged on October 8th, 1191, the right of the citizens to combine in a sworn association undertaking by oath to preserve the City and its liberties - the "Commune". At its head would be an entirely new officer known as Mayor.

In 1215 the Great Charter granted by King John at Runnimede accorded to the citizens of London all their ancient liberties and customs and the name of the mayor of the City appeared among those specially appointed to see that the terms of the Charter were strictly carried out. The year 1332 provides the first evidence in the City of London of a Common Council formed of ward representatives, elected on a wide franchise by the citizens.

Unlike other cities, London has no charter of incorporation. The constitution of the City is unique among British municipalities, the result of centuries of growth and development. It became the prototype to which lawyers pointed when they wished to explain the meaning of the word "Corporation". The development of this constitution is in the hands of the Corporation itself, and can be exercised by means of Acts of Common Council, a power enjoyed by no other local authority in the Kingdom.

*   *   *

The "privileges" that made London special

If London had gained its original feel for government under the Romans and used that experience to maintain some degree of authority in the face of onslaught from Saxon and Dane, its later powers would come from the special privileges bestowed by England's successive monarchs.

Such privileges were enshrined in royal charters which began with that of King William who, shortly after the Conquest, saw that in support from London lay his best chance of subduing and overcoming the strong antipathy of Saxon England. William's and all the subsequent charters were sometimes given as rewards, more often they were wrested from reluctant hands in return for London's political, military and (more often than not) financial support.

GHA historian Leonard Beecroft presented his paper on "The privileges of the City of London" in December 1947. He divided them into three groups: legal, ceremonial and administrative.

The most important of the legal privileges was the automatic status by Charter of the Aldermen as Justices of the Peace. This privilege was built up by five Charters, the earliest granted in 1444 and the latest in 1741. (A charter of 1638 gave the Mayor the right to nominate to the Lord Chancellor an Alderman as a Justice for Middlesex and another for Surrey but for the past two centuries the Lord Mayor had felt it imprudent to exercise this right!)

For seven hundred years the Lord Mayor has been a Commissioner of Gaol Delivery and Oyer and Terminer at the Central Criminal Court (the Old Bailey). Charters have laid down that none but London's citizens shall be justices over the men of London for Pleas of the Crown – such justices being Aldermen and certain City officers. The Lord Mayor is still named as principal Commissioner and takes precedence even over the Lord Chancellor.

Another legal privilege is the City Corporation's right to elect its own sheriffs, officers who elsewhere are appointed by the Crown – this rare privilege first granted to the citizens by Henry I in 1132.

Other rights were to appoint judges in civil matters and coroners for both the City and for Southwark, this last lapsing in 1926. Charters of James I and Charles I granted the City the right to claim all treasure trove and the goods of felons found within its walls.

Among ceremonial privileges Beecroft cites first the Lord Mayor's Procession which, since the 14th century, celebrates his admission to office; and then the ceremony at Temple Bar when the monarch enters the City – a submission of authority, the Lord Mayor's sword lowered, point downwards, upon surrender. All being well the Sovereign will reply with some such expression as that of Queen Elizabeth I: "No-one could better govern my Capital City". The Lord Mayor is then privileged to go before the monarch holding the sword aloft.

While a Charter of 1321 confirmed that the men of London could not be compelled to serve as soldiers outside the City – and when they did it was not to be regarded as setting a precedent – in the 16th century the Lord Mayor gave certain regiments permission to march through the City, drums beating, to enlist recruits for the French wars. To this day no troops may pass through the City without the Lord Mayor's permission.

Beecroft's paper lists many other ceremonial privileges – the right of Lord Mayor and Aldermen to attend a Privy Council at which the Proclamation is signed declaring the successor to the throne and for the Lord Mayor to attend the Coronation ceremony carrying the City sceptre. The Corporation has the privilege of presenting addresses to the monarch on the throne and receiving a reply from the royal lips. The City is also able to present petitions at the bar of the House of Commons.

Some City privileges have lapsed. Thus the City no longer appoints Coal, Corn, Fruit and Oyster Meters, nor does it collect four pence on every hundred of elephants' teeth imported or one penny on every hundredweight of gunpowder exported. No great loss perhaps.

As to the City's <u>administrative privileges</u>, Beecroft rightly says that the greatest of all is the right of governing that small but powerful area at the heart of the Greater London which for centuries has survived so many attacks made upon it and has maintained its own separate and special identity.

*   *   *

And what of "the Custom" of London?

If privileges came to London from the charters bestowed upon it by kings, so also the rather more intangible "Custom of London" – the basis of City law – was derived.

Irving Gane, Chamberlain of London, addressed this somewhat esoteric subject in November 1948 (there is no record as to which member of Common Council actually read it to the GHA).

Gane traced early confirmation of London's Customs to that famous Charter of Henry I in 1132 which enshrined, as it were, the laws and usages that had already become established in previous times.

In London, wrote Gane, the earliest surviving code of by-laws was the "Assize of Buildings" drawn up in 1189 (the year of London's first Mayor) which dealt with obstruction of views from windows by adjoining buildings. That and all the many subsequent customs of London were local laws existing immemorially, surviving because of their local value.

The whole nature of London's (and later the City of London's) quite special form of government, its aldermen, mayor, sheriffs and Common Council has evolved through custom and usage from Saxon times.

They were hard won and sometimes seized or "taken into the king's hands". The last such seizure arose out of a quarrel with Charles II who, in 1683, withdrew his own and all other royal charters, confiscating London's privileges and franchises. The Common Council was suspended and the Court of Aldermen filled with the King's nominees became the governing body of the City.

It was not until 1688 that London's rights and privileges were restored by James II seeking to win the City's support against the threat of invasion by William of Orange. One of William's earliest acts when he became England's king was to ordain that the Mayor, Commonality and Citizens of the City of London should for ever remain and be a body corporate and politick and should have and enjoy all "their rights, gifts, charters, grants, liberties, privileges, franchises, customs, usages, constitutions, immunities, markets, tolls, lands which they lawfully had at the time of the forfeitures" (by Charles II).

Customs, however, were never intended to be set in stone and Gane quotes as just one important change the Act of Common Council in 1856 which abolished all laws and customs prohibiting persons other than Freemen from carrying on business by retail or exercising any handicraft, trade or calling within the City.

*   *   *

The ancient office of Sheriff

The office of Sheriff is very ancient and historic far exceeding in antiquity that of the mayoralty, with holders of the office recorded since the time of Edward the Confessor in the 11th century. Indeed, under varying names it can be traced back to the 7th century and may be said to be of immemorial origin. So began Major Guy Richardson's account of the shrievalty to the GHA in March 1959.

The word "Sheriff" derives from the Saxon Shire-reeve, the title given to an officer appointed to administer justice within the shire or county. In London the title of sheriff was preceded by that of Port-reeve, "port" meaning city. William the Conqueror's famous Charter was addressed to the City's two foremost men: William the Bishop and Gosfrith the Portreeve.

It was Henry I's Charter of 1132 which granted the citizens of London the right to hold Middlesex for tax purposes and to appoint Sheriffs for both shire and city. A sheriff was by now head of the City's administration. From 1199 to 1888 the citizens would continue to elect sheriffs for Middlesex as well as the City. From 1888 two Sheriffs have been elected annually by members of the livery companies for the City alone, one usually an Alderman, the other a commoner.

Today the duties of the City Sheriffs are four-fold: to be present each day at the Central Criminal Court (the Old Bailey) to attend on the judges there; with the Remembrancer to present at the Bar of the House of Commons City petitions to Parliament; attend all meetings of the Court of Common Council and the Court of Aldermen; and to accompany the Lord Mayor at meetings and functions of all kinds.

*   *   *

The Court of Aldermen

It was, appropriately enough, the GHA President, Alderman Sir Frank Newson-Smith, who in September 1946 delivered a paper entitled "The Court of Aldermen", observing that reference to Aldermen could be traced back to the Saxon period in England as a whole, their pre-eminence by birth and family giving them an important role in the growth of cities and boroughs.

The first mention of an Alderman of London was in 1111 and Aldermanbury as a place-name in 1128. The wards of the medieval City were preceded by Saxon "sokes" which were the territorial holdings of individual Aldermen who, in the 12th century, became the head of each of the City's wards. Originally the wards were known only by the name of their alderman; thus the ward of Godwin, ward of Osbert and ward of Henry de Coventre.

The first full list of wards under established local names – Aldersgate, Bassishaw, Cripplegate – is dated 1285 although one or two, like Chepe, emerged later.

The roots of municipal government in the City are to be found in the activities of Aldermen within their wards, wrote Newson-Smith: supervising the watch, intimately concerned with legal matters and preservation of the peace, presiding at ward meetings for the raising of men, money and arms to meet demands royal, legal and municipal.

In London, Aldermen have always been elected by their wards, not appointed, as elsewhere, by the governing council and they held office for life until more recent times when, as magistrates, their term of office ended at the age of 70.

Unlike the early Court of Common Council, which met no more than four or five times a year, the Aldermen met in their Court almost daily. In the year 1600 meetings of Courts of Aldermen numbered 105 and in 1700 their minutes covered 620 pages as against only 44 for the Common Council.

There have been disputes between Aldermen and Commoners, the bitterest occurring in the 1720's when the Common Councilmen were seeking to extend the franchise to include non-freemen. Aldermen were totally opposed and took the opportunity to rule that however many Councilmen there were (210 at that time) any new legislation proposed by them had to be approved by the 25 members of the Court of Aldermen before it could be enacted.

The Aldermen had little difficulty in persuading Parliament to legislate in their favour and an Act of 1725 confirmed that the assent of mayor and aldermen was a pre-requisite for any new Act of Common Council. There was much bitterness among councilmen and the wider electorate.

That controversial decree of 1725 was eventually repealed twenty-one years afterwards, by which time there was a much improved relationship between aldermen and councilmen so that after 1746 the 25 aldermen and 210 councilmen were united in a supreme and effective organ of civic administration.[*]

The Court of Aldermen always had the final say as to whether a person newly elected by the ward as its Alderman was acceptable to them and a fair number have been vetoed over the years from taking this first step toward the mayoralty, a power now replaced by the requirement for aldermen to seek re-election at least every six years.

*　　*　　*

---

[*] "A miraculous survival" C. Douglas Woodward

The first Mayor of London

In King Richard's absence on Crusades it was his brother John who gave London the right to set up its Commune. This new form of civic government required a person of standing to be at its head. The title afforded to this position, borrowed from France where the concept of the commune had originated, was "maire" and John gave London its first such dignitary in 1189.

Historian Harold Hobbs related the story in his paper of October 1984 (surprisingly late in the GHA's existence, one might think, for such an important event in the development of City government) and in it expressing his profound disagreement with established thought as to the Mayor's inaugural date.

Hobbs was adamant that the origin of the mayoralty was between 1192 and 1193, even writing to Lord Mayor Kenneth Cork pointing out the error on the City State Coach of the beautiful scrollwork which refers to 1189. The City authorities, Mayor, Aldermen and Remembrancer held to 1189, pointing out that the 700th anniversary of the mayoralty had been celebrated in 1889 and that the 800th would be in 1989 – as indeed it was!

The first Mayor was a patrician figure who, according to Hobbs, was simply named "Henry", since neither he nor his forebears had any surname, early records describing him as 'Henry son of Ailwin, son of Leofstan'. For several hundred years however he has been known as Henry FitzAilwin.

Twelve years before his appointment as Mayor, he is recorded as an Alderman who owned property and lands not only in the City but in Kent, Surrey and Hertfordshire, his ancestors having held Manors at the time of Edward the Confessor. He was highly regarded as one of London's most important citizens.

An early reference to him as Mayor was in April 1193 when he was one of the five appointed as collectors of the enormous ransom of 150,000 marks for King Richard who had been captured on returning from his Crusade. The others were the Archbishop of Canterbury, Bishop of London and the Earls of Arundel and Warenne. Hobbs believed he would have lodged for safety in St. Paul's Cathedral with the oak coffers containing the gold.

FitzAilwin lived in a great stone house with courtyard and garden, close to where now stands the Mansion House near London Stone, the Roman mile-post centre of Londinium. It is interesting that a later Alderman kept his mayoralty in the same house in 1579-1580 and that the Salters Livery Company made it their hall.FitzAilwin himself is claimed by the Drapers as a liveryman of their company and he was probably both merchant and ship-owner. In his time the first stone-built London Bridge was erected.

He clearly enjoyed being Mayor and was held in high regard by King Richard and King John, retaining his office for 23 years until his death in 1212. Three years later, shortly before John was forced into signing Magna Carta, and already harassed by his barons, John granted the citizens of London a charter giving them, not the King, the right to elect a mayor of their own choice. Perhaps because of FitzAilwin's overlong tenure of office, citizens were now to elect a Mayor annually – their choice, subject to being approved by the Sovereign or his judges, a practice which continues to the present day.

As it turned out, while a good many 13th and 14th century Mayors reigned for just one year, others found reasons to be re-elected for at least a second or third term. Gregory de Rokesley remained in office from 1274 to 1281, seven terms in all and returned again for a final year in 1284. His eventual fall from favour led King Edward I to deprive London of its Mayor and to appoint as its ruling Warden the Governor of the Tower, a regime which lasted for thirteen years.

That most famous of Mayors, Richard Whittington, was elected four times, serving with considerable renown under three monarch – Richard II, Henry IV and Henry V – over a span of 23 years.

London's Mayors with Royalist leanings had a poor time of it during the Civil War and Commonwealth, three of them being imprisoned in the Tower, one dying as a result of his treatment.

*   *   *

Common Council gives the citizens a voice

By the year 1100, probably earlier, London's division into its wards was fully developed, each governed if not owned, by its Alderman. By 1127 however, twenty Wards had names of their own that are much the same as they are today. While the Folkmoot still took place in St. Paul's Churchyard, there were now Wardmoots, bringing citizens into touch with their Aldermen – and with each other.

Thus in May 1995 Geoffrey Rowley, Town Clerk, began his "History of the Common Council" (another paper which came surprisingly late – 50 years after the GHA came into being). Rowley observed:

"There came the breakthrough to real civic government when in 1189 we gained the right to have our own Mayor. So we had in place a Mayor running the City with the Aldermen – and with a vociferous citizenry behind them".

It became clear that from among that citizenry should be chosen leading representatives, to be consulted by Mayor and Aldermen in the governance of the City.

In 1332 a "Great Congregation" of citizens agreed at Guildhall that two persons should be elected by each Ward who, together, should make ordinances for the whole community". From 1376 this elected arm of the great congregation, now with the number of its representatives depending on the population of each Ward, became known as the Common Council.

Mayor and Aldermen would remain the dominant force in City government for a long time yet but, as Rowley said, "with the inevitability of gradualness", power moved from the Aldermen until the Common Council became the governing body for the City, the Aldermen forming part of it while retaining their own additional, separate duties. Rowley suggests that this change culminated at the end of the 18th century.

Thus it was that the City's support of the colonists in the American War of Independence was carried to King George III in 1782 by the Lord Mayor and Court of Aldermen, but in 1788 it was the Common Council which petitioned Parliament to abolish the slave trade and, in 1789, opposed Pitt's introduction of income tax.

*   *   *

The Court of Husting

The Court of Husting is the most ancient of courts of law with a history stretching back to Saxon times with evidence of its existence in the 10th century. The word "Husting" is of Anglo-Saxon or Scandinavian origin, signifying a court held in a house as opposed to assemblies such as the Folkmoot held in the open air.

This ancient body was the subject chosen for his address to the GHA by Historian Norman Hall in July 1975. It was curious, he said, in view of its indoor origin, that centuries later the term "hustings" was applied to the temporary, open-air platforms from which parliamentary candidates were wont to address their electors. In Guildhall, the place where the Court was held (and, indeed, still is on very rare occasions), the raised dais at its east end, is still known as the 'hustings'.

In a charter granted to the citizens by Henry I in 1132, it was decreed that the Hustings Court should sit every week on a Monday.

With the Court being the only one where civil disputes, pleas of land and offences against City ordinances could be settled, business grew and the Court was obliged to sit on Tuesdays as well as Mondays. But because of Henry's decree, sittings of the Court of Hustings were always recorded as having taken place on a Monday.

Mayor and Sheriffs sat as the judges, while the Aldermen, there to represent the citizens in their Wards, acted in the manner of a jury, and were ready to offer advice as to the law.

The work of the Court of Husting was gradually taken over by a new Mayor's Court which could meet as often as was needed and by the 18th century it functioned only as a registry for the enrolment of deeds, a function that survives to the present day. Although written evidence of titles was not peculiar to London, enrolments of documents of title in London were infinitely more numerous and have survived in quantity and richness unparalleled elsewhere.

Such evidence of ownership was of particular importance in the medieval City where frequent fires respected neither property nor evidence of ownership – and even in more recent times the security offered by such ancient registration of transfer of property can still be of value. Mr Comptroller and City Solicitor instanced the destruction by fire of Grocers' Hall in 1965. Had the Company lost all their title deeds they could have had recourse to the Hustings Rolls dating from 1431!

Then there was the microcosm of land registration as we know it today. In addition, the Court of Husting was responsible for the probate and enrolment of wills, a procedure undertaken in the City as early as 1230. As Norman Hall said, it has brought to the historian a rich source of information about London in the past, its people and topography. There are kept the wills of Richard Whittington, William Walworth (the Mayor who slew Watt Tyler) and Thomas Gresham, founder of the Royal Exchange.

*   *   *

The City and the Crown

London, with its ever-large population in comparison with the rest of England, and its wealth, had for long exerted its influence on the choice of kings. Even where its initial choice proved wrong, London managed to recover the situation. So that when Saxon Ethelred died and Londoners elected his son Edmund Ironsides to be England's monarch, the decision was soon overturned in recognition that Canute had become master of the country. A second election in London legalised the situation and Canute married Ethelred's widow.

Again, at the time of the Conquest, Londoners sought to maintain the Saxon line of kings by electing Edgar Atheling as king but were unable to back their choice with sufficient force against the strength of the Norman invaders. Londoners proved tractable, William was accepted and crowned, saw London as a useful ally and bestowed upon it his famous Charter.

An early king-making success for London was its election of Stephen in 1135 and its determined support of him against every attempt of Matilda to wrest the throne for herself.

While London's fancy for king-making had to yield to acceptance of the hereditary principle, the City remained a potent factor in settling the frequent royal disputes and rival claims of the 14th and 15th centuries. The opposition of a violent mob of Londoners was instrumental in the deposition of Edward II in 1327 and London played a crucial part in Edward IV's triumphant ousting of Henry VI in 1461.

Guildhall was somewhat less than triumphant at the hands of the Duke of Buckingham in 1483 when, on behalf of his master Gloucester, he bullied Mayor, Alderman and Common Council into acceptance of Gloucester as King Richard III. The new king, making his way to the throne, had never doubted that London held the key to his eventual success.

William of Orange regarded the City's call to him in 1688 as giving legitimacy to his eligibility to the English throne.

Lionel Denney's paper containing an account of the City's relationship – often tumultuous – with the Crown was read to the GHA on the eve of the crowning of our present Queen in March 1953.

Over the centuries it was the custom for the Lord Mayor, accompanied by a number of Aldermen, to be invited to attend the Privy Council and sign the Proclamation of Accession for a new monarch. The first signature on the accession proclamations of James I and Charles I was that of the Lord Mayor.

There followed the reading of the proclamation by the Lord Mayor accompanied by Aldermen and leading citizens, at various points in the City culminating at the Royal Exchange. In the coronation procession at Westminster Abbey, the Lord Mayor has always carried the City's Crystal Sceptre and been present near the throne, his place being next to the Garter King of Arms. Similarly the Lord Mayor and other City dignitaries have had places at Coronation Banquets where originally they claimed the right as "butlers" to serve the King from a cup of gold and to carry that cup together with a golden ewer away with them as the Lord Mayor's "fee".

Invariably in earlier times a new monarch would process through the streets of the City and from a viewing balcony in Cheapside watch the Lord Mayor's Pageant, following which he would be entertained at a banquet in Guildhall. From the accession of Edward VII in 1901 it has been the custom for the monarch to make a royal progress and to be entertained at a luncheon in Guildhall following a service of thanksgiving at St. Paul's.

In our own time members of the Royal Family continue to be visitors to the City, not only to banquets, but to all manner of occasions whether opening new buildings or being present at the functions of livery companies – Princess Anne has been the Master of three companies.

*　　*　　*

Two quite special Royal occasions

How the City greeted two very special monarchs on occasions outstanding in the history of England was the subject of another of the papers presented by Historian Norman Hall in October 1966. In it he recounted the victorious return to London of Henry V from his great victory at Agincourt in 1415 and the triumphant restoration to the throne of Charles II in 1660.

Hall opens his paper with a picture of the City at the beginning of Henry V's reign. Each of its 25 wards was controlled by its Alderman, much in the way of a manor. The Wall, kept in repair by the wards through which it ran, was still the City boundary, only along Fleet Street to the Palace of the Savoy had there been any outward expansion. To north and east, green fields provided a contrast to the narrow and crowded streets within which 20,000 citizens dwelt. There were gardens belonging to houses of the wealthy and to the numerous religious orders.

The Mayor was pre-eminent and when Dukes and Bishops came to the still incomplete Guildhall to seek money for Henry's bid to secure the throne of France, it was the Mayor – as the King's representative in the City – who occupied the central seat of precedence, the Archbishop of Canterbury and Bishop of Winchester to his right and the royal dukes to his left.

News of the victory at Agincourt reached London on 28 October 1415, three days after the battle. The celebrations began at Dover where Henry landed on 16 November, thence to Blackheath on 22 November. In the early hours of the 23rd the newly-installed Mayor, Nicholas Wotton (Hall tells us he was known as "Witless Nick"), the other 24 Aldermen, all in their scarlet finery and with 300 of the principal citizens wearing the liveries of their guilds, met the King at 10.00 a.m. and began their procession into the City. London Bridge was bedecked with banners for the occasion. On turrets either side of the drawbridge were figures of a man and his wife, the man holding a huge axe and the keys of the City, the wife in her best clothes. An image of St. George in full armour bore a laurel wreath studded with pearls on his head. Boys sang "with organs".

Having crossed the bridge, the whole procession passed through the crowded streets from east to west, past houses hung with carpets and tapestries, water conduits in Cheapside running with wine and the Eleanor Cross concealed within a mock wooden castle. As Henry passed there emerged from its drawbridge "a chorus of most beautiful virgin girls attired in white, singing with timbre and dance: "Welcome Henry Fifty, King of England and France".

At the west door of St. Paul's, sixteen bishops and abbots were assembled to conduct the service of thanksgiving and to lead the King in procession to the choir where he took Mass with the French lords, his prisoners alongside, and so to the wooden gate at Temple Bar, the Mayoral party escorting the King to Westminster.

The triumphant return of Charles II in 1660 was made through a City of the same shape and size but whose population had, in those 250 years, soared from 20,000 to 130,000. Charles was greeted at St. George's Fields, Southwark, by Lord Mayor Thomas Alkyne and the Aldermen, the Mayor knighted there by Charles in gratitude for the part played by the City in his restoration.

Within the City, Charles was accompanied, in John Evelyn's words, "by a triumph of 20,000 horse and foot shouting with inexpressible joy. The Ways strewed with flowers, bells ringing, the streets hung with tapestry, fountains running with wine. The Mayor, Aldermen and all the Companies in their liveries, chains of gold and banners. Windows and balconies all set with ladies. Trumpets music and myriads of people flocking".

On the 5 July 1660, says Evelyn: "The King went to the City feasted with as much pope and splendour as an earthly prince could do – but it rained". Norman Hall's last word was: "Had it been raining in September 1666 who can say what the City would have looked like today".

*   *   *

The Surrender of the Sword

It is a fallacy that the Monarch entering the City at Temple Bar has first to obtain permission of the Lord Mayor – so we are reminded by Philip Jones, Deputy Keeper of the Records in his paper to the GHA in July 1955.

The true significance of the proceedings can best be seen from the immediate action of the Lord Mayor.

He advances and proffers the City sword to the Sovereign and is thus signifying the Sovereign's omnipotence in the City and, by token, surrenders his own authority. He made such obeisance only to the Sovereign. The shutting of the gate, or the presence of a cord across the opening indicated that this is the City boundary, the area in which the Lord Mayor is supreme – until the Monarch arrives. Even the Heralds of the Sovereign were required to knock or seek admittance in order to make a royal proclamation.

The carriage bearing King or Queen does not halt without the bar but drives straight across the boundary and halts just within the City.

Jones's paper, after the opening, goes on to recount the origins of the ceremony with the sword, the first evidence of which was recorded in the grant of this privilege given to Coventry in 1387. The Mayor of that town was allowed to have borne before him a gilt sword "in the manner of London". No doubt that London's Mayor would have been the first to whom such privilege was granted – even if not recorded in a charter or any official document.

Jones concludes: Wherever the Lord Mayor meets the Sovereign (usually it is at Temple Bar), if the sword is present, it should be surrendered. Queen Victoria, returning it to the Lord Mayor in 1837, said it could not be in safer hands.

*　　*　　*

"Put not your trust in princes"

A positively unblinkered view of early relationships between the City and the Crown was delivered in October 1994 by Historian Major-General Pat McClelland who looked in particular at the dominant role played in such relations by the Tower of London (of which McClelland had latterly been the Governor).

William, Duke of Normandy, King of England, needed a peaceful, prosperous and supportive City and was willing that it should run its own affairs – but it had to be reminded that the King was all-powerful. So he had built a fort against "the restlessness of the vast and fierce population" – the White Tower which stood 90 feet high – the beginning of the Tower of London.

The Tower was the centre of his government, the most secure place in his kingdom. In his absence, control of the Tower was entrusted to its Constable, one of the highest officers in the land. Medieval Constables were invariably great Lords, sometimes Archbishops of Canterbury – always the King's man. McClelland tells us that among the Constable's many powers was total jurisdiction over the Jews of London including their protection against a hostile populace.

London during the 13th century saw frequent conflict with the Tower. In 1215, the year of Magna Carta, citizens and barons joined forces to take possession of the Tower whose Constable was Stephen Langton, Archbishop of Canterbury.

While the City emerged favourably from its disputes with King John, it was a quite different story during the reign of his son, Henry III, and grandson, Edward I. Edward, while still Prince of Wales, in retaliation for the undoubted enmity of the City towards his father, appointed the Constable of the Tower as governor of London. Mayor Fitz-Thomas was summoned to Windsor (under promise of safe-conduct), imprisoned and never heard of again. London was ruled by the Constable for four years. With a thaw in their relationship, Edward in 1270 allowed the City once again to elect a Mayor. On becoming

King two years later, Edward occupied himself with subduing the Welsh and the Scots, London being his main source of finance.

Hostilities broke out again when in 1285 the King's Justificers summoned Mayor Gregory de Rokesley and his fellow Aldermen to the Tower, ostensibly to give an account of how the King's peace had been kept in the City. The Mayor protested that by their ancient liberties they were not bound to enter the Tower for such "inquests" or to appear there for "judgement". Rokesley resigned the mayoralty and placed the Common Seal of the City in the hands of one of his colleagues. The now leaderless aldermen and other leading citizens, eighty of them in all, carried their protest to Westminster where they were promptly arrested and incarcerated although all except for the Alderman holding the seal, were released four days later.

Punishment was swift. On the King's instructions London was declared without a Mayor and taken into the King's hand. Sir Ralph de Sandwich was appointed to the dual role of Constable of the Tower and Warden of the City – his residence in Cornhill, something the citizens found particularly distasteful. This time the suspension of the City's franchise would last for thirteen years.

During the troubled reign of Charles I and the Civil War, three Mayors were imprisoned in the Tower for their independence of mind and royalist inclinations. The tables were somewhat turned at the time of the Restoration when Charles II appointed Lord Mayor Sir John Robinson to double up as Lieutenant of the Tower – the two offices combined in a person in whom Charles had total confidence.

*   *   *

The Office of Recorder of the City of London

Helping the Mayors, Sheriffs and Aldermen in their administration of the City were officers with such titles as Chamberlain, Recorder, Remembrancer and Town Clerk – uniquely in the City their designations still remaining today. For GHA Historians their histories have provided colourful material for after-luncheon speeches.

Sir Lawrence Verne, himself a recent holder of the office of Recorder, spoke in October 2000 about his earliest known predecessor, one Geoffrey de Norton to whom in 1298 the Mayor and Aldermen made a grant of £10 plus a 20 pence fee for every deed and will he wrote in the Court of Husting.

In fact Norton was already at that time not only a junior Alderman, clearly a man of some substance, but additionally he was one of the City's two Chamberlains. It would thus appear that the office of Chamberlain preceded that of Recorder but according to the next GHA paper the first known reference to a Chamberlain was not until 1330.

The second Recorder, John de Engrave, was given jurisdiction over both the Hustings and the Mayor's Courts and was required to declare orally the City's customs and privileges. The unique competence of the Recorder to declare what these privileges are was upheld by the House of Lords in the 1830's and recognised in the Court of Appeal as recently as the 1990's. Wengrave went on – the only Recorder to do so – to become Mayor, and the first of several to become a Member of Parliament. Recorders were treated as members of the Court of Aldermen and sat, as they still do, to the Mayor's immediate right. They were of necessity barristers-at-law.

The Recorder's status was greatly enhanced by a Charter of Henry VI which decreed: "The Mayor, Recorder and Aldermen past the chair (having served the office of Mayor) are made ex-officio conservators of the peace". The Recorder became a Justice of Gaol Delivery at Newgate, a judgeship thus being awarded. From that time on, a substantial majority of Recorders attained high judicial office or the

Speakership of the House of Commons. Verney remarks that for the last 200 years the holder of the office has tended to be someone who is near the end of his legal career.

The Stuart kings attempted to interfere in the selection of the Recorder, much to the City's resentment. In 1619 there was a declaration by the Lord Mayor that by ancient custom and usage of the City, Recorders have been and are elected by the Lord Mayor and Aldermen, a situation that still exists and was reinforced by legislation in the 19th century.

Today, the foremost duty of the Recorder is to act as the senior Judge at the Central Criminal Court, the Old Bailey. He is also in charge of the election each year of the Lord Mayor and is responsible for presenting him first to the Lord Chancellor in the House of Lords for the royal approval; then, on Lord Mayor's Day, to the Lord Chief Justice to declare his willingness to perform his obligations.

He acts as spokesman for the City in reading an address of welcome to a visiting Head of State who is being entertained in Guildhall.

Among his other ancient duties he acts as Returning Officer at the election of the Verderers of Epping Forest; he is a co-trustee with the Lord Mayor of two charitable trusts; he is Vice-President of the Sheriffs' and Recorder's Fund which assists prisoners and their families; he is on the Commission of Lieutenancy and the Courts of the Irish Society and the Honourable Artillery Company and is High Steward of Southwark.

*   *   *

The Chamber of London

In 1330 Chamberlain Henry de Seccesford was granted the sum of six marks for the loss of a horse while following the King on urgent City business – the first known reference to this office. In 1633 the Court of Aldermen allowed Chamberlain Robert Bateman some additional help at Guildhall in the making of freemen and enrolling of apprentices because of the many calls on his time at East India House, Bateman also being treasurer of the East India Company. In 1780, during the Gordon Riots, Chamberlain and Alderman John Wilkes was bullying a reluctant Lord Mayor into giving him a body of troops and directing the military defence of the Bank of England against the rioters.

These three glimpses of the not so trivial round and common task of some early Chamberlains came in a second paper by Irving Gane, now with a knighthood, in January 1962.Much of his paper was devoted to an account of the life of a Chamberlain of London in the mid-twentieth century, his attendance on the ceremonies and duties of the mayoralty and the meetings of the Courts of Aldermen and Common Council.

In particular, there are his dual tasks as treasurer and banker of the Corporation on the one hand and his direction of the Chamberlain's Court on the other, with its admissions to the Freedom of the City of more than a thousand people each year. Among them are notable recipients to whom the Chamberlain himself presents the Freedom. The most important of all, members of the Royal Family, visiting heads of state and other dignitaries receive the Freedom in Guildhall itself (not in the Chamberlain's Court) with the Chamberlain addressing the recipient in the name of the Corporation, a ceremony which reflects one of the highest compliments England can pay a distinguished person.

Gane's paper tells further tales of a Chamberlain's trials and tribulations of other days. For example, in 1643 at the height of the Civil War, he was called on to raise a loan of £150,000 for Parliament, £12,000 to fortify the suburbs against the Royal army and to equip four regiments of foot, one of horse and provide eleven pieces of cannon to help lift the siege of Gloucester. Not surprisingly at the end of the Civil War the Chamber of London was in debt to the tune of £220,000 – a fortune in those days.

After the depredations of the Great Fire, in spite of the City being granted a duty of 3 shillings for each ton of coal brought into the Port of London to help in re-building its streets, buildings, parish churches and St. Paul's, the Chamber was in even greater debt, some £750,000. It was this fact that gave the final push to the foundation of the Bank of England in 1694. At last the Chamberlain could lay down his role as Banker to the Government of the day and confine himself to the less-exacting function of Banker and Treasurer to the Corporation of London.

* * *

The Remembrancer

In 1571 with the City's written proceedings, its journals and repertories, being seven years in arrears, the Court of Aldermen appointed one Thomas Norton to bring the records up-to-date. He was a man of some substance in literary circles, a barrister who was counsel to the Stationers' Company and had served as a Member of Parliament. His first wife was daughter to Archbishop Cranmer. A tragedy he wrote had been performed in the presence of Queen Elizabeth. Norton was the City's first Remembrancer. For some two hundred years before that there had been a royal Remembrancer attached to the Exchequer charged with collection of debts owing to the Crown.

Thomas Norton's duties were quite different – the entering and engrossing of the City's books and reducing their content to indices and tables or calendars "whereby they may be more easily found". It may have sounded a routine task but as he was seen as a person of importance it was laid down that he was not to do anything prejudicial to the office of Town Clerk. Philip Jones, who presented this paper in October 1967, thought that the high-sounding title of Remembrancer was selected for Norton as being a man of some stature. His job was to "keep in remembrance" the City's important affairs, to act as the Corporation's memory.

In accordance with the practice of the period, Norton also served the Government not least in the persecution of Catholics including their examination under torture, his extreme Protestantism recommending him for this work.

After his death, there were moves in the Court of Aldermen to do away with the office. It was only a request from the Queen that led to the appointment of a second Remembrancer in 1587, one Doctor Giles Fletcher, broker to the Bishop of London and uncle of the dramatist John Fletcher. He himself had been a Member of Parliament and was, at Queen Elizabeth's command, sent as her ambassador to Russia to negotiate with the Czar, securing considerable concessions for the English merchants trading there.

The Deputy Keeper of the Records traces the ups and downs of Remembers through the early years of the office and the "curiously fluctuating attitude" of the Courts of Aldermen and Common Council to its incumbents. In the 18th century the office of Remembrancer, as with others, was offered for sale. Thus in 1760 it was purchased for £3,600 by Mr Brass Crosby, then a Common Councilman, later Alderman and Lord Mayor, the money paid into the Chamber of London.

By this time the Remembrancer's duties were becoming more clearly defined, his attendance upon Parliament described as the chief requirement. It is this aspect that has developed to the point where the Remembrancer is the accredited link between Guildhall and Parliament, the Remembrancer reporting to the Common Council on any legislation which could affect the City, explaining its significance and what action if any the City should take in its implementation. The Remembrancer will in turn, convey to Westminster any concerns of the Corporation that need to be considered in Parliament or Whitehall.

The other, and perhaps better known, side of the Remembrancer's duties is as head of Ceremonial. Philip Jones writes in his paper that the Remembrancer not only participates personally in many civic ceremonies but also bears responsibility for the arrangements beforehand, particularly those concerning entertainment of heads of state, members of the Royal Family and other distinguished persons, and with the masterminding of the Lord Mayor's Banquet. These responsibilities undoubtedly have arisen from the Remembrancer's special position as intermediary between Lord Mayor and Corporation on the one hand, and the Crown and High Officers of State on the other. They certainly require a high degree of recall of past procedures – the Remembrancer is now, more than ever before, the "memory of the City".

There have been forty-three Remembrancers since the office was created in 1571.

*   *   *

A particular Town Clerk

"It seems to be the case that few Town Clerks of the City of London have marked out notable places for themselves in the City's history" were the opening words of Alec Coulson's paper (July 1982) on a particularly famous one – John Carpenter – who held that office for twenty-one years from 1417 to 1438.

Carpenter, Common Clerk as the office was then called, served during the reign of Henry V and his conquest of most of France, and Henry VI during whose reign all France was lost except Calais.

He lived all his life in the City in a house at Billiter Lane, went to school in Threadneedle Street and in 1417 was elected to succeed the retiring Common Clerk having already worked at Guildhall for some years.

His first contribution to the City's history was his "Liber Albus", a compilation which brought together in a written record all the City's ordinances and usages which lay scattered throughout its books, rolls and charters. It was completed in 1419, a monumental contribution to the Corporation's archives. Later the book became known as the Liber Niger as frequent handling turned its binding from white to black. Preserved in Guildhall the book is a notable relic of the Middle Ages.

A key figure in the life of the City, many of Carpenter's influential friends appointed him as executor of their wills, most notably Richard Whittington, four times Mayor of London. In carrying out that will, Carpenter and his fellow executors re-built Newgate Prison, repaired St. Bartholomew's Hospital and contributed to the completion of Guildhall by lining the floor with Purbeck stone. They were also involved in erecting a library for the books and documents belonging to the Corporation on a site near Guildhall.

In Carpenter's own will, a bequest for the education of four choristers of the Guildhall Chapel led to the foundation of the first City of London School in Honey Lane Market off Cheapside.

John Carpenter grew in standing and influence and in 1431 the Corporation granted him a lease of property in Cornhill for 80 years at the rent of a red rose, the site now part of Leadenhall Market. After his retirement as Common Clerk in 1438, he accepted appointment as one of the City's four representatives in a Parliament which met first in Cambridge and then Westminster. John Carpenter's memory is much honoured at the City of London School and in St. Peter's Church, Cornhill, where he is buried. Unusually for the City, a street close by the site where the school once stood bears his name.

* * *

The Lord Mayor's three attendants

Traditionally there have been three Esquires in attendance on the Lord Mayor: the Swordbearer, Common Crier and Serjeant-at-Arms, and the City Marshal. The oldest and most historic is the SWORDBEARER. Appropriately his story was told at the first GHA meeting to be held at the Mansion House by invitation of Lord Mayor Cullum Welch who, in due course would become the GHA's second President. The paper was presented by Tom Kingsley Collett in December 1956.

Although the first mention of a City Sword was in 1387, it is difficult to name the very first of the Swordbearers since they went under the umbrella title of Esquire to the Mayor but John Credy was positively identified by that title in 1394 as was his successor John Hastyng. Historian Collett tells us that Swordbearer John Pencriche in 1426 was given not only a fee of four marks and reward of six marks but also the Town Clerk's house on the lower gate of Guildhall in which to lodge.

At that time the Swordbearer was appointed along with the Sheriffs and Chamberlain by members of the livery companies in Common Hall. Later the Court of Aldermen took it upon themselves to make the appointment and in the 17th century Lord Mayors seized what had become a valuable perquisite, Swordbearers being entitled to a fee from other City officers, and for this expected privilege having to pay the Lord Mayor as much as £4,000 upon their own appointment. Of this sum the Lord Mayor would retain two-thirds, the remainder going to "City's Cash". As the takings grew ever more lucrative, Common Council passed an Act by which the office was sold to the highest bidder with all the proceeds going to City's Cash.

Eventually all such arrangements came to an end and the Swordbearer, like all other officers, was paid a salary.

The Swordbearer was confirmed as head of the Lord Mayor's household by the Court of Alderman in 1502 and so continued almost up to modern times. His remit was wide, not least in acting for the Mayor in settling the days for meetings of the Courts of Aldermen and

Common Council and the nature of the business placed on their agendas. In 1838 it was resolved he would be in charge of all such matters even to having the agendas printed and delivered to the Keeper of the Guildhall for distribution to Aldermen and Commoners – duties now residing with the Town Clerk.

These attendants on the Lord Mayor have for long been engaged in the ceremonial surrounding him in all his civic duties, beginning on his first public appearance when Sword and Mace are carried before him into the gilded coach at the start of the Lord Mayor's procession in November. And at every meeting of the Common Council they precede him through Guildhall to the dais where he will preside, Sword and Mace being laid below him while the Council is in session.

But over and above these special occasions the Swordbearer or one of his two colleagues will accompany the Lord Mayor on most of his hundreds of engagements during his year of office including his overseas visits to promote the City across the world.

Until very recently it was they who were in sole charge of making all the detailed arrangements for these engagements – opening an exhibition, presenting an award, marking some special occasion. However, with the increasing size, scope and nature of the Lord Mayor's programme, particularly in regard to business initiatives, it has been necessary to increase the resources and experience needed to manage the programme to the best advantage.

The second of the Lord Mayor's Esquires was the COMMON CRIER AND SERJEANT-AT-ARMS, he who carried the Mace.

In his paper of December 1958, Philip Jones told that the earliest City mace was not the heavy "weapon" of later days but an antique treasure from Anglo-Saxon times known as the City Sceptre, its crystal shaft eighteen inches long topped by a gold coronet. The crystal sceptre is now used only at the admission of a new Lord Mayor at Guildhall and carried by him at a new monarch's Coronation ceremony.

By the early part of the 16th century a more serviceable mace was being carried by the Serjeant-at-Arms before the Mayor. He has also always performed the duties of Common Crier and seems in that part of his responsibilities to have done quite well for himself, occupying one of the gates of the City, usually Aldersgate, rent-free.

When in 1344 it was ordained that only the King's serjeants should be permitted to carry silver maces and others be limited to copper ones, Edward III made an exception for the City of London whose sergeants should bear maces of gold, silver or silver gilt.

Forty-six Common Criers and Serjeants-at-Arms are listed in Philip Jones's paper up to 1958 and there have been seven since then. The first was Thomas Juvenal who served in that office from 1291 to 1309. Among them was Henry Hodges who achieved the high office of Alderman for Cripplegate in 1657 but returned to being in addition Serjeant-at-Arms a year later; for more than the past hundred years they all held high military rank.

Today the Common Crier and Serjeant-at-Arms still carries the Mace and still cries out in stentorian tones at the start of each meeting of Common Council: "Oyez, Oyez, will all Members rise in their places" before the Lord Mayor utters the City prayer "Domine dirige nos".

THE CITY MARSHAL completed the trio of ceremonial officers of the Lord Mayor's Household, a somewhat later creation in Elizabethan times. Historian Cyril Lewis gave this paper in May 1965.

With large numbers of unemployed – "masterless men" as they were called – their number swollen by soldiers and sailors discharged after the Armada, concern was increasingly felt as to the disorder arising in cities and towns, particularly London.

A royal proclamation of 1589 gave vagrants two days grace to appear before a Justice of the Peace and obtain a "passport" to travel to their place of birth after which time they would be punished by "marshal lawe". In November the Common Council appointed one Richard Young, grocer, to execute the office of provost marshal for the City and Liberties and to have for salary 10s a day and another 10s for disbursement to ten attendants.

Two subsequent provost marshals were Aldermen, indicating the importance attaching to the post and in 1595 the Queen, not the City, appointed Sir Thomas Wilford ordering that "he punish by death on the gibbet such vagrants who proved incorrigible". (Were the City authorities considered too soft-hearted?) Later the Recorder declared that the Queen had no authority to appoint provost marshals in the City – but that was long after Elizabeth had departed the scene.

The earlier marshals' duties included supervision of ward constables, that orders concerning the plague were enforced, that beadles performed their lantern lighting, and that young housewives selling oysters unless they were licensed be taken up and punished as vagrants. In 1605 came a first reference to the marshal's taking part in the Lord Mayor's Show.

In Queen Victoria's reign, with the introduction of a City police force, marshals were relieved of their role in maintaining public order leaving them to concentrate on ceremonial duties and attendance on the Lord Mayor. The past practice of having an upper – as well as an under – marshal came to an end in 1857 when Lord Mayor Thomas Finnis decreed that one was sufficient to maintain the pageantry of his office.

In recent times the City Marshall shared with Swordbearer and Serjeant-at-Arms the secretarial duties of the Mansion House. His ceremonial duties include the marshalling of civic processions, the most important of which is his leading role in the Lord Mayor's Show. He escorts any troops who are privileged to march through the City.

*   *   *

The Gates of the City

Of all architectural survivals none can be more immediately evocative of the past than a city's gates and walls, declared Historian Hugh Wontner in this paper he delivered in 1972, shortly before becoming Lord Mayor. But unlike the citizens of York or Carcassonne, Londoners must do without these aids to historical imagination. We make do with the names of streets or the wards in which the gates were once situated.

When the Romans built their wall around Londinium soon after 200 AD they provided gates at those points where important roads led to other parts of Britain: Aldgate straddling the road to Colchester; Bishopsgate on the route to Lincoln,' Newgate going west to Silchester and northwest to Verulamium, Ludgate also leading to the west.

The oldest was Cripplegate, built before the wall as an entry and exit point to the Roman fort established in the north-west corner of the city in the first century. A sixth point of exit, Aldersgate, was inserted into the wall in later Roman times.

King Alfred is believed to have repaired the wall in making London the centre for his military activities against the Danes but virtually nothing is known about the wall and its gates until the 13th century when the City archives tell of the medieval fortifications erected upon their Roman foundations.

There remained six gates, now far more elaborate structures, and supplemented with smaller posterns. London Bridge was defended by massive gates at either end, that on the City side defended also with a drawbridge. It was on this "Drawbridge Gate" that the heads of traitors were displayed on poles – an appropriate location it was thought since it was here that rebels and people with a grievance such as Wat Tyler or the later Gordon Rioters would seek entry to the City.

In 1282 ordinances made by the Mayor and Aldermen provided that during the day when all the gates were open two serjeants of "experience and eloquence" were to keep watch at each of them on all passing in and out lest evil should befall the City. At night, after curfew was rung the serjeants were to lie in or near their gates. During the night men from each of the wards were appointed to maintain an armed watch on each of the gates. Nothing was left to chance in securing the City's safety against attack. Murage (a tax) was levied from time to time on goods entering the City for the repair of the wall and gates.

When in 1471 the men of Kent led by Thomas Faconbridge rose against Edward IV they tried to force London Bridge, Aldgate and Bishopsgate but were repelled with considerable loss of life. Falconbridge was later captured, executed at York and his head sent to London to join others on the Drawbridge Gate.

There were happier occasions when, for example, newly repaired and richly hung Ludgate housed minstrels for Mary Tudor's royal progress through the City before her coronation. London Bridge was the way of welcome back into the capital for medieval sovereigns returning from campaigns in France. Notably in 1660 King Charles II was greeted by Lord Mayor and citizens in Southwark and conducted with great acclamation across the Bridge and through the streets of the City.

The gates provided comfortable and sought-after dwelling places, most famous of occupants being Geoffrey Chaucer, poet and customs official, to whom in 1374 the City granted the habitation over Aldgate and a cellar beneath – the only conditions being that he kept his quarters in good repair and would give temporary possession back to the civic authorities if the City was in danger of attack. Christopher Fulke who lived over Cripplegate as Serjeant and Common Crier was allowed to stay in residence free of rent on his retirement.

Several of the City gates with their stout walls were used to house criminals. Newgate and Ludgate became the principal prisons, continuing in use as such for many years. Ludgate was the gaol for freemen imprisoned for debt, Newgate for the worst class of criminal. Conditions then were dreadful and Richard Whittington left instructions in his will to rebuild it, wishes carried out by his executors in 1423. The ruinous gate and gaol of Newgate was demolished and a new one constructed.

Wontner, owner of the Savoy Hotel, told the assembled historians that a forebear, John Wontner, presided over a somewhat different property being Governor of Newgate as well as Master of His Majesty's Gaols from 1822 to 1833.

Later there came smaller passage ways through the wall known as posterns, one of which became Moorgate giving access across the Ditch to the Moor Fields and in 1653 three new posterns were created at the northern ends of Coleman Street, Basinghall Street and Aldermanbury. A larger and more impressive Moorgate was erected in 1672.

So much for the wall and its gates. But with the expansion of the City boundaries into those areas known as the Liberties, the City limits were marked by "bars" placed across major roads. They took the form of posts, rails and a chain as at Holborn and Whitechapel. The most famous of them, Temple Bar, leading into The Strand and Westminster began in this way but as early as the 14th century it had become a solid gateway structure serving also as a prison. Rebuilt after the Great Fire it was demolished in 1878 as an obstruction to traffic and languished in Theobalds Park, Cheshunt, until its rescue by the City Corporation and re-erected as the splendid entrance to the new Paternoster Square.

The Temple Bar memorial stone surmounted by a bronze dragon of 1880 marks the western entry into the City and two further dragons holding the City arms salvaged from the sadly demolished Coal Exchange stand at the boundary on the Thames Embankment. More modern dragons define entrances elsewhere into the City.

Long before the removal of Temple Bar it was decided that all the famous gates should go because of their hindrance to ever-increasing traffic. In 1760 the process was begun and the City Lands Committee at Guildhall advertised for sale the stonework and other materials of the first three to be pulled down – Aldgate, Cripplegate and Ludgate. They went to one Benjamin Blackden for a total of £396.10. How sad and indeed short-sighted that we did not retain at least one of them as a national treasure – just think of the appeal to tourists of such an outstanding piece of the City's history.

* * *

City Lands Committee and its Chairman, The Chief Commoner

From early times Mayor and Aldermen who invariably were property owners in their own right, laid claim also, for the City, to extensive tracts of land running alongside the wall – the ramparts within and the ditch without. What had become hallowed by custom was given legal recognition by Henry VI's Charter of 1444 which confirmed the citizens' rights to all soils, commons, streets, ways and other places of the City, together with the profits of the same, and they may improve and enjoy the rents of the same for them and their successors for ever.

King Henry had dealt the City a pretty good hand wrote Historian Wallis Hunt with masterly understatement in his GHA paper read in 1986. The City's meagre holdings of land had become the basis for its future wealth.

Thirty years after Henry's Charter, Edward IV also in need of substantial financial assistance, came to an arrangement which, in return for wiping clean the slate of his indebtedness of £13,000, empowered the City to acquire land through devise and purchase. For much the same reason Charles I in 1638 confirmed the rights of the Mayor, Commonalty and Citizens to all houses, messuages and edifices and their site and foundation, and all watercourses, gutters and easements which are now erected, built or enjoyed in, upon or under any void grounds, wastes, commons, streets, ways or public places and in the banks, shores and waters of Thames.

It is of course the "sites" that would, with the passing years prove ever more valuable, a high proportion of the City's Cash derived from them.

In the early Middle Ages administration of the City and its property holdings lay exclusively with the Mayor and Aldermen. By the mid-1500's they had delegated control of property to the Chamberlain then, thinking better of it, they resumed direct control through a committee of aldermen to which four commoners were added in 1563.

With increasing pressure from a now increasingly important Common Council for more direct involvement in administration of the City's lands it was decreed in 1592 that all future leases would be granted in the name of the Lord Mayor, Commonalty and Citizens, under the City seal. Management would be in the hands of a committee comprising four aldermen and six commoners. Thus the City Lands Committee was born, holding its first meeting on 9th May 1592.

The City Lands Committee, always acknowledged as the Corporation's premier body, would continue brilliantly over the centuries the maintenance and development of an increasingly great property portfolio, mainly situated in the City but spreading out into affluent areas of the West End.

The City Lands Committee had always worked closely with Bridge House Estates and its substantial income deriving from the tolls, trade and bequests of property associated with the City's four bridges across the Thames. In 1969 Bridge House Estates was merged with City Lands, to become an ever more powerful and effective source of the City's wealth, provider of the private resources used to finance the City's schools, the great open spaces of Epping Forest, Burnham Beeches and Hampstead Heath, and the hospitality afforded to visiting heads of state.

It was seen as highly appropriate that the Chairman of this prestigious committee should be recognised as someone quite special in the Guildhall hierarchy and so it was that in 1880 the City Lands Chairman became designated as the "Chief Commoner". Very early in the existence of the GHA the "Title and Office of Chief Commoner" was chosen as the subject of a paper by Lt. Col. Cullum Welch (later Lord Mayor of London). He reminded the assembled Historians that the Chairman/Chief Commoner presides as trustee for the citizens and is charged to ensure that the common estate of the citizens is carefully preserved for the enjoyment of generations of commoners to come.

*　　*　　*

Richard Whittington

Strangely enough the City's most famous of Mayors was not selected as a subject for attention by the GHA until 1979, but in May of that year Historian Alan Lamboll paid full justice to this remarkable man.

Lamboll speaks first of Dick Whittington, the pantomime hero and his cat, the poor orphan employed as kitchen scullion who runs away but is summoned back by Bow Bells, makes his fortune and married his master's daughter. A charming story that first appeared, says Lamboll, 150 years after Whittington's death.

The real story is somewhat different but no less remarkable.

It would seem that Richard Whittington was born in the 1350's at Pauntley in Gloucestershire, third son of a local knight, Sir William Whittington. As a third son he had to make his own way in the world, which he was well able to do. Still in his early twenties he was in London and sufficiently established to be among those citizens contributing to a civic loan, albeit a modest sum. By 1384 he was a Common Councilman at Guildhall, in 1393 he was elected Alderman of Broad Street Ward and only a few months later he was chosen as Sheriff.

Whittington was a member of the Mercers' livery and three times its Master. His trade as a mercer in the early years of his career would lay the foundations of his great wealth. In the 1380's and 1390's he is known to have supplied velvets and other rich materials to royal favourites and courtiers. In 1389 came the first record of his sale of two cloths of gold to King Richard II. In 1392-4 the Royal Wardrobe spent £13,000 of which a quarter was due to Whittington for fine cloths. Richard, when he was deposed in 1399, owed Wittington £1,000 for goods supplied to the Wardrobe and money and personal loans – money repaid by order of his successor, Henry IV.

Whittington continued to supply mercery to the courts of Henry IV and Henry V including the trousseaux of Henry IV's daughters Blanche and Philippa.

By the late 1300's he had moved into the world of royal finance and was seriously lending money as well as supplying goods to the crown, while his civic career had entered a new and important phase. In 1397 on the death in office of Mayor Adam Bamme he was appointed by Royal decree to serve out Bamme's year of office – an unusual departure since mayors were normally elected by members of the Guilds, but clearly demonstrating King Richard's regard – and gratitude.

After this royal appointment Whittington went on to be elected Mayor as was customary by the livery on three further occasions in 1397, 1406 and 1419, indicative of the esteem in which he was held by London's citizens as well as the trust placed in him by the three monarchs who ruled England.

In the first year of Henry IV's reign he was one of three Londoners who, in recognition of the important part played by the City in the King's accession to the throne, were appointed members of Henry's Council.

A merchant prince rather than man of extensive estates, the most important of his properties lay in the parish of St. Michael Paternoster where in 1402 he acquired the tenement to the north of the church where he lived for the remainder of his life. He married Alice, daughter of Sir Ivo Fitzwaryn, a Dorset knight.

His benefactions were legend. He contributed largely to the re-building of St. Michael Paternoster – this perhaps also being an act of piety to provide a fitting place of burial for his wife and later for himself.

The re-building continued until he died in 1423 and was completed, according to his wishes, by his four executors, his will being proved in the Court of Husting.

Richard and Alice had no children and his will holds no kinsmen, friend or member of his household in individual remembrance. Only the four executors, of whom John Carpenter, Town Clerk of the City, was the chief, are individually named. Whittington's charitable gifts had begun in his lifetime and his will lists some thirty bequests: to the poor, to inmates of hospitals, to prisoners in gaols, for the fabric of churches and the repair of highways. The residue was left to his executors to dispose of in charity for the good of his soul. While it is probable that Whittington may have indicated to John Carpenter projects he would like undertaken there is no reference to them in his will so, as Lamboll says in his paper, they may have been initiated by the executors themselves.

The principal benefactions were the re-building of Newgate Gaol, the building of the south gate of St. Bartholomew's Hospital, the establishment of a library at Guildhall and the founding of the Whittington College of Priests in St. Michael Paternoster and the Whittington Almshouses for thirteen poor men and women.

One tale not told in Lamboll's paper about this remarkable man, the wealthiest merchant of his age, four times Mayor of London and great philanthropist indicates that there was yet another side to him.

When Henry V brought his French princess back to London as his wife Whittington celebrated their nuptials with a great banquet in Guildhall in the course of which he threw on to a fire blazing in the middle of the hall promissory notes from the king to the worth of £60,000. A favourite of kings he himself was capable of royal gestures.

*   *   *

The Lord Mayor's Banquet

If Richard Whittington is the most famous of City mayors, there are no two events in the City's calendar better known or more celebrated than the Lord Mayor's Show and the Lord Mayor's Banquet; and no-one better placed to write about the Banquets than Alderman Sir Hugh Wontner who presented this GHA paper in October 1973, just a month before his election as Lord Mayor and thus presiding at his own Banquet at Guildhall on Monday 12 November. He also happened to be the owner of the Savoy Hotel.

He wrote: It is inconceivable that on the occasion of a new Mayor's accession to office and his procession through the streets there would not have been a dinner or feast held in his house or the Hall of his Company. Such a dinner is mentioned in the famous book of City customs, "Liber Altus", compiled by John Carpenter, town clerk in 1419.

According to the "Great Chronicle" Lord Mayor Sir John Shaa was the first to hold his feast in Guildhall, in 1501, although other records suggest that Guildhall was used for that purpose in the previous century – its construction having begun in 1411 with completion not all that long afterwards.

Hugh Wontner begins his history of the banquet during the reign of Queen Elizabeth: The Privy Council demanding in 1580 why "the ancient and honourable Feast of the Lord Mayor" had been omitted that year without the Council's permission. He goes on to say that the first banquet for which we have details was that of Mayor Robert Pankhurst in 1634 and tells us of the curious seating arrangements with the Lords of the Council and other great dignitaries on the platform of the Hustings at the eastern end of Guildhall, the Lord Mayor and Aldermen on a dais at the Western end.

Such separation dates from earlier times when it was the custom for a newly-crowned monarch to watch the procession from a balcony in Cheapside and then to be the Mayor's principal guest at the Banquet which followed. On many later occasions when the

Sovereign was present this division continued into the early 19th century.

The first banquet bill of fare which survives is from 1634 which tells of brawn, boiled pullets, pheasants, herons and hare, soused capon and carp, venison pasty, cold tongue pie, fresh salmon and lobsters, after which came some exotic puddings for those able to consume them.

From 1671 to 1677 Charles II was a constant attendant at the banquets. On these royal occasions the Lord Mayor paid £300 and the Sheriffs £150 each towards their total cost of some £1,400. As well as charges for food and wine there were the expenses of "fitting up" Guildhall: flambeaux, torches and candles, rushes, herbs and perfumes, ribbons for the arms of serving men and guards, refreshment for the retinues of distinguished guests.

The narrow confines of Guildhall Yard presented problems of access and only the coaches of the King and Queen, royal Dukes, Ambassadors, the Lord Chancellor and the Aldermens' ladies were allowed to enter the yard.

In 1689, the first Lord Mayor's Day after the accession of William and Mary, the Common Council invited the King and Queen and selected members from both Houses of Parliament to the Banquet to mark the City's major role in bringing William to the throne. A subscription list among Aldermen and Councilmen raised over £2,000 including the Sheriffs' £150 apiece and the Lord Mayor's £300.

King George IV missed the 1820 banquet because the trial of Queen Caroline, which he had engineered, was highly unpopular in the City. Similarly, William IV's attendance in 1830 was put off because of fears of unrest caused by agitation over Parliamentary reform. The youthful Queen Victoria in 1837 was the last sovereign at a Lord Mayor's Banquet. Since the time of Edward VII it has been customary for a new monarch to attend a coronation luncheon in Guildhall.

George I's Banquet in 1714 was notable for the purchase of a considerable quantity of wine: 1,290 bottles and 354 flasks of claret,

70 flat bottles of burgundy, 252 bottles of French white wine, 168 of old hock, 276 of Canary, 132 bottles of white Port and 276 of red. Clearly a good party although some surplus bottles were later sold off to the Lord Mayor and members of the organising committee.

Music was increasingly important and in 1727 the instrumentalists came from London's leading theatres – the Opera House, Drury Lane and the Theatre Royal in Haymarket. Music was composed by Mr Handel, the Court composer.

Food was becoming more cosmopolitan and for George III and his Queen in 1781 there were chicken à la reine, tongues Espagnole, fillets de lambe à la Conté, artichokes à la Provencale and Mille Feulles. An innovation which would become the hallmark as it were of Lord Mayor's banquets was turtle soup.

The Banquet of 1772 was somewhat exceptional not on account of George III's presence but because of a riot outside Guildhall. The new Lord Mayor, James Townsend, had been preferred by the Court of Aldermen rather than his rival, John Wilkes. Partisans of Wilkes broke into Guildhall Yard where they put out the lamps, tore down a temporary wooden portico and set fire to it. The ringleaders were arrested, tried next month at the Old Bailey and, surprisingly enough, found not guilty.

Until 1815 the banquets were illuminated by oil lamps and candles and, when that year, the Hall was first lit by gas the arrangements seemed even more perilous than before with a complicated system of pipes installed to feed fourteen gas chandeliers. The committee responsible for the entertainment would dine together beforehand to view the fitting up of Guildhall. After the introduction of gas lighting they attended a rehearsal of the lighting arrangements the night before the banquet, this event developing into the "Lighting Up Dinner" that continues to the present time.

The Lord Mayor's Banquet was ever an occasion for toasts and for the number of important people present. In the latter part of the 19th century the Banquet became the occasion for a major speech by the Prime Minister as is still the custom today. That of Gladstone in 1881 was devoted to the Irish question and South Africa. Altogether that night there were thirteen toasts (and replies) in addition to the loyal toast to the Queen and the Royal Family. They were to the Army and Navy, Foreign Ministers, Her Majesty's Ministers, the Lord Mayor, the late Lord Mayor, the House of Peers, the Lord Bishop of London, the Judges, House of Commons, the Aldermen, the Sheriffs, the Bar, and the Lady Mayoress – something of an endurance test for all those present.

Today there are but three toasts – and replies – Her Majesty's Ministers, the late Lord Mayor (in whose honour the Banquet is given) and the Lord Mayor and Sheriffs (the hosts). The speakers are the Lord Mayor and late Lord Mayor, the Prime Minister, the Lord Chancellor and the Archbishop of Canterbury. The two Sheriffs have two minutes each from either end of the top table.

Where once the banquets were funded by subscriptions and grants they are entirely paid for by the Lord Mayor (half the very substantial cost) and the two Sheriffs (quarter each).

*   *   *

PART TWO
THE GREAT INSTITUTIONS OF THE CITY

The Bank of England

Throughout the centuries England's prosperity has largely depended on the commerce of London, and kings and governments have looked to the City of London for the money they needed to run the country, secure the kingdom against invasion and fight their wars.

As the business of government and commerce became more sophisticated, methods for the financing of loans had also to be developed. Merchants of enormous wealth such as Richard Whittington who had once financed kings were superseded in the 16th and 17th centuries by City Livery Companies, notably the Goldsmiths, and the Chamber of London in Guildhall who were acting as bankers in lending money to the Crown, to Parliament and trading concerns such as the East India Company.

Banks, public and private, came into existence in order to provide finance in sufficiently large sums to meet the needs of London's ever-increasing commercial activity.

The author of this paper of December 1949, Alderman Edmund Stockdale (Lord Mayor ten years later), drew particular attention to the role of the City Chamberlain as banker to Government – a role that almost certainly took up considerably more of his time than running the City's own finances and his supervision of the Chamberlain's Court.

When Crown or Parliament needed money he was approached for an immediate loan. The loan was collected by the Chamberlain from individuals, sometimes by an assessment upon the Wards or Livery Companies. Guildhall would make up any shortfall. These sums were repaid by the Exchequer from the proceeds of taxes.

During the whole of the 17th century the strain on the finances of the City Corporation increased. The Chamber gradually ceased to lend but was compelled to continue borrowing on its own account. By 1633 the City's debt had risen to £179,000 and in 1666 to £238,000. Came the Great Fire of that year, itself cataclysmic, and together with ever-growing interest charges raised the City's debt to £650,000 by 1690.

The City no longer able itself, because of this mounting debt to finance Crown, Parliament or even private commerce, was now at the forefront of efforts to establish a national bank which could undertake these tasks.

The Bank of England was incorporated by Act of Parliament in 1694 as an undertaking by 1,268 sharcholders, its immediate purpose being to raise some £1,200,000 to the Government of William III for his wars with France in the Low Countries. A Royal Charter enabled the bank to operate as a joint-stock bank with limited liability. Of the original 26 members of its Court of Directors, ten were City Aldermen. Alderman Sir John Houblon was appointed the Bank's first Governor in 1694. Sir Gilbert Heathcote doubled up as both Governor and Lord Mayor, Governor from 1709 to 1711 and occupying the mayoralty from 1710-11. He was the last Lord Mayor to ride on horseback in his own Show! Clearly a man of stamina.

The Bank's quarters for the first few months were in Mercers' Hall and then at the hall of the Grocers' Company. In 1732 the Bank purchased as its permanent home, Sir John Houblon's mansion in Threadneedle Street, where it was rebuilt in the Palladian style and occupied in 1734 having been worked upon by four of England's architects, notably Sir John Sloane.

Stockdale in his GHA paper turns finally to the Bank's connections with City livery companies which, he says, are so voluminous that as a single example he instances the Grocers. It was in their hall that the Bank was located for 40 years before its move to Threadneedle Street and, appropriately enough, Houblon its first Governor was a Grocer.

Another Grocer, Sir John Barnard, helped the Bank steer clear of possible financial disaster during the invasion of the Pretender in 1745. He was instrumental in collecting the signatures of leading City merchants who bound themselves to accept the Bank's notes in payment of all debts. In World War One with Government stocks greatly increasing, the Grocers' Company again made their hall available to the Bank as overflow accommodation for the extra business.

*   *   *

The Royal Exchange

The Royal Exchange vies with the Bank of England as its most famous institution and is certainly of greater antiquity, its location and the streets radiating from it already defined in Saxon times. Bargains were struck and negotiated in shops, homes and taverns located in this area – but there was no central market or exchange.

In the great port of Antwerp such an exchange had been created in 1515, improved in 1531, where merchants guaranteed credit and raised loans. It was visited by Sir Richard Gresham, a London Mercer dealing in cloth and tapestries for Cardinal Wolsey and, later, for Henry VIII. He saw the enormous potential for a similar institution in London.

A man of great standing in the City – Master of the Mercers' Company and a past Lord Mayor – he urged on Thomas Cromwell who was the Lord Privy Seal that a Bourse be set up in London. He estimated its cost at £2,000 of which he offered to pay half. But nothing came of this initiative.

It was Richard Gresham's son, Thomas, who would eventually bring off its achievement.

Thomas Gresham, also a Mercer, graduate of Cambridge, trader in France and Flanders, Royal Agent for Edward VI and Queen Mary, favourite of William Cecil and recognised for paying off the Crown's debts with a knighthood, he owned Osterley House in Middlesex and dwelt in a great house around a courtyard in Bishopsgate. In 1565 he proposed to the City that a Bourse be established and the Lord Mayor and Aldermen agreed.

A site north of Cornhill was purchased from the Dean and Chapter of Canterbury for £3,532 involving the demolition of 40 houses. Money came from some 20 not altogether enthusiastic livery companies encouraged to contribute by Lord Mayor Sir William Garrard, and 742 individuals who hoped for a good return on their investment. Work began in 1566 and was largely completed three years later.

The London Exchange was modelled on the one at Antwerp with an open courtyard, an arcade and some 100 shops above. It had a bell tower to announce the hours of trading and topped by a golden grasshopper, the Gresham family crest.

Queen Elizabeth visited the building in 1571, lavishly entertained afterwards in Gresham's Bishopsgate mansion. She ordered her herald to sound the trumpet and proclaim the name of the bourse to be "The Royal Exchange and so to be called henceforth and not otherwise".

In the shops you could buy all kinds of rich wares and fine commodities as well as mousetraps, birdcages and lanthornes. Merchants did their business in the courtyard and the earliest surviving life insurance policy was drawn up there.

Gresham in his will left the Exchange jointly to the City Corporation and the Mercers' Company, the rent helping to finance a new Gresham College with its seven professors, to be established in his house in Bishopsgate. The Corporation and the Mercers would form a Joint Grand Gresham Committee to run the Exchange, all these arrangements continuing to the present day.

But in 1666 that first Royal Exchange was gutted in the Great Fire with Pepys saying how it "did run down the galleries filling them with flames and the court with sheets of fire" and Evelyn describing how he clambered over "heaps of yet smoking rubbish... the ground under my feet so hot it burnt the soles of my shoes".

Guildhall believed the Exchange could be restored using what was left but in the outcome petitioned Charles II for 300 tons of Portland stone for a completely new building. The second Royal Exchange almost followed the design of the original structure, the tower over the entrance crowned by the Gresham grasshopper. Early occupants inside were Royal Exchange Assurance and Lloyds of London.

Fashionable shopping had by then moved away from the City to St. James and Mayfair. The essayist Richard Steele complained that beggars, vendors of trash and wenches had jostled out the honourable merchants and substantial tradesmen.

In January 1838 disaster struck again. The flames of this second great fire could be seen 24 miles away at Windsor. After two competitions to select an architect for the rebuilding the design of William Tite was chosen. It involved the acquisition of additional land and the demolition of a number of neighbouring buildings including the church of St. Bartholomew-by-the-Exchange. A new portico was modelled on that of the Pantheon in Rome with eight huge Corinthian columns. In the centre of the pediment a figure representing Commerce holds the Charter of the Royal Exchange.

Prince Albert laid the foundation stone in 1842. Two years later the opening by Queen Victoria was made a state occasion, the Queen being provided with a throne by the Lord Mayor from over the road in the Mansion House.

An early addition to its front was Francis Chantrey's statue of the Duke of Wellington around which Armistice Day services would later take place.

The courtyard was roofed over in 1883 and the walls of the ambulatory magnificently decorated with twenty-three painted panels depicting scenes and people from England's history– Alfred the Great, William I granting London its first Charter, King John placing his seal on Magna Carta, Whittington and Thomas Gresham.

Trading on the floor of the Exchange came to an end at the start of the Second World War. Since 1945 the Royal Exchange has been theatre, home for the Guildhall Museum and the location of the London International Financial Futures Market.

This admirable paper was presented in June 1999 by Historian Tony Moss, a recent GHA Secretary.

*

In 1992 this Grade I listed building was presented with the City Heritage Award for its magnificent refurbishment – with new richly-coloured barrel vault roof over the courtyard (replacing one that leaked), and two new upper floors skilfully introduced to provide badly-needed office space for Guardian Royal Exchange Assurance.

With elegant shops enclosing the great courtyard the Exchange remains one of the City's finest structures and totally faithful to its long history.

*   *   *

Insurance in the City of London

Alderman Tony Hart who read this paper in October 1988, himself a distinguished loss adjuster, reminded the assembled Historians that Babylon had preceded London as originators of insurance 4,500 years earlier.

After this modest disclaimer he treated his audience to a whirlwind history of insurance as it spread first to Phenicia where it was called "bottomry", then to Greece and Rome.

Evidence has it that in 1310 a chamber of insurance was set up in Bruges where merchants met to insure their goods against marine and other risks while in Italy there existed in medieval times a system of marine insurance. He might have added that insurance of ships and cargoes was almost certainly being undertaken in England in the Middle Ages and that in the 1680's London was getting a good share of marine business. Ship owners, captains and merchants were gathering at Edward Lloyd's coffee house in Tower Street, near the Pool of London, which became the centre for shipping insurance.

Hart was, however, concerned with insurance of buildings, particularly against the risk of fire. Insurance tends to follow a need and so it was that after London's densely-populated narrow streets, their wooden houses packed together, were devastated in the Great Fire of 1666 there came the first initiative to provide insurance against fire.

Oddly enough, wrote Hart, it was the City Corporation who took the first steps during the early 1670's, seeing fire insurance as an appropriate and profitable activity. Lengthy committee discussion was, however, rapidly overtaken by one Nicholas Barban, a doctor turned building speculator after the Fire, and it was he who having got wind of the Corporation's project established his own Fire Office in 1681 and was the virtual founder of the fire insurance business. In six years he wrote some 5,000 policies for houses in London. Soon there came competitors and by 1720 there were six fire offices doing business, the best-known being the Amicable with its famous Hand-in-Hand fire mark, and the Sun.

A great sight in the City streets were their horse-drawn pumps whose splendidly uniformed firemen would gallop to blazes but only to extinguish fires on those buildings which carried their office's Fire Mark.

Gradually fire insurers expanded their activity to cover buildings in the rest of the country and, in addition to buildings, offered protection for goods and chattels. Competition came from companies in the provinces and beyond like Norwich Union, the Hibernian in Ireland and the Caledonian in Scotland. But the City remained the centre for fire and general insurance, and by the first half of the 20th century accommodated some seventy companies now, sadly, reduced by mergers and takeovers to a mere three or four.

Hart, in his paper, apologises for the fact that lack of time prevented his talking about Life Assurance and Lloyds and hoped that another Historian might deal with them in a following paper. To date no volunteer has yet come forward.

* * *

The Baltic Exchange

When Alderman Charles Trinder read his GHA paper in July 1968, the Baltic Mercantile and Shipping Exchange occupied one of the most handsome buildings in the City. Although completed in 1903 it was a wholly Victorian triumph – pink granite exterior with triple-arched entrance within, beneath a great glazed dome, a hall of marble, mahogany and stained glass. The Baltic was the last survivor of its type and style in the City. In 1992 it was severely damaged by the IRA. It could have been rebuilt but was not, its members finding more pedestrian accommodation.

If that building was unique so, indeed, is Baltic Exchange itself as a City institution, the only truly international shipping exchange where most of the world's chartering of freight is arranged and more than half the world's shipping is bought and sold.

While everyone knows that Lloyd's originated in Edward Lloyd's coffee house in the late 17th century, the Baltic goes back even earlier – to the Virginia Wine House in Threadneedle Street early in the reign of James I. The wine house became the Virginia and Maryland Coffee House when coffee was introduced into England about 1650, then came another change of name in 1744 when its sign proclaimed the Virginia and Baltic – indicative of the vast imports of tallow for candle-making from the Baltic ports.

In 1810 the merchants in the Baltic trade moved their meeting place to the Antwerp Tavern which was renamed the Baltic Tavern. At that time there was great speculation in commodities and frequently high financial loss, particularly in tallow. So for their own protection and to regulate conduct among the traders, the frequenters of the Baltic Tavern turned themselves into the Baltic Club of 300 subscribing members – a first manifestation of the Exchange as it came to be.

In 1857 the Baltic moved to South Sea House in Threadneedle Street and grew steadily in business and prestige. With ever increasing imports of grain and raw materials and expanding exports of coal and manufactured goods the Baltic became firmly established as the world's freight market.

Meanwhile another group of merchants, ship owners and captains trading with the Near and Far East and Australia, had come into being and, meeting in the Jerusalem Coffee House, formed a London Shipping Exchange. Early in the 1900's the members of the two exchanges, their interests overlapping, amalgamated as the Baltic Mercantile and Shipping Exchange at its splendid new premises in St. Mary Axe.

Trinder describes in great detail the activities of the Baltic's 2,500 members – shipping, dealing in grain, dealing in oilseeds and vegetable oils, aircraft chartering. Far and away the most important of these is the Baltic's handling of the world's sea-borne trade with, for example, China as one of the largest charterers of ships under many different flags, all handled on the Baltic in London.

With Britain purchasing so much grain the UK held a predominant position in the movement of grain throughout the world, all organised by the Baltic's traders. Similarly all the principal shippers, crushers and brokers of vegetable oils and oilseeds are members of the Exchange, the products in which they deal including margarine and cooking fats, animal feeding stuffs, paint and linoleum.

Enquiries about aircraft chartering were reaching the Baltic as long ago a 1925, the first air charter (from Croydon to Cologne) being signed in 1928. The end of the Second World War left a pool of aircraft and pilots eager to operate commercially and the Baltic seized this new opportunity with a hundred operating companies of all nationalities having their representation on the floor of the Exchange.

*   *   *

The City Livery Companies

Guilds, bringing men together in religious as well as trading organisations, existed in many European countries but nowhere more early, in such large and powerful number and destined to endure for so long, than in England, chiefly of course in London, ever the centre of England's trading activity.

So the guilds, which became the livery companies, would clearly rank highly in the GHA's scheme of things – not least in that every member of the GHA was himself a liveryman.

Not surprising therefore that early in the GHA's existence, March 1948, Historian William Morris should have presented such a splendid account of the City Livery Companies.

Their origin is lost in the twilight of Saxon antiquity (he began) with references to them in the Chronicles of King Alfred, and their greatest prosperity in the Middle Ages. They constitute a unique survival of institutions once general throughout Europe and which continue to flourish to the present day.

The term "livery" is derived from the wearing of a distinctive dress or livery by members of the Companies in the 14th century, the gowns parti-coloured in bright hues.

The full titles of the more ancient Companies were derived from the saints of the various Fraternities – thus the Grocers Company was referred to as the Fraternity of St. Anthony, the Goldsmiths as the Fraternity of St. Dunstan. The Livery Companies are relics of medieval civic life standing for the five great points of fellowship: charity, citizenship, commerce, comradeship and conviviality. Members sought to maintain a high standard of craftsmanship and honest dealing and that newcomers should be well trained and capable workmen.

As they increased in wealth and power the Guilds began to organise their crafts and "misteries" so as to form complete monopolies and prevent competition from all outsiders, particularly foreigners who had taken root in London and throve on imports from

Holland and Italy. The "German Steelyard", out of which grew the Hanseatic League, had established itself early on a site now occupied by Cannon Street Station and fought for its existence until it was finally overwhelmed and destroyed.

The early Guilds ruled their crafts with a rod of iron. Masters and Wardens drew up ordinances giving them absolute power over standards of workmanship, wages of journeymen and treatment of apprentices. They petitioned the Crown for Charters giving them legal powers to regulate their trades.

The first of the Guilds were concerned with basic needs – food and clothing, bread and wool. The Weavers are mentioned in 1130 and the Bakers in 1156. The Butchers, Cooks, Clothworkers and Pepperers (later Grocers) followed soon after. By the year 1500, 25 Guilds had Royal Charters and eleven of them – Mercers, Grocers, Drapers, Fishmongers, Goldsmiths, Skinners, Merchant Taylors, Haberdashers, Salters, Ironmongers and Vintners (and a little later the Clothworkers) arranged for themselves the special privilege of being called the "Twelve Great Companies" as, indeed, they are still known.

In the 13th and 14th centuries the behaviour of the Guilds degenerated with stories of armed battles on the London streets mostly concerning the precedence of Companies. In 1340 a battle between apprentices of the Skinners and Fishmongers left many badly injured. The Drapers Company accused the victualers, notably the Fishmongers, of using their monopolistic powers to drive up the price of food.

Despite such setbacks the Companies continued to flourish and even persuaded Edward III that it was they, not the Wards of the City, who should provide the elected members for the Court of Common Council – a system that remained in place for ten years.

The Guilds' early meetings were held in the Master's house or a church to which they were attached. As they grew ever more prosperous they began to erect the beautiful halls that were such a splendid feature of the City until nearly all were destroyed in the Great Fire of 1666. Twenty-three halls were rebuilt but many of them were destroyed or damaged in the air raids of 1941 and 1942.

Edward III with his admiration for the Guilds was the first monarch to become a member of a City Company, the Merchant Taylors. Since his day it has become common for the Sovereign to be enrolled as a Freeman of one or another of them. The present King George VI (wrote Morris in 1948) was a Freeman of several and Princess Elizabeth as she then was took up her Freedom of the Draper's by patrimony, this being one of her father's companies.

An outstanding event in the history of the Livery Companies was their involvement – enforced rather than willing – in the Ulster plantation ordered by James I to combat Catholic uprisings there. Pressured by the king, the Common Council in 1613 decreed the formation of the Honourable the Irish Society to settle what would become County Londonderry with English and Scots. The cost of the plantation would be met by the Companies who, unlike James, saw no profit for themselves in this venture. Reluctantly the Twelve Great Companies plus a few of the lesser ones were driven to participate.[*]

The Companies have always been in the forefront of charitable giving and in the establishment of schools and for hundreds of years provided men and materials for England's defence against foreign invasion. At the time of the Armada they furnished 38 ships fully armed and manned and a force of 10,000 soldiers. They were long regarded by England's sovereigns (and mayors) as a kind of reserve Treasury.

Where there were once a handful of Guilds there are now well over a hundred Companies, including among the latter, the Tax Advisers, Management Consultants, Hackney Carriage Drivers and Firefighters with still more in the pipeline.

Many of the old Companies like the Goldsmiths and the Fishmongers continue the links with their craft or trade. Some, like the Tallow Chandlers have "adopted" their modern successors such as the oil industry.

---

[*] "A Miraculous Survival" C Douglas Woodward

Today the Companies remain an integral part of City governance, as they always have been, in having the right of electing on Midsummer Day the two Sheriffs of the City and, on Michaelmas Day, the Lord Mayor.

*

In a comprehensive and masterly review of "The Rise and Decline of Guilds" Historian Tom Hoffman, in his paper of June 2006, spelled out the history of the guilds from the reign of Henry I to the Municipal Corporation Act when almost all the guilds in England were required to surrender the last remaining areas of control they still exerted over trade and industry (but see also the final paragraphs of the above paper). Hoffman uses the Tilers and Bricklayers Company as a specific example.

* * *

The Stock Exchange

Derek Edward's paper, read to the GHA in April 1996, is something of a requiem to the vanished glories of an institution he held in great esteem and affection and of which he, himself, was a distinguished member.

The paper opens with a picture of the Stock Exchange as it once was in Throgmorton Street, all bustle and activity, scurrying clerks, top-hatted stockbrokers moving between market and their offices, jobbers having left their pitches and heading for refreshment to the Coal Hole, Birch's Bar, Slaters or Lyons. (Brokers dealt on behalf of clients; Jobbers traded only with brokers).

How different today is Throgmorton Street. No market place, no bustle, little romance. It all disappeared in October 1986 with what became known as Big Bang and its deregulation, laments Edwards, but first he goes back much further, 400 years in fact, to "days of adventure and discovery" when the first joint-stock companies were formed in the 16th and 17th centuries.

These were the days of the Muscovy Company "the Mysterie and Companie of Merchant Adventures for the Discoverie of Regions, Dominions, Islands and Places Unknown". It was formed in 1553 and £6,000 was raised to equip and fund three ships that sailed out of Deptford in May. Only one survived, its commander having negotiated a treaty with the Czar, Ivan the Terrible, allowing free trade for English merchants.

It was the funding and issue of shares for the venture which was the basis for future offers of shares by public subscription and the emergence of an organised market of brokers and jobbers. Such business was carried out in the Royal Exchange but brokers were ordered to leave (because of unruly behaviour) and they took themselves off to Jonathan's and Garraway's coffee houses. About this time in the late 17th century financial speculation on an explosive scale led to the bursting of the South Sea Bubble. Clearly a more regulated system of shareholding was required.

The Stock Exchange finally came officially into being in 1773, first at the New Jonathan's in Threadneedle Street and then, in 1802, in purpose-built premises in Bartholomew Lane. They came in time to cope with the vast growth in Britain's industrial development and the raising of capital for railways, canals and every form of commercial activity. In 1853 the Exchange was rebuilt to become one of the City's handsome Victorian buildings, marble-lined and with a galleried trading floor. Membership of the Exchange had grown to 4,000 by the year 1900.

There followed thirty years of dramatic change with the great South African gold rush and a period of speculation with fortunes made and lost, the Great War during which War Loan and Victory Bonds kept the Exchange busy. The boom years of the 1920's hardly interrupted by the General Strike of 1926 and fuelled by the trade in industrial shares and in mining groups of South Africa, Western Australia, Northern Rhodesia and Ceylon.

In 1929 came the Wall Street crash with the start in Britain too of the Great Depression of the 1930's. Within the Stock Exchange, writes Edwards, members continued to trade and interest grew in the more domestic speculation such as in gramophones and records.

The Second World War and its aftermath was seeing a new professionalism taking place, something that became particularly noticeable following the opening by the Queen of a new Stock Exchange in 1973. It was, said Edwards, a much more orderly market place and with rather better systems for dealers to communicate with clients around the world. The dreaded sound of the hammer wielded by the senior waiter that signalled the failure of a member firm was now of the past.

(Derek Edwards who was concerned with the workings of the Stock Exchange did not touch upon the change in its style of architecture: from Victoriana to concrete brutalism – but there, it was all part of the greatly changing scene).

The Christmas of 1974 was a time of bad news, the market having fallen dramatically against a background of high inflation, union confrontation out of control, strikes and conflict. Major companies were said to be on the point of bankruptcy. On the Feast of the Epiphany, 6 January 1975, trading began an upward turn and to help deal with increasing volumes of business an entirely new computerised clearing system, "Talisman" was introduced.

Although a central trading floor remained, many members of the Exchange were now doing business in their own offices. Finally, in 1986, Big Bang saw incorporation of member firms, mergers and acquisitions taking place, the purchase by foreign banks of trading names in existence since the 18th century. The flood gates were open. Great dealing rooms were constructed in the new "banking factories" of the City, their dealers sitting in front of screens dealing through the latest computer systems.

The market closed. Its chambers and traditions disappeared. An era ended on 27 October 1986.

"O tempera, O mores!" was Edwards' final epitaph.

Postcript: There is now a smaller but seemingly successful new Stock Exchange as one of the more elegant constituents of the new Paternoster Square. It remains for another GHA Historian to write about it.

*   *   *

Chartered Accountants in the City

As one would expect from the lips of Brian Jenkins (the current President of the GHA) his address to the Historians in July 1991 (three months before becoming Lord Mayor) was as amusing as it was erudite.

Among the stories he told, poking gentle fun at the profession of which he has been so notable a member was the remark by Mr George Carman QC in Ken Dodd's trial for tax fraud "that comedians are not chartered accountants but sometimes chartered accountants are comedians". And, then again: "I spent many years seeking methods to offset the baleful effects of John Cleese's infamous description in one of his films "Our experts describe you as an appallingly dull fellow, unimaginative, timid, spineless, no sense of humour, drab and awful. And whereas in most professions these would be considered drawbacks, in accountancy they are a positive boon".

But now to business.

The accounting profession, like engineering and surveying, grew with the industrial revolution. Confidence in the proper use of funds was indispensable to the raising of investment capital, and this the accountant increasingly provided. Indeed the work of accounting and audit goes back very much further. In the City the annual appointment of auditors by Mayor, Aldermen and Commonalty is recorded from 1298 and the livery companies invariably had their accounts audited.

It was the huge demand for capital and the growth of joint stock companies, particularly during the age of railway mania, that really led to the growth of accountancy as we understand it. Large amounts of capital and complex procedures clearly required improvement in book-keeping. More companies becoming involved inevitably meant more bankruptcies.

The surge of work led to unscrupulous men believing that all they had to do to become accountants was to put a plate on their door in order to become rich. Clearly there was a need for the more honest practitioners to combine and introduce rules of professional conduct and recognised standards. The first steps to these ends were taken in 1870 when an Institute of Accountants was formed in Moorgate Street.

From the start with its 63 members confined to well-to-do City firms the Institute was exclusive. There was also a competing Society of Accountants admitting members from the provinces. Initially the Institute had sought incorporation by Royal Charter but this move in 1870 was turned down. By 1890 the climate of government opinion had changed and the Institute having merged its interests with other accounting bodies obtained its Royal Charter as the Institute of Chartered Accountants in England and Wales in May that year. Clients were advised to look for the initials of FCA (Fellow) or ACA (Associate) after the name of their accountants.

The Institute's first premises were in Copthall Buildings in Moorgate but soon it saw the need for more imposing quarters. John Belcher who had designed the splendid Mappin & Webb building opposite the Mansion House was commissioned to design Chartered Accountants Hall which opened in 1893 in a handsome building lying between Moorgate and Copthall Avenue and there it remains to this day. Appropriately, Accountants are the only learned profession, Jenkins told Historians, to have their headquarters in the City of London.

Two of the most influential men in the early days of the profession were the founders of what is now the largest firm in the UK – Coopers & Lybrand Deloitte. William Welch Deloitte set up in practice, aged 27, in the City in 1845 when the steel pen was supplanting the quill and letters were still sealed by wafers. William Cooper set up in business in 1854 taking two rooms close by Mansion House.

The vast growth of Britain's commercial activity and investment to all parts of the world in the 19th century was also the catalyst for the spread of accountants to every corner of the globe; where capital went, chartered accountants would follow. Deloitte's set up their first overseas office in New York in 1890 followed by outposts in Buenos Aires and Johannesburg.

The foundations had been well and truly laid for the vast growth of accountancy that would occur in the 20tt and 21st centuries, so much of it driven as ever by the great accountancy firms of the City of London.

*   *   *

A History of the Port of London

If Roman Londinium began as a military encampment it soon became, thanks to its situation on a great tidal river, a place of commerce with ships bringing in oil and wine, pottery and fine cloth, and carrying away vast quantities of corn. For Historian Reginald Philp who read this paper in August 1948 the Port of London's story was really the story of London's river, its "liquid history".

Wharves were there in Roman times both along the open river and inside the creeks draining into the river – later known as the Fleet and Walbrook. A port continued during the years of the Saxons and, says Philp, the coming of St. Augustine in 597 saw a developing wine trade which he perhaps indulgently, ascribes to a growing demand for sacramental purposes. The monk Bede wrote that in the year 604 London was the mart of many nationals coming to it by sea and land.

The trade of the port increased during the 7th and 8th centuries as the Saxons came to realise the value of this ready-made centre for seaborne trade. With the coming of Christianity and the building of a first cathedral dedicated to St. Paul in 604 the river and port were the means to import materials for its construction. This was ever more the case when that first cathedral built mainly of timber was destroyed by fire and a new one of stone was built between 675 and 685.

With the growing popularity of wine by the middle of the 10th century there was a call for new dock facilities and these were provided by a group of merchants from Rouen who settled in Dowgate and built a dock for the unloading of casks of wine from Bordeaux.

Early in London's history the unity of city and port was marked by the name of Portreeve given to its chief citizen – the dignitary to whom with the Bishop, William the Conquerer would address his Charter. Over the centuries the river and its maintenance for shipping was vested in Mayor, Commonalty and Citizens.

The Mayor's central role in this is evidenced by his holding quarterly Courts of Conservancy and in his conducting an annual "view" of his jurisdiction from Staines down to Upnor and Canvey

Island. Philp records that the last of the mayoral barges used for such an expedition was the "Maria Wood" built in 1816 for some £5,000 and sold in 1859 to one of the Aldermen (it is not known for how much).

Not surprisingly one of the Lord Mayor's titles down to the present day is Admiral of the Port of London.

The Roman galleries at the Museum of London show Londinium as having even then a quite advanced system of docks which developed over the centuries but Philp writes that towards the end of the 18th century conditions had become chaotic. With very rich pickings indeed from East and West Indies robbery and pilferage were rife. "Disappearances" in 1797 were put at about £500,000.

So in 1795 a meeting of West India merchants launched their proposal for the first of the great new London docks, the West India, being followed by the East India and many others, the last being St. Katherine's and Surrey Docks on the south side of the river. From the Pool of London by the Tower down to the Isle of Dogs both sides of the River were largely given over to docks.

Philp records that by the 1850's however cut-throat competition among the dock companies had cast a blight over Docklands. A Royal commission recommended that there should be one over-riding authority to take total control. Eventually the private companies were swept away, and a new Port of London Authority created.

Philp expressed his regret that the City Corporation had not itself become the agency for the supervision of Docklands and thus continuing what had been its historic role – and would, indeed, have been a logical development of its existing ownership and control of the food markets. "But like incorporation of the suburbs into the City, such an expansion was beyond the vision of the citizens of those times", he wrote.

*

In August 1960 another Historian, Tom Kingsley Collett, provided a sequel to Philp's 1948 paper. It was a detailed and technical account of the Port of London Authority's oversight and management of the docks from its creation in 1908 to the time of his paper, 1960.

The PLA was a mammoth undertaking as shown by its labour force of 10,000 of which 2,150 were the permanent labourers – the dockers – added to which was the "casual labour" taken on each day when extra hands were required to load or unload ships.

Over this half-century new docks such as the King George V were built and Tilbury was much extended. The vast amount of damage wreaked by war-time bombing had to be repaired or renewed.

Collett reminds us of the magnitude of the docks operation with 550 cranes at work and 140 miles of railway track linking up with the main line services of British Railways.

The years since Collett read his paper to the GHA witnessed the self-inflicted destruction of London's docks by a series of devastating strikes. The loss of the docks as a viable industry has seen the quite astonishing transformation of these once highly-industrialised stretches of London's riverside. Now all is apartment blocks. If any semblance of the docks remains it is warehouses converted to flats and occasional bits of the old docks salvaged to provide decorative features for local residents.

* * *

The Corporation of Trinity House

On the north side of Tower Hill, overlooking the Pool of London, heart of Britain's maritime trade, stands Trinity House, that attractive Georgian-style building which, though blitzed in the Second World War, was faithfully rebuilt to Samuel Wyatt's original design of 1793.

Here is the headquarters of a Guild of great antiquity whose governing members under their Master are responsible for ensuring that the ships of all nations approach Britain's shores and harbours in safety. Trinity House is the authority which supervises the running of lighthouses, lightships, buoys and beacons around our 2,350 miles of coastline.

The author of this very detailed and impressive paper in April 1964, Historian Sir Gilbert Davis, was well-qualified for the task, educated at Dartmouth Royal Naval College and war-time officer in the Royal Navy, before working in the City and a 23-year stint as Common Councilman. Just before he wrote this paper he was Chief of the Admiralty Ferry Crew Association, a body of civilian part-time seamen that grew out of the great rescue operation by the armada of little ships at Dunkirk.

It would appear that in the 17th and 18th centuries there were four guilds of mariners known as Trinity Houses, none in the City itself. They were situated in Deptford, Dover, Hull and Newcastle, all of them places closely associated with the sea and ships. Samuel Pepys records in his "Naval Minutes" that the Hull Trinity House dates from as early as 1354. The first Charter given to "The Corporation of Trinity House of Deptford Strond" by Henry VIII was in 1514. It was this Charter to the Lodesmen (pilots) and mariners of Deptford that brought into being the Guild of Trinity House. But even further back in history, Davis reminds us, the oldest light beacon for the guidance of sailors is that well-preserved tower built by the Romans and still standing at Dover Castle.

Like many livery companies Trinity House has its early roots in religious orders, possibly with the Fraternity founded by Archbishop Langton of which it was written: "Godly disposed men who for the suppression of evil persons bringing ships to destruction by the showing of false beacons, do bind themselves together in the love of Lord Christ, and in the name of the Master and Fellows of Trinity Guild, to succour from the dangers of the sea all who are beset upon the coasts of England, to bind up their wounds and to build and light proper beacons for the guidance of mariners".

Under Henry VIII's Deptford Charter a local man, Sir Thomas Spert, became the first Master of the new Corporation of Trinity House. Later, he was to be Captain of Henry's ship the Great Harry, the beginning of a long relationship between the Royal Navy and Trinity House. The other important connection was with the City Corporation because the Mayor, Aldermen and citizens were conservators of the Thames and Medway and the Corporation's Navigation Committee were in frequent communication with the "Elder Brethren" of Trinity House as the senior members and administrators of the guild were known.

In 1588 the Brotherhood was called upon to assist in the nation's defence against the Armada. The Master arranged the fitting out of thirty merchant ships supplied by the City and the livery companies, an obligation to be repeated over the years as the Navy found itself short of fighting ships.

The Charter of James I in 1604 contains the first actual mention of Elder and Younger Brethren, with an establishment of 31 of the former. Younger Brethren, while they were mariners or closely associated with the sea, had no duties except to vote in the election of Master and Wardens. In this Charter there also comes the compulsory pilotage of shipping in London approach waters. Trinity House already had rights of beaconage, including lighthouses but it would be another 250 years before the Corporation was able to take all lighthouses within its care.

For Cromwell the Corporation with its Royal Charters smacked too much of earlier privilege although ships still had to be guided to safety; Trinity House lost its title and became a kind of government department. The Restoration reinstated the Corporation with a new

Charter from Charles II, his only proviso being that anyone with the slightest whiff of republicanism should not be elected to their ranks.

As in the time of the Armada, Trinity House was again called in to assist when the Dutch invaded by way of the Thames estuary. Blockships were sunk in Gallions Reach to prevent the Dutch attempting to raid London. The Brethren also manned the defences at Gravesend. Later, Gravesend became the largest pilot station in the world with some 200 pilots available for duty.

Pepys wrote in his Diary in June 1667: "Down by water to Deptford, it being Trinity Monday, when the Master is chosen". Eventually, as men of high rank become Masters, the tenure of office grew much longer than just one year.

Pepys became ever more closely involved himself with Trinity House. He was made a Younger Brother in 1662 and an Elder Brother in 1672. The following year he was elected a Warden and a few months later became Master. It all linked with his appointment as Secretary to the Admiralty.

One of his achievements was to persuade King Charles to found a Mathematical School for forty boys at Christ's Hospital. Trinity House was being entrusted with the task of licensing navigators and pilots and clearly a knowledge of mathematics was important for such men. (Later it transpired that the idea of the Mathematics School was that of Lord Mayor Robert Clayton and that it was he who first persuaded Pepys – and the Duke of York – to suggest it to the King).

As the years went by the range of responsibilities of Trinity House grew ever wider. The Elder Brethren found that not only boys had to be given instruction but their teachers as well and also the very Masters serving on ships of the Royal Navy. Trinity House became a teaching and examining body. They found themselves saddled with some curious tasks, one being the selection of British consuls for foreign ports. An Act of Parliament of Queen Anne in 1705 gave Trinity House the right to rebuild Eddystone Lighthouse.

In 1797 the Elder Brethren were charged with quelling the notorious mutiny of the Nore by rebellious sailors. This they achieved by removing all buoys and beacons and destroying all sea-marks. Within a week the mutinous sailors, at risk of grounding and wrecking if they attempted to sail, were forced to capitulate.

In 1803 the Brethren went to war again to counter the threat of French invasion. They commanded and manned ten frigates as a barrier of floating forts. With a total force of 1,200 men and 250 guns, each frigate had two Elder Brethren aboard as commanders. They were called the "Trinity House Royal Artillery Company".

In 1822 an Act of Parliament placed the many privately-owned lighthouses under the ownership of Trinity House, a move that at long last gave the Brethren the unified control over this vital service.

When Davis gave his paper in 1963, administration of Trinity House was in the hands of an Executive Board comprising the Deputy Master and the Elder Brethren, and presiding over them the Master, usually a Royal Prince, at that time the Duke of Gloucester, now Prince Philip, Duke of Edinburgh. The senior Elder Brother in 1964 was Sir Winston Churchill who had been elected to Trinity House in 1913. He would certainly have enjoyed the Elder Brother's rank of Captain and the uniform closely resembling that of the Royal Navy. He wore it on an official visit to France and when asked by the leader of the reception committee as to its provenance, Churchill replied in his impeccable if literal French that it was the uniform of an Elder Brother of the Trinity. The reception committee bowed deeply and their leader was heard to murmur in awed tone "Mon Dieu".

*   *   *

The Old Bailey where once was Newgate

Victor Durand Q.C. was a notable barrister practising in criminal cases, usually for the defence, at the Old Bailey – or to give it its proper title, The Central Criminal Court. So that when in August 1959 as Common Councilman and Historian he presented this paper to the GHA he spoke with considerable authority. But, perhaps finding the Bailey all too familiar he devoted most of his talk to its notorious and dreadful predecessor on this site, Newgate Prison.

Newgate was the principal entrance into the City from the West and as was the custom with city gates it was utilised as a gaol when required. Another gaol was at Ludgate. The necessity for a larger Newgate arose from the rebuilding of St. Paul's in the 12th century when congestion around it made the gaol at Ludgate untenable. "It is a cynical reflection" wrote Durand "that the rebuilding of this House of God indirectly created the terrestrial inferno of Newgate gaol, a repository of so much human suffering and sorrow". The suffering would continue for seven hundred years. Prisoners later transferred from comparatively salubrious Ludgate to Newgate died off so quickly that Ludgate had to be re-opened at least to serve as a prison for debtors.

Medieval Newgate fell to Wat Tyler who released some of its inmates in 1381 and was rebuilt to the wishes of Richard Whittington. Appalled by the conditions there he said when he was Mayor for the fourth time: "Everyone is sovereignly bound to be tender of the lives of men whom God had so dearly redeemed".

His wishes were carried out by his executors led by Town Clerk John Carpenter who obtained the King's licence to demolish Newgate and build a new prison there in the 1420's. Some kind of water supply was provided but to use it the inmates had the keeper's extortionate charges to pay. The weight of a prisoner's chains also depended upon the price he could pay for "easement of irons".

While the Court of Aldermen repeatedly forbade the keeper from charging for such "favours" their orders were generally ignored. The office of keeper was in the gift of the Sheriffs and openly sold in the market. One keeper, a Captain Richardson, bought his office for £3,000. Having parted with so much money a keeper would naturally set about recoupment by extortion from those in his charge.

In 1750 an epidemic of gaol fever carried off the Lord Mayor, an Alderman, an Under-Sheriff, two Judges and some 50 others, all of whom had attended the April Sessions. These took place in the neighbouring Sessions House, forerunner of the Old Bailey, in which Newgate prisoners came for trial. Clearly something had to be done about the disease endemic to the prison.

Whittington's Newgate continued until 1767 when George Dance (creator of the Mansion House) was commissioned to design a more healthy and commodious gaol. It was described in Pevner's City of London volume as architecturally a masterpiece, while Dance's "terrifying rhetoric of incarceration still haunted the imagination". A new Sessions House was also designed by Dance.

Hardly had Dance's Newgate and Sessions House been completed than they were fired by the rampaging Gordon rioters in 1780. Some 300 of the inmates were freed. Dr Johnson came next day to view the scene and described how he saw the rioters plundering the Sessions House with no interference by the authorities whatsoever. "Such is the cowardice of a commercial place" was his verdict.

The year 1784 saw the first public hangings outside Newgate's walls in substitution for the centuries-old site at Tyburn. This change of venue was decided on by the Sheriffs, one reason being that the prisoners inside "would derive a useful lesson of duty and obedience and a strong admonition from the presence of the heavy hand of justice so near the walls". Dr Johnson objected on the grounds that executions were intended to draw spectators and certainly the crowds grew ever larger. In 1807 twenty-eight persons were trampled to death when a large wagon, serving as a grandstand collapsed. Public hangings continued until 1868.

Newgate was demolished in 1902 as was the Sessions House adjoining it and the new Central Criminal Court, the "Old Bailey" was built on the site they had for so long occupied, its great dome surmounted by the statue of Justice holding its scales. Originally there were four court rooms including the well-known Court No. 1, scene of so many famous trials. In 1941, not long before the GHA's foundation, a bomb destroyed part of the building.

Durand, in 1959, had observed that crime was increasing. When the opportunity presented itself in the 1960's the City Corporation built a large extension of fifteen additional courtrooms, the better to ensure that the Central Criminal Court keeps abreast of this continuing increase.

Durand's final paragraph links old and new: "By day the Old Bailey impresses the visitor with its despatch of judicial business. By night when the last prison van has returned to the still overcrowded prison establishments, the Old Bailey leaves one with a feeling that here must still writhe in spirit those thousands who, before our time, just managed to breathe in the dank dark horrible depths below the marble halls now covering the past.

*   *   *

The City of London Police

The two authors who examined the history of City policing – Cyril Lewis with his paper of December 1959 and Wimburn Horlock's of December 1993 – traced it back to the time of the Norman conquest but, more realistically, saw its early foundations in the "Watch and Ward" of medieval days. Its day and night patrols of part-time (and unpaid) watchmen were drawn from householders in the City's 24 (later 25) Wards, all of whom were obliged to take their turn in patrolling the streets of their Ward.

However, it was an enactment of 1737 that really ushered in a form of policing as we recognise it today. While the Ward watchmen still remained, the City now had a body of 68 paid men employed specifically to patrol the streets; man "station houses" at important points such as the Mansion House, London Bridge and Fleet Market' and generally preserve the peace.

In 1784 following the Gordon Riots, this small force was slightly augmented although Horlock said its only legacy to police history was its uniform of top hat, blue frock coat and blue trousers. Lewis was rather more complimentary: "The Act of 1737 with little modification controlled the policing of the City of London for over a century".

At any rate the City's example was viewed favourably by a Parliamentary Committee which in 1812 said: "If it could be successfully initiated in Westminster and its Liberties and other adjacent parishes, considerable benefit might be expected". Lewis believed that it was from this early City force that Sir Robert Peel, the Home Secretary, formed his plan for the creation of one force for the whole of the Metropolis.

Peel's first attempt for a paid force was rejected by hostile public opinion. Largely in English minds there remained a lasting image of the atrocities of the French secret police during the Revolution, wrote Horlock.

"But Peel was no fool and his next draft bill placed the City itself with the rest of London under the control of the proposed

Commissioner, knowing that the Whig opposition, close allies of the City, would regard this as an attack on its privileges. In the wake of the inevitable outcry Peel agreed to drop that part of the measure on condition that the remainder was unopposed". Certainly Peel had no intention of crossing swords with the City.

So it was that in 1829 his "Act for improving the Police in and near the Metropolis" was passed into law. It covered all of London except for the City which retained its own independent stance based on its historic privileges.

It was, however, recognised in Guildhall that the City's existing force, whatever its part in prompting Peel's actions, needed considerable improvement. By 1838 the City had its own strong police force of 500 men.

In 1839 a further attempt was made in Parliament to amalgamate the two forces but a petition from the Court of Common Council to Queen Victoria met with immediate success and the proposed merger was heavily defeated.

There followed a City Corporation Bill in Parliament for the reconstitution of the City Police and for preservation of attendant rights and privileges. The City of London Police Act 1839 established the system which has continued with no fundamental changes until the present.

As with the City Corporation itself the City Police has retained its own separate identity and has to date warded off various attempts to fuse it with the Met (with which it maintains a friendly relationship) during the 19th century, and to abolish it altogether through LCC and GLC times, the last attempt being made by Paul Boateng before he moved from the GLC to Westminster.

It is a tribute to its efficiency – and positive value – that this small force in England's smallest local authority should have survived the mergers and streamlining of the country's police forces from nearly a hundred down to forty-three – and with yet more mergers threatened. Its usefulness was confirmed during the Blair government when its fraud squad was enhanced by making the City Police the lead body nationally in this area of policing.

Wimburn Horlock describes the annual inspections of all police forces by H.M. Inspectors of Constabulary as being no "rubber stamp". The author of this volume remembers being told a few years ago by H.M. Chief Inspector that the annual visitation to the City invariably recorded a standard of excellence.

*   *   *

The Coal Exchange

Unlike the other City institutions described in this section of the book the Coal Exchange is no longer to be seen and admired since it was demolished in 1962 to allow for the widening of unlovely Lower Thames Street. And although Alderman Lionel Denny's paper was read to the GHA in November of that same year its title was not the Coal Exchange but the "Coal Market", his early pages devoted to the long history of London's coal trade.

As Lloyds began in a coffee House and the Stock Exchange at meetings of brokers in the open street, so the coal merchants gathered together in an open space behind the wharves of Billingsgate – the only landing place available for the ships carrying heavy and bulky cargoes such as coal. "Roomland", as the space was called, was where the earliest market in coal was conducted.

With Roomland being used by other traders – not least those selling and buying fish – the coal merchants in order to avoid the crowds moved to adjoining streets and, more particularly, went to the River with two or three Thames lighters fastened together to make shops and warehouses. This practice soon caused congestion on the river and led to its prohibition.

In 1682 the inhabitants of Billingsgate complained that the coal traders had moved their meeting place in Billingsgate to Monument Square. The Court of Aldermen induced the traders to go back to their Billingsgate space which was somewhat improved. But by 1731 the coal dealers were so bothered by fish-women, wheelbarrows, porters and quarrelling coal-heavers that they again moved to Monument Square. Once more Roomland was improved for them but having to meet in the open, with the constant smell of fish around them, the traffic and the bustle and dirt of dockside would never suit the increasingly prosperous merchants of the coal trade.

So in 1761 John Biggin and thirty-four other coal factors and merchants formed themselves into the Coal Factors Society and soon afterwards bought two houses on the north side of Thames Street and built themselves a first Coal Exchange. There was dislike both at Guildhall and in Parliament for the fact that the market was no longer open to everyone, solely for the members of the Coal Factors Society.

Eventually an Act of Parliament in 1803 enabled the City Corporation to purchase the Exchange, the money coming from a duty of 1d per ton of coal landed. A free open and public market for the sale of coal under the control of the City of London was opened in January 1805. Denny noted that the Coal Exchange had thus been in the hands of the Corporation for 157 years when he delivered his GHA paper.

In the mid-1800's, a time when the Corporation was engaging itself in a massive programme of building construction and redevelopment of the City streets, it was decided to build a new and far grander Coal Exchange.

John Bunning, the Corporation's notable architect, was given the project. His plan was in the form of a circular "temple" supported by 32 Columns occupying the whole site between St. Mary at Hill and St. Dunstan's Hill and would have cost £170,000 which, the Corporation's Coal, Corn and Rates Finance Committee found excessive. (Denny says that had it been built it is likely it would not have been necessary to demolish it in 1962 for the widening of Thames Street since it was sited that much further north).

A second scheme costing £44,000 was adopted but as is the way of these things the eventual cost was some £100,000. The new Coal Exchange, completed in 1849 if not quite as splendid as Bunning's first proposal was nevertheless a magnificent addition to the City's Victorian architecture – with "Italianate exterior, all iron and glass within, and domed hall encirculed by richly ornamental galleries" (Pevsner).

The Exchange was badly damaged during the War and first-aid repairs undertaken to keep the building in use. By 1947 and the nationalisation of the coal industry the real business of the Exchange had gone. Where once between 400 and 500 had attended on the floor of the market, now there were less than a dozen. In spite of the lack of business, further repairs were carried out and in October 1950 Lord Mayor Sir Frederick Rowland re-opened the Exchange so that a market could be held there once a month. Its main use was to provide office space for the various organisations concerned with the coal industry. Coal was still Britain's major source of heat and power.

Oddly enough the Corporation had submitted a scheme for rehabilitation at a cost of some £60,000 but ministerial consent was refused because of the proposed road widening of Lower Thames Street which was part of London's post-War planning. From 1958 the Corporation were committed to demolition. Thus began the four-year battle to save the Exchange.

These post-War years were not favourable to conservation projects. The famous Euston Arch had its champion in John Betjeman and still was lost. Once the Corporation had given up there were few champions for perhaps this rather better example of Victoriana. Consideration of architectural merit was raised by the Royal Fine Art Commission who suggested that at least the best parts of the Exchange could be erected elsewhere.

There were suggestions for finding an alternative use and applications were received from the British Theare Museum Association, the Toy Museum and the British Puppet and Model Theatre Guild. It was in fact used for a time by Bernard Miles's Mermaid Theatre Trust and as a training ground for the City's police dogs.

Three alternative road schemes for Lower Thames Street were presented to Parliament, one of them involving the removal of Watermen's Hall – all were turned down.

As 1962 and road widening came closer, attempts at rescue became more desperate – and impractical!

Alderman Denny, probably no great conservationist himself, was right to defend the reputation of the City Corporation in its exercise of patience and restraint. Most of the villainy lay with the Government of the day, the Transport Ministry totally determined on its straight, wide southern route along Thames Street.

There was no City Heritage Society nor Save the City in 1962 – and even when they were there in the 1980's they could not alas save Mappin and Webb from the bulldozer.

*   *   *

Smithfield and Billingsgate Markets

In his paper on the London Food Markets, July 1950, William Bonsor reminded the GHA that they were entirely "retail" in origin with countryfolk bring their produce to the City for housewives to buy.

The most notable was the Stocks Market established in 1282 to provide money for the maintenance of London Bridge. It was sited right at the heart of the City at the junction of Cornhill, Threadneedle Street and Poultry – indeed where the Mansion House stands today. There the citizens could buy meat and fish, fruit and vegetables.

Stalls were leased to the traders, the income going to the Bridge. The Stocks Market, with its filth and stench increasingly offensive to its neighbours, was closed in 1737 – in time for the creation of the new residence for future Lord Mayors.

It is the wholesale markets of Smithfield and Billingsgate, however, that feature among the great institutions of the City, both of them centuries-old but still flourishing today. The fish market felt obliged to vacate its traffic-laden Thames Street site for new quarters in Canary Wharf though its old and splendid building remains as a place for conferences and similar events. The meat market is still there in Smithfield where once was the cattle market and, with its recent outstanding refurbishment, looks set to be there for a long time to come.

*

SMITHFIELD, THE CATTLE MARKET

The first GHA study of Smithfield was presented in May 1984 by Historian Betty Masters who traced its beginnings to the 12th century and the weekly sale there of fine horses on a smooth field outside the Western Wall. There was also a more workaday market for the cows, sheep and pigs required to feed the population and the work-horses needed as beasts of burden. This cattle market would continue in being for nearly 700 years.

The City regarded this open space of "West Smithfield" (to differentiate it from the other Smithfield in the east) as part of its common soil. It claimed pickage – a toll for breaking the ground for the setting up of stalls – and took a strong line against encroachment by any buildings. The City's immemorial title to the market was confirmed by charters of Charles I and Charles II. The market was ever a source of considerable revenue.

The history of Smithfield is rich in so much else, interpolates Betty Masters – the killing there of Wat Tyler at the hands of Mayor William Walworth; a place of further executions where William Wallace, leader of the Scots was hung, drawn and quartered and where in the 16th century, in the name of religion, many men and women, both Catholic and Protestant, were burnt at the stake. Somewhat more agreeably Smithfield was the home of Bartholomew Fair.

There is no evidence of market buildings in the central open space of Smithfield but from the middle of the 16th century there were sheep pens with lofts over them and the pens were paved "at the City's expense, so that cattle owners and buyers might walk there handsomely".

The number of animals driven through the streets to Smithfield was high. In 1790, 104,000 cattle and 750,000 sheep and by 1810 there were 132,000 cattle and 963,000 sheep, many coming long distances. Such long journeys did little to improve the quality of the meat and there was little concern in those days as to the welfare of the beasts. Conditions in the twice-weekly markets, with beasts closely packed together and sometimes delays of several days in their slaughter, would be considered horrific by modern standards, observed Betty Masters.

The driving of such large numbers of beasts not only through the streets of the City but also of surrounding areas including Westminster and Islington caused great nuisance with its consequent filth, noise and congestion. Regulations concerning the driving of cattle and the routes they should take were issued with some frequency by the City authorities, probably to little avail.

In 1850 the market was said to hold at any one time 30,000 sheep, 500 calves, 1,000 pigs and 4,000 cattle. Not surprisingly therefore the

City faced growing demands from the inhabitants for the market's improvement – or better still its removal. The butchers, graziers and buyers also sought improvement and, indeed, its enlargement. The City Corporation had always to bear in mind that its cattle market was a vital source of food supply for its own citizens as well as surrounding districts.

Parliament, after some years of agitation and procrastination, dismissed all thought of "improvement" and legislated for removal. In 1851 the Corporation was given six months to agree that the cattle market be moved from Smithfield. In 1852 a 72-acre site was chosen at Copenhagen Fields in Islington and City Architect Bunstone Bunning commissioned to create the market building. Smithfield was closed in June 1855 and the new Metropolitan Cattle Market opened by the Prince Consort two days later. The total cost was £440,000. It was to remain as a cattle market run by the City Corporation until 1963 when the site was sold to the London County Council for housing.

*

SMITHFIELD CONTINUED

It would be another 25 years before the Smithfield story would be taken up again, and in a rather different style, by Historian Michael Welbank in October 2009.

In fact he returned to the years just before the removal of the cattle market, poking not so gentle fun at the City Corporation who, he said, were rather less concerned with the nuisance aspect of the market than the threat to its annual £1m income from the levy on each beast entering the market. He quotes from a letter in "The Times":

Smithfield for Ever! Long live the Common Council
The Common Council have again stood forward nobly in defence of their own congenial Smithfield. They have treated with a becoming and characteristic disdain, the petitioners of the petitions who have again presumed to petition for some abatement of the sanguinary and

stercoraceous glories of their ancient Smithfield – some mollification of that slaughter loving giant who wieldeth night and day the pole-axe and the knife in the very centre of civilised and intellectual London: who causeth its conduits to be ruddy with the blood of bullocks and sheep and ever changeth the complexion of Old Father Thames himself.

Eventually, as described in the earlier account, the Corporation secured the rights to build at its own expense, run and retain the revenues of any new cattle market outside the City, and so the Caledonian Cattle Market came into being.

With that move accomplished, City Architect Dunstone Bunning turned his hand to designing a Meat Market on the old site. It was Bunning, wrote Welbank, who first saw the opportunities arising from the new Metropolitan Railway and the Chatham and Dover Line coming into Farringdon. He persuaded these two "very reluctant" railway companies to take up the idea of a branch freight line into the new market. Negotiations took ten years but in the end Bunning got acceptance and produced a design for a new meat market sitting over a criss-cross of subterranean railway lines. And then, in 1863, poor Bunning died, not least from overworking on his Smithfield Market project.

Horace Jones was appointed in his place in 1864 and it was an outside firm of architects who were first commissioned to build the new market. But, wrote Welbank, rather mysteriously in 1866 Horace Jones was given the job. He was a man brimming with self-confidence which, in the light of his architectural accomplishments for the City, was entirely justified.

He quickly took up the earlier Bunning designs and developed them into the building we have today. The foundation stone for the new Smithfield was laid in the year of his appointment. The Central Meat Market opened for trade a year later in 1867.

*

BILLINGSGATE

Sam Sheppard, who delivered his paper on the fish market in November 1969, had spent his working life as a trader at Billingsgate and was thoroughly steeped in his subject. He laced his account with anecdotes about the characters and events he recalled there such as the November Fifth when red and green fire and loud bangs came from the curing bay where a pile of herrings were being turned into that one-time delicacy, the bloater; or the wake of an erstwhile colleague when candles around the coffin fell over and ignited the corpse and the fire brigade was summoned.

Like Smithfield, Sheppard told his fellow-historians, Billingsgate originated not as an organised market but as an open space, on a wharf in the case of the fish market. Its main competitor was Queenhithe and both markets had what were known as "roomlands" adjacent to the wharves to accommodate the landing and display of their cargoes of fish. The term "gate" implied a watergate and Sheppard hazarded a guess that before the Norman Conquest there could have been a Saxon owner of this site called Billing or Belling. The fish market is at least as ancient as Smithfield it seems.

At any rate facilities at both Queenhithe and Billingsgate were much improved by the reconstruction of the waterfront and docks where more and bigger ships could tie up. While Queenhithe was originally the chief market for waterborne foodstuff, at Billingsgate in medieval times one could buy a great variety of products – wine, leather, poultry, salt, cheese and butter. There was a corn market there too, in 1300. Fish was just one of the things on sale. But in 1699 it was laid down by statue that Billingsgate should serve as the chief market in the City for fish.

Common Council decreed somewhat earlier that century that a ducking stool should be set up at Billingsgate so that wenches who unlawfully frequented the market could be punished by ducking – a bit of extra fun for the fish traders and their customers if not the girls themselves!

Sam Sheppard entered the family firm at Billingsgate straight from school on Armistice Day 1918 when they found it impossible to recruit a lady assistant to run their office – the surroundings were not particularly attractive. When asked by a Press friend after he had worked in the fish market for fifty years what had been the greatest change, he thought it was the absence of horses. In 1918, and long afterwards, all traffic was horse-drawn.

Postcript: The author of this volume recalls his own experience of the fish market as a member in 1972 of the Billingsgate and Leadenhall Markets Committee as it was then called. In particular I enjoyed the early-morning tours of inspection led by the Clerk and Superintendent, Charles Wiard, a one-time Olympic rowing star. We picked our way through the stalls to admire some of the exotic catch just in from Far Eastern waters alongside the eels and octopi. These visits concluded with breakfast in the Superintendent's office at which the central feature was a Dover sole on the bone spilling over the edges of a very large plate. I had ambitions to become the Committee's Chairman but as a very new Common Councilman I was being over-ambitious!

*   *   *

The City's Bridges

The City owns and maintains four road bridges across the Thames: London Bridge, Tower Bridge – that iconic structure that is best known of them all, Blackfriars and Southwark Bridges. Then there is the recent footbridge (the one that wobbled) linking St. Paul's with the Globe and Tate Modern, built to celebrate the Millennium. GHA Historians have given their attention to London, Tower and Blackfriars bridges but have neglected Southwark. But even Southwark got a mention in a paper devoted to yet another bridge, one that was never built.

*

LONDON BRIDGE

Today's London Bridge is a mere 38 years old, but in origin it is far and away the oldest of them all. While there is no record of a Roman bridge, it is hard to believe that the Romans, great bridge-builders as they were, did not create a crossing into Londinium. But, as Historian Sidney Fox tells us in his paper of October 1951, there certainly is evidence for a Saxon bridge of the 10th century – a woman having been drowned there for witchcraft in 980. A series of wooden structures were built and repeatedly destroyed by fire in Norman times and then, in 1135, Henry I, City merchants and the Church commissioned Peter de Colechurch, the chaplain of St. Mary's, Bermondsey, a priest with engineering capabilities, to build an entirely new and stronger bridge.

His first bridge was of elm, still vulnerable to fire, and after only ten years he proposed rebuilding in stone, a prodigious undertaking, it would be the first stone bridge in Europe since Roman times. Again, City and Crown agreed upon its necessity, but some 30 years would elapse before work began in 1176. This great 19-arch structure was completed in 33 years, its substantial cost leading to complete transfer of ownership and upkeep from the Black Friars of Bermondsey to the

City. In 1201 it was King John who addressed London's first mayor as to completion of the bridge and the erection on it of houses and shops, the rents from which would pay for its upkeep.

Colechurch died in 1205 four years before completion of his great work, its final stages completed under the direction of Mayor Serlo le Mercer. Into this first true London bridge Colechurch had introduced as a central feature a chapel dedicated to the martyred Thomas à Becket. The road to his shrine in Canterbury Cathedral began on the bridge and it was in the chapel that pilgrims stopped to pray at the start of their journey.

With many repairs, partial rebuildings and widenings, Colechurch's London Bridge would endure for more than 600 years as one of the great sights of Europe.

Fox, in his paper, told of its extraordinary history, the pageantry associated with it, the welcomes afforded to many of England's monarchs on their arrival at Southwark to assume the throne or fresh from victories in France. It was there they would be greeted by Mayor, Aldermen and the Guilds in all their finery, banners waving, to be led in triumph across the bridge and through cheering City streets.

There were less welcome arrivals of rebels bent on doing mischief to Crown and City whose heads would be impaled on the gates at the northern end of the bridge.

Attached to its chapel was the Bridge House which administered all the money raised by the bridge from tolls, levies and benefactions. The bridge was held in high regard and over the years received gifts of land and properties. As early as the 13th century it acquired lands in St. George's Fields, Southwark, formerly held by the Prior of Bermondsey and grants of meadows and mills in Stratford and Peckham. From the 14th century to recent times the Bridge House Trust was increasingly in possession of great wealth from many sources, not least properties it owned within the City. From time to time the Bridge House Fund provided help for worthy causes in need of financial help – St. Bartholomew's Hospital was one. In particular, after the Great Fire the City Corporation was able to borrow £16,000 to help restore its public buildings. For some 300 years the Trust provided "benevolences" to Lord Mayors and Sheriffs towards the cost of the Lord Mayor's Banquet.

In 1951 when Sidney Fox wrote his paper he could say that the Bridge House Estates were still intact and meeting their primary charges of maintaining the four bridges. Recently, however, the City Corporation decided, in view of the almost embarrassingly large income enjoyed by Bridge House, to establish in its place a new City Bridge Trust administered by the Corporation as trustees of a wholly charitable foundation which has become London's largest grant-giving body.

*

There are postscripts to this main strand of the history of London Bridge.

First when Colechurch's famous structure could no longer suffice despite repairs, partial rebuilding and several widenings. In June 1825 the foundation stone was laid for a new bridge designed by architect John Rennie with its five elegant elliptical arches and superstructure of dark granite. That occasion is commemorated by Historian John Bird in his paper of 2007 entitled "A ticket to attend the laying of the first stone of the new London Bridge".

Rennie's bridge spanned the Thames for 136 years from 1831 until it could no longer be sufficiently widened or strengthened to meet the ever-increasing volume and weight of traffic.

A third London Bridge designed by Horace King the City Engineer (alas an office like that of City Architect that no longer exists). It was almost double the width of Rennie's bridge and beautiful in its own way if rather more utilitarian in appearance.

But the story of Rennie's bridge was by no means at an end. For Common Councilman Ivan Lucking, London Bridge was the embodiment of the history of London and the thought of it being demolished was not to be borne. He had the quite brilliant idea of selling it and, with his own long experience of American business, where better to find a purchaser than in the United States.

Against all the odds and in the face of City scepticism Luckin did find a buyer – Robert McCulloch, Chairman of the McCulloch Oil Corporation of Los Angeles. He was in the process of creating in the Arizona desert a new residential city and tourist attraction. He saw London Bridge as a wonderful central feature and promptly had a river diverted over which London Bridge could extend in all its glory. When the author of this volume made the very last of the City's annual inspections of the bridge in 1995 he found that London Bridge at Lake Havasu City was much more clean and sparkling in that crystal-clear and dry Arizona air than it had ever been across the Thames.

"Ivan Luckin and the sale of London Bridge" was read to the GHA in June 2008 by Historian Archie Galloway.

*

BLACKFRIARS BRIDGE

Until the 1750's old London Bridge provided the only crossing of the Thames. Then in a rush came Westminster, Battersea, Kew and Richmond bridges. In 1753 Common Council resolved, by the narrowest of margins, "that the building of a bridge between London Bridge and Westminster Bridge would be of great advantage to the landholders, owners of houses and traders in the City and of general utility and convenience to others". Blackfriars was the chosen area, the bridge going from the end of Fleet Ditch to the opposite Surrey shore, its estimated cost £185,000. Cynics said it would be worth all the money if only to rid Blackfriars of its bawdy houses, pawnbrokers, gin shops, strolling prostitutes, thieves and beggars.

The City was not particularly well-off at this time, having just built the Mansion House, repaired the Royal Exchange, being about to remove all the City Gates and, having taken away the houses on London Bridge, lost the lucrative rents thereof. The City was therefore empowered by Parliament to borrow up to £160,000, the loan to be repaid by future tolls: 2s for a coach drawn by six horses, 1s 6d for coaches drawn by four horses, 1s for wagons and carts, 1d for horses, mules and asses and 1d for each foot passenger.

The dignity of the City required the new bridge to be of stone not wood, the greater expense to be met by floating an additional loan of £144,000 on the City's bond. Fines on aldermen refusing to serve the office of sheriff produced another £19,000 for the bridge.

Lord Mayor Sir Thomas Chitty laid the first stone of Blackfriars Bridge in October 1760 (it was originally to be named after the great statesman of the day, William Pitt, but by the time it was completed Pitt had fallen from favour). The bridge was opened for foot passengers in 1766 and fully opened for vehicles three years later. There were problems resulting from the economy with which the project was carried out, the cost being £261,000 compared with the £400,000 spent on Westminster Bridge. In 1780 the toll houses at either end were burnt by the Gordon rioters.

The architect, Robert Mylne, felt great affection for his bridge and built himself a handsome residence on the site of what would become Blackfriars Station. Magnificent views of St. Paul's were ruined by the ugly railway bridge built alongside it and the beauty of the bridge itself not enhanced by extensive repairs that became necessary in 1833.

Eventually with the stonework in a most dilapidated state and the offensive sight and smell from animal carcases and putrid vegetable matter discharged from the Fleet Ditch beneath it, the bridge was rebuilt by James Cubitt between 1864 and 1869 at a cost of another £400,000.

The bridge, together with that other great improvement, Holborn Viaduct, was opened by Queen Victoria in November 1869. It remains there today, the oldest of the City's bridges across the Thames.

This paper was one of those written by Philip Jones, Deputy Keeper of the Records and was read to the GHA in March 1954.

*

TOWER BRIDGE

It was Historian David Clackson who recounted the story of Tower Bridge in his paper of April 1980.

Even by the mid-1850's traffic over London Bridge, Blackfriars Bridge and the privately-owned Southwark Bridge (of which more in the next section of this chapter) had increased to such an extent that another crossing, to the east of London Bridge was required, By 1875 the call for either a bridge or a tunnel had become urgent and a variety of schemes were being considered in Common Council. All this was at a time when London was saddled with a Metropolitan Board of Works which came up with its own scheme for a bridge and sponsored by them in a Bill to Parliament. It was opposed by both the City Corporation and the Thames Conservancy Board as restricting most of the river traffic coming into the Pool of London.

It was at this point, in 1878, that City Architect Horace Jones concentrated on the design of a low-level bridge on the bascule principle with a centre span of three hundred feet bridged by hinged platforms to be raised by steam or hydraulic power. It would provide a wider and unobstructed passage for shipping compared with a swing bridge coupled with ease and speed of working. Architecturally he said, somewhat modestly, it would produce "a picturesque effect". So was born the design for London's greatest landmark after St. Paul's, the most astonishing bridge the world had ever seen: Tower Bridge. Alas, that design was at first rejected by Common Council.

In 1884, however, the scheme for a bascule bridge came back to Common Council and with the admirable expedition that could occur in Victorian days, Common Council agreed to proceed, the Remembrancer was instructed to promote a bill to Parliament, the bill went rapidly through all its stages to receive Royal Assent in August 1885 and in September Common Council authorised work to start. City Engineer Horace Jones and John Wolfe Barry, the eminent engineer, began work in April 1886, their design basically the same as the one rejected eight years earlier. The main difference was that provision was made for pedestrians on a high-level walkway reached by lifts.

The foundation stone was laid by the Prince of Wales in June 1886 and opened by him in June 1894 to thunderous cheers from the enormous crowds assembled there and the roar of guns at the Tower.

Tower Bridge, ever one of London's greatest sights, thanks to a proposal by Ivan Luckin (the man who sold London Bridge) has also become one of its great tourist attractions, with its own exhibition and its upper walkway a magnet for many thousands of visitors throughout the year and a place for quite spectacular receptions.

In 1994 the author of this volume and his wife were among those privileged to meet another Prince of Wales at the celebration of the 100th anniversary of Tower Bridge and to continue those celebrations in the Royal Yacht "Britannia" sailing on the River below.

*

AND A BRIDGE THAT NEVER WAS

Before the building of Tower Bridge was being discussed, another proposal to ease traffic congestion across the Thames was put forward in 1852. It was for a road bridge in the area of St. Paul's which would have the added benefit of opening a new vista to Wren's masterpiece. The City Engineer's comment was that if the comparatively underused Southwark Bridge could be given more use it might supercede the necessity of the proposed project.

Southwark Bridge had been built in 1811 as a private venture charging tolls for its use but had never provided sufficient easing of congestion. In the 1860's, after protracted negotiations, the City Corporation purchased the Bridge which was then freed of tolls. But the siting of the approach roads and their steep gradients kept traffic away. At the turn of the century a traffic census shows London Bridge and Blackfriars Bridge each taking 19,000 vehicles a day, Tower Bridge (which had to be opened for ships) 14-15,000 and Southward only 4,000.

Historian Colin Dyer whose paper this was, in May 1983 remarked that this "unsatisfactory bridge" seems to have been used as a sort of red herring whenever the question of an additional bridge was mooted. A Royal Commission said "in no district of London is congestion greater or relief more urgently needed" than the City. Nothing happened and the years dragged on. At last, in 1909 – 57 years after it had first been proposed – the Bridge House Estates Committee recommended that a new 80 feet wide bridge should be sited between Southwark and Blackfriars Bridges (and, that Southwark Bridge should be reconstructed).

By this time the Bridge House Trust was vastly in debt having had to borrow substantial sums for building Tower Bridge and widening Blackfriars and one critic said the Committee must be obsessed on spending money to contemplate any further expenditure. But debates in Common Council continued (at great length), a new bridge was favoured and the Royal Institute of British Architects was consulted. That body said that for aesthetic and architectural reasons the bridge should come out opposite the south door of the central transept of the Cathedral – exactly as suggested in 1852.

Again, there were problems, the Committee feeling that the bridge would thus come to a dead end in St. Paul's Churchyard. They also received representations from neighbouring Wards asking that a swimming bath should be incorporated in any scheme for the new bridge. While the new trams were already crossing other bridges (a tram route was proposed for Blackfriars Bridge) the City did not envisage trams going over the new bridge.

By the time the scheme was presented in a Bill to Parliament there were twenty-one petitions presented against it. The Dean and Chapter were concerned that works so near the Cathedral might harm the structure. But in August 1911 the bill passed all its stages to become the City of London (Bridges) Act. It took into account many of the objections that had been made including the wish of the London County Council that the St. Paul's Bridge should indeed carry trams which, upon reaching its north end would go underground to a terminus under Cheapside. Who was to pay for the terminus remained a problem unsolved.

114

Following past form work to improve Southwark Bridge came first, this being completed in November 1913. The Bridge House Committee then announced an architectural competition to decide who would design St. Paul's Bridge. The winner was George Washington Browne and the fact that the runner-up was no less than Charles E. Barry indicates the quality that might have been. Although war had broken out that summer of 1914, in December Browne and Barry were appointed joint architects. But war stopped further progress.

By 1921 the work on Southwark Bridge was completed and it re-opened in June. Although there was a new Act of Parliament for the St. Paul's Bridge (on which a large sum had already been spent in compulsory purchase of land and buildings) and there was such enthusiastic support for the project, bureaucracy won the day so that in 1926 anther Royal Commission would recommend that the bridge should be abandoned in favour of an astonishingly mad scheme for a high-level bridge stretching from Southwark to Holborn Viaduct! Not surprisingly Bridge House Estates ruled the mad bridge and other wild ideas as quite impractical.

It was Mr Hore Belisha (of the beacons) who read the obsequies in 1934 – discussions were even then still going on:

"Had the St. Paul's Bridge been built when the statutory powers were in force a most desirable traffic artery would have been provided. Under the altered circumstances, however, the Ministry see no prospect of a revised or modified proposal meeting with Parliamentary or public favour".

Requiescat in Pace.

*　　*　　*

PART THREE

CITY OF ALL THE VIRTUES: CHURCHES, HOSPITALS AND HEALTH CARE, SCHOOLS AND ENTERTAINMENTS

St Paul's and the City before 1300

Historians of the GHA have researched and read some 25 papers devoted to social aspects of City life across the centuries and they are reviewed in this third section of the GHA history. The Cathedral of St. Paul quite properly takes precedence although, curious to relate, Wren's great masterpiece has not itself been chosen as a major topic.

'The phrase St. Paul's and the City perhaps most often calls to mind aspects of that complex relationship between about 1400 and now, including such topics as Londoners' devotion to the site, its role as a symbol of their own and the nation's identity (especially during the Second World War), the link between cathedral and the City's fraternities and guilds, civil ceremonial and the highly-charged sermons at St. Paul's Cross'.

Thus did the esteemed Professor Derek Keene open his paper of 2005 on what he called the equally interesting, but less well-recorded, earlier centuries in which the cathedral helped shape the identity and institutions of London.

In 604 Ethelbert, King of Kent based in Canterbury where the archbishopric was established, founded St. Paul's as a cathedral to serve the East Saxons of whom he was overlord. Keene believes it was within the footprint of present-day St. Paul's and that a royal palace lay just to the north. He points out that it was not until Edward the Confessor's rebuilding of Westminster Abbey as a burial church in the late 11th century that the palace was moved outside the city walls.

Well into the 12th century bishops had an important role as representatives of the king in the governance of cities. It was one of the traditional attributes of a good bishop that he should look after the material as well as the spiritual interests of the citizens. At the time of the Conquest it was Bishop William to whom King William's charter was addressed. Londoners came to believe that the bishop had been instrumental in negotiating a good settlement between the Conqueror and the City, his tomb in St. Paul's becoming the destination of annual pilgrimage.

St. Paul's was the focal point of London, its open space between cathedral and palace being a place for assemblies of Londoners in the presence of the king and sometimes to elect a new king. Here, at the site of the folkmoot, was St. Paul's Cross and the neighbouring belfry which summoned citizens to its meetings. In 1216, when it was clear that the promises of Magna Carta were not being properly fulfilled, sermons were preached there urging the citizens to oppose King John.

Cathedral and bishop were involved in the foundation of many of London's parish churches with the result that the City had a very large number of priests and clerks. To provide them with support and regulation Bishop Gilbert, around 1130, founded a fraternity of London priests. As the parishes grew stronger they began to serve as useful subdivisions of the much larger wards into which the City was divided.

St. Paul's also interacted with the commercial life of the City. The cathedral promoted trade with its bringing in of produce from its estates to sell and buying in return goods made in London. By the later Middle Ages the nave of St. Paul's was a place for trade of all kinds not least where the advice of lawyers could be purchased. The cathedral was associated, too, with the production of coinage and its regulation, a number of the canons working as moneyers. Keene believes it was this association with production of coin that brought the City's goldsmiths to set up in nearby Cheapside.

On a loftier note Keene tells us that a particular feature of this cathedral, unlike others, was the powerful sense of presence there of its patron saint. Also unusual was the way in which the citizens regarded St. Paul as their patron and were content that bishop and clergy should act as their leaders in the 11th and 12th centuries. The magnificent seal of 1220 depicts St. Paul with a sword, stern protector of the City. The obverse shows the citizens under the protection of another saint, St. Thomas, a Londoner born in Cheapside who had been murdered in his cathedral at Canterbury fifty years earlier. His parents' tomb in St. Paul's would, too, become a place of veneration.

During the 13th century it was the cathedral's processional ceremonies that had the greatest impact on the life of the City and its inhabitants. Outstanding of these events were the processions of Whitsun when the clergy of London, Middlesex and Essex assembled on successive days at some distance from the cathedral and then processed through the streets of the City to great services there. The clerics were accompanied by their parishioners, these gatherings numbering tens of thousands. In due course the processions acquired a civic component – Mayor, Sheriffs and Aldermen.

St. Paul's became the destination for other kinds of procession: assemblies to elect a king, to welcome a king back from the wars or a royal bride. In such ways the cathedral almost from the date of its foundation articulated the public spaces of ceremonial display in the City, above all in Cheapside. The citizens and, still more the mayor and aldermen at Guildhall, could thus express their role as the embodiment of the chief city and capital of the realm.

*　*　*

St. Paul's Cross

St. Paul's has dominated the City from the summit of Ludgate Hill for over thirteen centuries. Its lofty and stately structure has served as a rallying point for both religious and secular purposes. What more natural than that the citizens should assemble close by the cathedral at their folkmoots and on other public occasions – to receive commands, to rejoice or weep, to protest or just to stare and wonder. Thus Philip Jones opened his paper on St. Paul's Cross in January 1949. It was a good topic, deserving of such early GHA attention.

Originally a stone cross standing on a rostrum of stone steps (date unknown) it was replaced after storm damage in 1450 as a pulpit cross of timber mounted on stone steps.

This preaching cross beneath the shadow of the cathedral has, through the centuries, witnessed the leave-taking of kings en route to wars in France, the reading of proclamations and papal bulls, the public penance of heretics and sorcerers and the preaching of famous sermons.

As the meeting place of the folkmoot it is mentioned in January 1242 when Henry III met the assembled citizens to "ask their leave" to pass over the sea to Gascony. Relations between king and citizens were not of the best (royal financial demands on London were ever fierce) and in 1262 a wary Henry demanded oaths of allegiance there from Mayor Thomas Fitzthomas.

St. Paul's Cross was the place for all manner of proclamations – the announcement of the king's nominee for the office of sheriff; military victories across the seas, royal marriages and births, all proclaimed to the citizens summoned there by the great bell of St. Paul's. It was also a place for public degradation with traitors and heretics cursed by the Dean of St. Paul's with bell, book and candle. Lady Markham appeared there clad in a white sheet of penance in 1617 for marrying one of her servants during her husband's lifetime.

Political sermons preached by clerics were not uncommon. Dr. Shaw's famous sermon preached at the Cross in 1483 on the theme that Edward IV and his sons (the princes in the Tower) were all bastards, paved the way to the throne for Richard III.

Mayor and aldermen attended sermons and other events at the Cross from the early 15th century and for their comfort against the weather an awning was erected to shield them from the rain, and rushes flowers and perfumes were provided to protect them from the smells. The aldermens' ladies were lodged in a little house built beside the Cross.

The end for St. Paul's Cross came in 1643 by order of the Long Parliament of that year. Philip Jones in his paper says it "could have been" rebuilt in 1907 since a King's Counsel, H.C. Richards, bequested £5,000 for its restoration – or if that were impracticable for a memorial. The Dean of St. Paul's opposed the suggestion of restoration and so it was that the present memorial was erected. Its inscription reads:

"On this spot of ground stood of old 'Paul's Cross' whereat amid such scenes of good and evil as make up human affairs the conscience of church and nation through five centuries found public utterance. The first record of it is in 1191 and it was rebuilt by Bishop Kemp in 1449 and was finally removed by order of the Long Parliament in 1643. This cross was re-erected in its present form under the will of H.C. Richards to recall and to renew the ancient memories".

*　　*　　*

The Churches of the City of London

This paper of Sir Frederick Tidbury-Beer was actually entitled "Notes on some of the Guild Churches" of which he dealt in detail with just half-a-dozen. So, with apologies to Sir Frederick, this review looks at his introductory survey of all the City's parish churches as they were in December 1952 when he read his paper.

London was ever a city of churches and as far back as the latter half of the 12th century there were, according to the chronicler Fitzstephen, 126 parish and 13 conventual churches spread across the City. Tidbury-Beer believes that the large number was to some extent made up of household oratories belonging to the nobility, their properties of several acres eventually becoming parishes.

At the close of the 16th century Stow records 123 churches of which 106 were within the walled City. The Fire of London destroyed 87 of them, 35 of which were not replaced. Wren, in addition to St. Paul's, rebuilt 49 of the City churches as well as St. Clement Danes in the Strand and St. James's in Piccadilly.

By the beginning of the 19th century the total number of churches had been reduced to 70, the earliest Wren church to be demolished was St. Christopher-le-Stocks in 1781 but the Victorian City, with its massive rebuilding programme, saw 16 more Wren churches and three others destroyed.

In 1939 there remained 47 City churches of which 30 were Wren and no fewer than eight were from before the time of the Great Fire of 1666. Wartime bombing, chiefly during the raids of December 1940, resulted in the destruction of 18 churches, mainly Wren but also three of these ancient pre-Fire buildings. City and Church authorities put in hand, at the earliest possible moment, a most commendable programme of restoration and new building although in 1952, when Tidbury-Beer delivered his paper, much was still at the planning stage.

There were to remain 40 churches in the City, 24 staying as parish churches and 16 becoming "Guild" churches. So of the 47 churches existing in 1939 only seven were not being replaced. Three would disappear – St. Alban, Wood Street (although in a later post-script its tower would be preserved); St. Mildred, Bread Street; and St. Stephen, Coleman Street. St. Augustine, Watling Street was to be incorporated in a new Cathedral Choir School; Christ Church, Newgate would be a diocesan headquarters and assembly hall (in the outcome it would be neither but its tower would be kept as an architect's office and residential apartments, the shell of its nave becoming a beautiful garden); while the fate of St. Swithin, London Stone and St. Anne and St. Agnes in Gresham Street remained undecided. St. Anne and St. Agnes was rebuilt (thanks to an intrepid vergeress who kept it open even when the City Surveyor had served a dangerous notice on it) in accordance with Wren's original plans – "a refreshing red brick interlude in the modern mediocrity of Gresham Street" John Betjeman tells us in a more recent report. St Swithin's was sold off in 1960. One of the Wren churches destroyed in 1940 was St. Mary, Aldermanbury, its stones sent to Fulton, Missouri and rebuilt there as a memorial to Sir Winston Churchill.

Tidbury-Beer's tally of churches emerging from the War was 40 while the current existing total of City churches is, in fact, 38. Those 38 were not always safe. In the early 1970's Alderman Sir Edward Howard, not entirely tongue-in-cheek, thought it would be a good idea to ship some of them, stone-by-stone, to the United States. In 1992 came a more serious threat, from the Church itself. The report of Lord Templeman claimed there were far too many churches in the City and that either new uses would have to be found for them – for example as halls for livery companies – or they would need to be closed down.

There was an immediate rallying round to save all the churches under threat and their eventual reprieve would be announced by a new Bishop of London, Richard Chartres. The new "Friends of the City Churches" has done much to ensure that churches without a Sunday congregation would be open during weekdays for services, music and as places where workers and visitors could find peace, quiet and beauty.

One of the City's smallest and most ancient of churches, St. Ethelburga, Bishopsgate, which had survived the Great Fire and War-time bombing, was destroyed by an IRA bomb in 1993. It has been appropriately rebuilt, using parts of the remaining structure, as a centre for reconciliation.

THE "GUILD" CHURCHES

In 1952, faced with so much of the City in need of rebuilding, repair and restoration, and with a much diminished residential population, it was accepted that not all the City's churches could carry on as once they had been.

Legislation that year allowed churches regarded as redundant and in danger of being closed, to continue in being by providing a weekday ministry. Some of the churches assumed quite new roles such as places for music and discussion groups, or advice centres. Most would continue to provide a religious presence holding regular weekday instead of Sunday services, their congregation drawn from people who work in nearby offices.

The City's 15 Guild churches come under the jurisdiction of the Bishop of London but have to rely for funds on the generosity of the congregation, local business firms, one or more of the livery companies and from visitors.

The Guild churches are as follows:

All Hallows, London Wall	St. Andrew, Holborn
St. Benet, Paul's Wharf	St. Botolph Without, Aldersgate
St. Dunstan-in-the-West	St. Ethelburga, Bishopsgate
St. Katherine Cree	St. Lawrence Jewry
St. Margaret Pattens, Eastcheap	St. Martin Ludgate
St. Mary Abchurch	St. Mary, Aldermary
St. Mary, Woolnoth	St. Michael, Paternoster Royal
St. Nicholas, Cole Abbey	

*   *   *

The Royal Hospitals

With Henry VIII's dissolution of the religious houses, great distress was being suffered by the sick, disabled and helpless poor. There had been four great houses for these unfortunates. St. Helen's was given by the king to the Master of the Jewels as a dwelling house; the others, being laid waste, were: St. Mary of Bethlehem outside the Bishop's Gate, the Priory of St. Bartholomew – although the hospital struggled on when the priory was suppressed; the Hospital of St. Thomas the Apostle in Bermondsey which was then a liberty of the City.

In 1538 with the fear of plague and the presence of a host of destitutes, Lord Mayor Sir Richard Gresham petitioned King Henry that he and his brother Aldermen might be given the governance of the hospitals of St. Mary, St. Bartholomew and St. Thomas for the aid of the poor, sick, blind and aged. The petition also reminded the king that the churches and lands of the Grey, Black and White Friars were vacant and might be put to humanitarian use. Henry's response was unfavourable.

However in 1543 the plague returned and conditions in London grew worse. Just before setting sail for war in France, he issued letters patent establishing a new hospital of <u>ST. BARTHOLOMEW</u>. Soon afterwards he endowed the hospital with property to the yearly value of 500 marks, the City binding itself for the annual payment of a like sum. Four weeks before his death the City was granted the house of the Grey Friars and Christchurch, Newgate, together with the church and property of St. Bartholomew as well as the governance of BETHLEHEM Hospital. Citizens and livery companies were taxed to provide for the maintenance of the poor and sick. The Court of Common Council provided income from the profits of public weigh-houses and fees derived from imports of wine and fish.

By 1552 aldermen and senior councilmen had been appointed governors for the hospitals of St. Bartholomew and ST. THOMAS. Lord Mayor Sir Richard Dobbis caused appeals to be made for the existing hospitals and for a new one to be known as CHRIST'S HOSPITAL for poor, fatherless and helpless children. An appeal to the ailing Edward VI brought his father's hardly ever occupied palace of BRIDEWELL into City ownership as yet another hospital.

So it was at the time of Edward's sisters, first Mary and then Elizabeth, that the City Corporation was in possession of three hospitals for the sick – Bart's, Thomas's and Bethlehem (the latter for the mentally sick); a school, Christ's Hospital; and at Bridewell a workhouse or place of correction for vagrants, and where children could be taught useful trades. Ordinances laid down rules for the election of governors and their duties as well as those of matron and nurses, cooks and porters.

It was always intended that the educational establishments should be complementary. For example, the bread for Christ's Hospital was baked at Bridewell, while some boys came daily from Christ's Hospital to learn trades at Bridewell while younger children from Bridewell went to Christ's for schooling.

The 18th and 19th centuries found the medical hospitals of St. Bartholomew, St. Thomas and Bethlem growing vigorously and including important medical schools. With Thomas Guy founding his own hospital in a wing of St. Thomas's and St. Thomas's itself receiving nearly £300,000 from the railway developers for its site, the two hospitals separated, with the new Guy's staying in Bermondsey and St. Thomas's moving to the Albert Embankment.

Bethlem, which had moved into palatial premises in Moorfields, found in the 1770's that its building was structurally unsound and accommodation was found for its over 200 inmates in a new building at St. George's Fields, Lambeth. In more modern times the building became the Imperial War Museum.

Bridewell Royal Hospital, a mixture of school and house of correction, eventually became a common prison, while the educational side was renamed King Edward's School to be moved in the 1860's to Witley in Surrey.

Christ's Hospital has continued to flourish with the main school being established at Horsham in Sussex with Aldermen and Common Councilmen members of its governing body. The Lord Mayor attends the annual speech day in state and the scholars, boys and girls, provide one of the most popular marching bands in the procession on the day of the Lord Mayor's Show.

The paper on the City's five Royal Hospitals was presented in July 1973 by former Lord Mayor Sir Lionel Denny. He also paid tribute to Thomas Vicary who, as Serjeant-Surgeon to Henry VIII, Edward VI, Queen Mary and Elizabeth I, and the man who brought together the Barbers' and the Surgeons' Livery Companies in 1540, had much to do with the early practice of surgery in the Royal Hospitals.

*   *   *

The Hospital of St. Bartholomew

Of all the Royal Hospitals, the foremost and the one most closely associated with the City was and is St. Bartholomew's. Most appropriately this paper was read at the hospital in March 1987 by one of its notable surgeons, Historian and Alderman John Chalstrey who, when he served as Sheriff, would before his stint at the Old Bailey, perform an urgent operation or two at Barts. He went on to become Lord Mayor in 1995, the only surgeon to serve in that high office – and a very good mayor, too.

So he was able to greet fellow historians with the words "Welcome to the ancient and Royal Hospital of St. Bartholomew". Ancient it certainly was, having existed on this site for 864 years. However, although the Hospital has had a Royal Charter for the last four centuries, its original founder, Rahere, was no king but a king's jester who became a monk.

Rahere, by his intelligence and ready wit, gained entrance to the houses of City merchants, thence to those of the nobility and eventually to the Court of Henry I. Worldly and sinful he went on pilgrimage to Rome, fell ill and was cared for in a monastery dedicated to St. Bartholomew on an island in the River Tiber. He prayed to God for forgiveness of his sins and promised that if he recovered and returned safely to London he would found a hospital for the sick poor of the City of London. In Rome or on his homeward journey a vision of St. Bartholomew told him that his planned foundation should be built in Smithfield and dedicated to the saint.

Rahere took holy orders, becoming an Augustinian monk and King Henry granted him land in Smithfield which was dedicated by the Bishop of London in 1123. Rahere's past popularity and current influence with King, courtiers and City merchants must have been considerable, their support such that the great priory church and adjacent hospital were completed in only six years.

Rahere became the first Prior and spent the remainder of his life at the head of his foundation. He died in 1143 and was buried on the north side of the high altar in the priory church where his tomb may still be seen.

The medieval hospital grew to become an important shelter for the sick poor and foundling children. Gradually it was endowed with much wealth and valuable property, becoming an institution of great social significance. An early benefactor was the wealthy and powerful Henry Fitz-Ailwin, first Mayor of London, appointed in 1189.

Occasionally the quiet routine of the monks, and the sisters who worked in the hospital, was disturbed – no more so than in June 1381 when Wat Tyler and his followers, fresh from their rampage through the City streets, must have terrified the monks, nuns and patients as they streamed past the hospital.

Three days after their first appearance a meeting had been arranged at Smithfield for the rebels to meet the fourteen-year-old Richard II and City dignitaries led by Mayor Sir William Walworth. Here it was that fearing an attack on the King, Walworth's dagger thrust toppled Tyler from his horse and then to be more seriously injured by one of the King's entourage. The wounded rebel leader was carried into the hospital and laid in the chamber of the Master but the Mayor had other ideas for one who had been responsible for many brutal deaths in the City. He ordered Tyler to be dragged out into Smithfield and beheaded.

The monastic status of Barts changed abruptly during the reign of Henry VIII. Following the King's rift with the Church of Rome, all monastic possessions were taken by the Crown, the Priory of St. Bartholomew suppressed and the monks driven out. Many of the buildings were destroyed leaving little more than the chancel which became the parish church we know as St. Bartholomew the Great.

Thanks largely to sustained pressure by Mayor, Aldermen and Commoners, Henry was prevailed upon to sign an agreement granting to the City "The Hospital formerly known as St. Bartholomew and hereafter to be called the House of the Poore in West Smithfield in the suburbs of the City of London, of King Henry VIII's foundation". This long and clumsy title was never used by the public, only in legal documents. But it was not until the National Health Service Act of 1948 that the hospital again officially became St. Bartholomew's.

There had been five chapels in the medieval hospital but only one was retained after the Reformation and this would become the church of St. Bartholomew-the-Less. Because the hospital precinct was and still is a City parish, St Bartholomew-the-Less is a parish church (along with its big neighbour St. Bartholomew-the-Great) with its own vicar who also holds the title of Hospitaller.

When in 1546 Mayor, Aldermen and Commonalty became rulers of the hospital, the four aldermen and eight councilmen who had previously negotiated with the king became its first governors and began to appoint recognised physicians and surgeons, the latter having to be liverymen of the Barber-Surgeons' Company.

Chalstrey tells of two famous Barts physicians. One, Dr Roderigo Lopez, was appointed in 1586 physician to Queen Elizabeth but later accused (falsely probably) of attempting to poison her. At his trial (in Guildhall) evidence was produced that he had received money from King Philip of Spain which, together with his foreign name and a reputation for being skilled in poisons, was enough to find him guilty of treason. He was hanged, drawn and quartered at Tyburn in 1594. Chalstrey observes that to date Lopez is the only member of the hospital staff to have ended his life on the gallows.

A more celebrated physician was William Harvey who discovered the circulation of the blood and in his 35 years of service from 1609, his brilliance as a doctor, researcher and teacher, brought great fame to St. Bartholomew's.

At the end of the 17th century Barts consisted of an irregular collection of buildings inside a maze of alleyways and small squares, the buildings largely of timber, lath and plaster, much of it in disrepair. The governors of that time initiated a programme of rebuilding with the construction of the gatehouse which is there today. It was flanked by tenements which were let to provide the hospital with an income.

Between 1730 and 1769 the noted architect James Gibbs designed four elegant buildings in the classical style. The first was the North Wing containing the Great Hall, its soaring staircase decorated with the famous murals painted by Hogarth who was a governor of the hospital.

The East and West wings though both transformed internally are the buildings of James Gibb. His South Wing was rebuilt in the 1930's to become the King George V Block. During the Second World War there was much air-raid damage with the Medical College buildings largely destroyed. Their reconstruction was only completed in 1980.

*

In June 2001 Sir John Chalstrey presented a second paper on St. Bartholomew's on the subject of the hospital's funding from its earliest times. Its special interest is that it provides an up-dating of the hospital's circumstances from that dire moment in 1992 when the Government of the day was persuaded that London had too many hospital beds and proposed that Barts should be extinguished. With a change of Government in 1997 that decision was reversed with Barts alas ceasing to be a general hospital but becoming a world-class centre for the investigation and treatment of cancer and cardiac problems.

Chalstrey presented this second paper at a GHA meeting at the Mansion House held there at the invitation of the Lord Mayor, Sir David Howard. In his opening words, Sir John said his paper had been inspired by the decision of the Lord Mayor that Barts would be the beneficiary of his charitable appeal that year – a splendid boost for the fundraising programme to support the vast costs entailed in rebuilding the Royal London Hospital at Whitechapel as well as the development of Barts at Smithfield.

* * *

The City's Famous Schools

ST. PAUL's SCHOOL, attached to the cathedral, can lay claim to having the most ancient roots, almost certainly there before the year 650. As Historian and Alderman Sir Alexander Graham said in his paper of February 2001, King's Canterbury dates from AD 600 and St. Peter's York from 627 and St. Paul's would not have been far behind in having a school. William Fitzstephen described St. Paul's in 1174 as the City school par excellence.

However, wrote Graham, a quite new school was founded by John Colet, dean of St. Paul's in 1509 although he did, to begin with, make use of the buildings of the old school in St. Paul's churchyard. The Mercers' Livery Company was directly involved in its foundation, endowment and direction.

The high master and chaplain were chosen by the Mercers, the first high master being William Lily at an annual salary of £34 13s 4d. The school was to number 153 scholars – far and away the largest school in the kingdom, Eton and Winchester each having 75. St. Paul's, unlike other ancient and famous schools, was not for the poor. To enter, scholars had to be able to read and write English and Latin and their families had to provide them with books and wax (not cheap tallow) candles.

Thomas Becket, son of a Mercer, had been a scholar of the old school, now there were many more including one John Clement, a protégé of Thomas More, who would become president of the College of Physicians. The first old Pauline to become a sheriff and then Lord Mayor (1556) was Thomas Offley. Among the school's famous pupils were John Milton, Samuel Pepys, G.K. Chesterton and Viscount Montgomery.

Like the cathedral, the school was destroyed in the great fire of London but was rebuilt even before Mercers' Hall was restored. In the 18th century, as with other great schools, St. Paul's suffered from falling numbers of pupils at a time when the Mercers' Company were experiencing financial problems. However, with a new High Master appointed in 1748, school numbers were back to the statutory 153.

In the middle of the 1800's the Clarendon Commission's inquiry into England's nine great schools was critical of St. Paul's as the only one that did not teach music or drawing. Also its system of nomination of scholars by members of the court of the Mercers' was criticised as being too exclusive. There were other growing problems – the noise from St. Paul's Churchyard and the lack of playing fields.

Eventually, in 1877, a new high master, Frederick William Walker, was responsible for carrying out the recommended move from St. Paul's Churchyard to Hammersmith where the school was able to expand to 600 boys. The handsome new building was designed by Alfred Waterhouse, an old Pauline. St. Paul's girl's school was founded in 1904. In 1968 with the old buildings no longer adequate, St. Paul's moved to a riverside site at Barnes.

As it approaches its 500th anniversary the school, so long a great City institution, has for 134 of those years not been in the City but clearly from Sir Alexander Graham's account of its history the warmth of its relationship with the City – not least through the Mercers – remains very much alive.

THE CITY OF LONDON SCHOOL, accepting that St. Paul's was truly founded in 1509, is oldest of the great City schools by more than 60 years and where St. Paul's is long gone from the City is still very much present as one of the City's great institutions. Its history was recounted by David Clackson in May 1961.

When perhaps the most famous of Town Clerks, John Carpenter, died in 1442 he left a bequest that four children at a time should be educated and maintained in perpetuity. Stow put it more exactly: "He gave tenements to the City for the finding and bringing up of four poor men's children with meat, drink, apparel, learning at the schools, universities, etc. until they be preferred, and then others in their place for ever". They were to be called "Carpenters' Children".

This was the beneficent, if modest, origin of the City of London School which, as such, was actually founded in the early part of the 19th century.

In 1827 the Court of Common Council had before them a recommendation that the current four boys who were to benefit should be sent to Tonbridge School in Kent. But one of the Councilmen argued instead for the foundation of a day school in the City so that a greater number of children could benefit from the charity money. With the backing of the Chairman of the City Lands Committee, later Lord Mayor Warren Hale, the City of London School became a reality in 1837. Hale was the first Chairman of the School Committee, an office he held for 33 years.

From the start its curriculum was liberal and progressive, its headmasters chosen by a panel of eminent professors, with the school quickly making its name at the universities and by the 1850's having established itself, particularly at Cambridge, as an educational force.

The "Illustrated London News" had a picture of the prize giving day ceremony in 1843 recording that school instruction included the English, Latin, Greek, Hebrew, French and German languages, besides book-keeping, geography, mathematics and history. Its liberal curriculum was matched in its admission policy being open to dissenters of every shade, Protestant and Catholic, Jew and Gentile – something of an unusual policy in early Victorian days.

The original school buildings were in Milk Street but by the 1880's were no longer adequate and the school moved in 1883 to the splendid Victorian building on the Thames Embankment that it would occupy for the next hundred years.

The school, wrote Clackson, was fortunate in the number and variety of scholarships and benefactions with which it was endowed. The most revered of benefactors was Henry Beaufoy whose generosity was marked by the governors with a holiday on his birthday, April 23, a date he shared with Shakespeare. Touched by this gesture Beaufoy presented the school with another £1,000 for prizes to encourage the study of Shakespeare. The City of London School was among the first to teach English Literature comprehensively as part of its curriculum.

Inevitably, over the years, there has been debate as to whether a bustling and traffic-laden city is the right place for a school. Clackson quotes a famous "Old Citizen", Lord Oxford and Asquith on the subject: "Instead of those spacious surroundings under which the life of most public schools is carried on, we spend our days within the sound of traffic of Cheapside... years ago when Manchester Grammar School and the City of London School were winning scholarships at Oxford and Cambridge and leaving the old foundations far behind, an explanation for this phenomenon was that town-bred and town-educated boys brought into everyday contact with the sights and sounds and life of a great city mixed knowledge with actuality and reality".

Playing fields would become a necessity and grounds at Beckenham, Catford and finally at Grove Park, provided for the sporting activities of the school's 850 pupils.

When David Clackson presented his paper he was applauding the fact that talk of moving the school to another part of the City had been shelved. However, when the large area between Fleet Street (its newspapers all gone) and the River was increasingly sought after by banks, dealing houses and other financial institutions, the temptation for Guildhall to capitalise on that valuable site was too great. The façade and part of the space immediately behind it remain as a reminder of the school's Victorian grandeur.

The City of London School was reborn in Blackfriars, still on the riverside, in a handsome enough modern building designed by the last of the City Architects, Stuart Murphy, and of course its facilities are far beyond what was possible in a Victorian building, however splendid.

*

Historian Alex Coulson in July 1972 provided the GHA with some fascinating byways of City history with his paper on Early Benefactions to the school.

When the boys attended their first assembly in the new building in January 1883, that morning the school governors brought with them

Sir Polydore de Keyser, owner of the Royal Hotel which adjoined the school premises, and destined to become Lord Mayor in four years' time – the first Roman Catholic to hold that office since the Reformation. Anxious to establish good relations with his new neighbours he arranged for a cartful of apples and oranges to be emptied in the playground at the noon break. The building in Milk Street from which they had come had no such thing as a playground, let alone one with apples and oranges in it. And imagine, a grand hotel on the Embankment at that time. Even more of a City celebration it was Sir Polydore's hotel that in 1914 was the venue for the inaugural meeting of that venerable institution, the City Livery Club.

Both the City and the school had, since the 1830's, been far more liberal in their attitude towards Jews than most of England's governing class. Two of them, David Salomons who became the first Jewish Lord Mayor in 1855 and Baron Lionel de Rothschild who in 1859 was finally permitted to take his seat in the House of Commons as one of four Members of Parliament representing the City of London.

Salomons founded a scholarship at the school for pupils going on to Oxford, Cambridge and London Universities. Rothschild gave £2,000 to found a scholarship to be awarded on 26 July each year to mark the day he took his seat on the Commons.

Strange to relate the other two famous City schools, the City of London School for Girls and the celebrated conservatoire, the Guildhall School of Music and Drama, have yet to find GHA Historians to recount their origins and highly successful progress.

CITY OF LONDON FREEMEN'S SCHOOL came into being in 1854 as an Orphans' School to care for and educate the children of a Freeman who had died. Indeed, from time immemorial, the guardianship of the orphans of Freemen had devolved by "the custom of London" on the Mayor and Aldermen. The establishment of an Orphans School in the mid-1800s was merely a modern manifestation of an ancient City custom. Thus wrote Historian Gervase Wood in his paper to the GHA in June 1947.

The origins of the Orphans' School were of a harsher nature – the London Workhouse created by Act of Parliament in 1662. Here vagrant and parish children could benefit from "a pattern of that happy mixture of industry with instruction so much to be desired in all nurseries set apart for the children of the poor" – the words from an all-too-self-satisfied report of the times.

Early in the 19th century, with the London Workhouse becoming redundant, its properties and endowments could be sold off and the proceeds put to better use. In 1829 an appeal was made to the Court of Common Council to add to the income from the workhouse funds and to set aside the money for the education of sons of poor Freemen. The wheels turned exceeding slow and it was not until 1854, largely due to the efforts of Councilman Warren Stormes Hale (who had already established the City of London School) that the Freemen's Orphan School was opened – not in the City, but at Brixton.

There, it carried on for the next sixty years with some 70 boys and, later, with the addition of 60 girls. In 1926 when the school was moved from Brixton to Ashtead Park in Surrey the Governors, supported by the Board of Education, believed it would be to the advantage of the orphan scholars to be mixed with children coming from more fortunate homes. Hence the beginning of accepting fee-paying boys and girls both as day pupils and boarders. At the time Gervaise Wood read his paper there were 190 pupils – 145 paying school fees and 45 Foundation scholars. Whether Foundationers or fee-payers, all the children are sons or daughters of City Freemen and it is a nice touch that the proceeds from all the fees paid by those gaining the Freedom of the City by redemption go towards the cost of running the City of London Freemen's School. The school is otherwise financed from the City's cash.

THE SIR JOHN CASS FOUNDATION is the last of the City's schools to have had a GHA paper devoted to it, a primary school close to Aldgate with a 300-year-old history. So who was Sir John Cass, and why did he establish a school in Portsoken all those years ago, these were the questions posed by Historian Geoffrey Lawson and answered in his paper of March 1999.

John Cass was born in Rosemarie Lane (now Royal Mint Street) in February 1661, the son of a carpenter who would become Master of the Carpenters' Livery Company, a prosperous contractor and supplier to the Navy. After William of Orange acceded to the throne in 1688, the Cass family fortunes waned and both John and his father became much involved in the Tower Hamlets Militia which, for some reason, was closely associated with the Jacobite cause. In 1692 the Stuart Court in exile planned with sympathisers in England to launch an invasion, the Commander of Tower Hamlets Militia promising to raise a regiment of cavalry and two of militia around the Tower of London.

The attempt was doomed from the start, the ringleaders tried for treason and executed while adherents like the Cass father and son, although suspected of complicity, were able to extricate themselves. But their involvement certainly delayed the emergence of John Cass into public life.

It was at the end of the 17th century that fortune began to smile on him with his appointment as Deputy Lord Lieutenant of Tower Hamlets. Over the years he played a prominent part in the political, social and commercial life of London – Member of Parliament, an Alderman and Sheriff of the City, Master of two livery companies, prosperous landowner and businessman.

He was always more concerned with City rather than national politics and successful electioneering in the City in those days required extensive philanthropic activity with the charity school movement a particular favourite with those aspiring to high office. Indeed, charity schools proliferated in London during the second half of the 1600's. In a city packed with people and teeming with children, wrote Lawson, parishes competed with each other in setting up schools, the number reaching 130 with over 5,000 pupils.

So it was natural enough for John Cass to found, fund and build yet another school, this one to serve Portsoken Ward. All he asked was that the parish would contribute £20 a year towards the salary of a master, an offer eagerly accepted. He was given a piece of land south of old St. Botolph Church on the west side of Houndsditch. The project put into effect the terms of a will that Cass had made in 1709 stipulating his intention to build a school "to instruct 50 boys in reading, writing and arithmetic, and 40 girls to write and cast accounts, to read and learn plain sewing."

The school was built in 1709 but Cass's hopes to become the Portsoken Alderman would take another two years and four elections before they were fulfilled.

It was a time of quite bitter strife in national politics between Whigs and Tories. In the City the division between the Court of Aldermen, Whigs to a man, and the Common Council which had a Tory majority. Cass was something of a champion for the Tory cause.

In a first aldermanic election in 1709 Cass won a substantial majority of the votes but his candidature was rejected by the Court of Aldermen.

The Tories' response later that year was to nominate Cass as one of the City's parliamentary candidates and after a turbulent campaign Cass was elected.

The following year Cass fought a second aldermanic election in Portsoken, was elected, but again rejected by the Court of Aldermen. A third election followed soon after with Cass again elected (oddly enough together with a second candidate). The Aldermen, true to form, selected this other man who immediately disqualified himself by admitting he could not raise the £15,000 required to meet the costs of becoming an alderman.

Cass's persistence was finally rewarded in 1711 when in a fourth attempt he was again elected and the Court of Aldermen lacked the courage to bar him yet again, although they had the right after three elections to fill the aldermanic vacancy with their own nominee.

So John Cass was at last the Alderman for the Ward of Portsoken as well as being a Member of Parliament.

The formal opening of his charity school early in 1711 was, in Geoffrey Lawson's words, more than just a lavish ceremony. It was, in effect, a popular demonstration of support in the City for the Tory-Anglican cause. The celebratory service was conducted by the High Anglican and Tory hero Dr. Henry Sacheverell and attended by 60 peers and 40 M.P.'s – a remarkable inauguration for a small charity school on the City's edge. The school was, however, at the heart of Cass's rise to fame and fortune.

He was knighted by Queen Anne in 1712 and prospered as a shareholder and member of the Court of the Royal Africa Company which was primarily concerned with the slave trade. In 1713 Sir John Cass was one of the candidates for Mayor, moving his allegiance to the Skinners' Livery as a more influential company but in the event he failed to secure the Tory nomination.

His career in the House of Commons continued for a while but his final years were devoted to charitable activities and he considered that his charity school would be his most enduring monument.

The Sir John Cass Foundation as set out in his will was finally established in 1748 and has continued ever since, one of the very few survivors among charity schools. In its fine building in Duke's Place facing the church of St. Botolph, Aldgate, it is the only state school in the City of London catering as it always has done for the children coming from less affluent and ethnically mixed homes in the area.

*   *   *

Towards a cleaner, more healthy City

In a city so often visited by the plague, thought was given from earliest times, at least in the most basic of ways, to keeping its streets free of filth.

John Morton's paper for the GHA in March 1947 on <u>THE PUBLIC HEALTH DEPARTMENT OF THE CORPORATION OF LONDON</u> had as its starting point a requirement of 1280 "That each Alderman cause to be elected in Wardmoot four reputable men to keep the pavements from obstructions such as dung in the streets...". The responsibility actually fell on individual householders who all too often failed in their duties. Records of 1309 reveal a sorry state of affairs: "Seeing that the people do cause the ordure collected in their houses to be placed in the streets and lanes of the City whereas they ought to have it carried to the Thames or elsewhere out of the town", an ordinance was passed forbidding such practices.

The Plague of 1665 with its enormous death toll followed by the Great Fire of 1666 resulted in the rebuilding of the City. Part of this process was that the Court of Common Council, in 1668, appointed London's first Commission of Sewers, a body that would continue to function for 230 years, gradually taking on more and more responsibilities to protect the health of the citizens. The Commissioners, at least to begin with, were the Aldermen and deputies (senior councilmen) from each of the City's wards.

An Act of Parliament in 1897 transferred to the Corporation of London all the rights, powers and duties of the Commission which, in its final 50 years, had spent £2,500,000 on street improvements, £200,000 in the erection of artisans' dwellings, and £88,000 on the creation of a cleansing department. It had also acquired land at Ilford for a City of London cemetery so that there could be an end to burials within the City's vastly over-crowded graveyards.

Another major development in health care had come in 1848 with the City's appointment of a <u>MEDICAL OFFICER OF HEALTH</u> – a story recounted to the GHA by George Challis in January 1989.

John Simon, born in the City in 1816, surgeon and pathologist at St. Thomas's Hospital, who was appointed by Common Council (on a part-time basis) worked in the City for seven years. It was said of him that he drained the streets properly for the first time, abolishing the practice of cesspools under houses. Opponents were many and in Common Council they were called the "Filthy Party", their leader nicknamed "Defender of the Filth". One example of his foresight was the acquisition of land in 1853 for a City cemetery in Ilford.

His talents were widely recognised with his later appointment as Medical Officer to the Privy Council.

Sir John Welch's paper in October 1985 on <u>THE SEWERS SERVING THE CITY OF LONDON</u> paints a much broader picture of improvements to London's sewerage problems culminating in Sir Joseph Bazalgette's creation of a London-wide drainage system during the mid-1800's, a system which served the City up to the present time with its vast programme of renewal which is evident in the excavations all around us.

A side-line in Sir John's paper is his account of England's first water closets that came in 1592, brainchild of Sir John Harrington, a godson of Queen Elizabeth I. By the late years of the 19th century the introduction of W.C.'s to the City and elsewhere (Thomas Crapper's name forever associated with the process) represented a great advance in sanitation. But it was Bazalgette's sewers that would eventually rid London of the threats to health from all-too-frequent outbreaks of typhus and cholera.

*   *   *

Bringing a water supply to the City

Was Col. William Dove known by his fellow Historians to enjoy a glass? At any rate he introduced his paper in September 1954 with the words: "Strange as it may seem to members, the subject of my talk today is water".

His address on the "Water Supply of London" suggested there were few problems from Roman times to the 12th century. The Thames, Fleet River, the streams of Walbrook, Lambourne and Sherbourne together with various springs provided an adequate supply. The problems arose as London's population grew. It became necessary to pipe water into the City.

A great conduit, built in 1274 when Henry le Galeys was Mayor, brought water from Tyburn to a large leaden cistern in Westchepe. Other conduits followed, one built by John Walworth, tavern owner in Fleet Street, and when he died he bequested his tavern for the upkeep of the conduit, an expensive process for the lead pipes which carried the water needed constant repair.

Throughout the 15th century numerous conduits were privately built to provide water for different parts of the city but the responsibility for supplying the citizens with water really lay with the City Corporation. In 1439 the Abbot of Westminster granted the Corporation the use of springs in Paddington and this supply was later supplemented from springs in Tyburn and Marylebone. Once a year Lord Mayor, Aldermen and other City dignatories would make a "state visit" of inspection to all three conduit heads combining their visit with some hunting followed by dinner.

In 1582 one Peter Morice introduced a water wheel into the Thames to operate pumps that could deliver water to most parts of the city. A year later the Fishmongers' Company constructed their own pumping engine to convey Thames water to Old Fish Street.

Then in 1606 the Corporation was empowered by Parliament to bring water to London by means of an aqueduct from the springs of Chadwell and Amwell in Hertfordshire but the enormous cost of the project was too much for Guildhall and it was left to a private citizen, Hugh Myddelton, to undertake the task at his own expense on condition that he receive any financial benefits. Work began in 1609 in the teeth of opposition from landowners along the route. In 1611 when the aqueduct was within a few miles of London, Myddelton's money ran out and he appealed to King James I for financial help, the City apparently unwilling to contribute. James agreed to bear half the cost of the work – provided he received half of any future profits.

So it was that the "New River", 38 miles in length from Amwell to New River Head in Islington, was completed and on Michaelmas Day 1613 was officially opened by Lord Mayor Sir James Swynnerton. Also present that day was Hugh Myddelton's brother, Sir Thomas, who would be elected Lord Mayor the following year.

The New River Company was not an immediate financial success, prompting the King to relinquish his half share in return for a perpetual rent charge of £500 a year. It continued to be paid at the time of Dove's paper to the Metropolitan Water Board and now, presumably to Thames Water.

*   *   *

Disposal of the Citizens:
Corporation Cemetery and Crematorium

Tony Moss's paper of February 2005 began with the reminder that in the year of the Great Plague the number of burials was 60,000 with Samuel Pepys much concerned at the 326 in his parish churchyard of St. Olave Hart Street. With destruction of 35 churches destroyed in the Great Fire, and never re-built, burial space was further reduced. The City's ever-rising population made the pressures on burial space a problem of increasing magnitude. Conditions in some City churchyards were deplorable.

By the mid-1850's urgent action was called for. At that time the responsibility for burials lay (as with so many aspects of public health) with the Commissioners of Sewers. The Surveyor to the Commissioners and the Corporation's Medical Officer of Health each reported in 1853 that burials in crowded cities should be abolished. A cemetery had to be created well outside the built-up area. It was estimated that a space of 100 acres would be required to cope with some 64,000 burials over a 20-year cycle.

In the event Common Council agreed to purchase 200 acres of land from Lord Wellesley at Little Ilford in Essex, this larger area helping parishes east of the City which were also short of burial space. The cost was a little over £30,000.

The site was the old Manor of Aldersbrook, its grounds already improved with a lake and hermitage. In 1786 the manor house had been demolished, replaced with a farmhouse, the land given over to farming.

William Haywood, Surveyor to the Commissioners of Sewers, was given responsibility for the layout of the cemetery and some of the more important buildings. Contracts were let in 1854 for enclosing the first 98 acres and at the year's end contracts for the Episcopal and Dissenters' chapels, the entrance archways, porter's lodge and superintendent's house. The contracts for a catacomb (on the site of the drained lake) and the roads were finalised in 1855.

Construction work was completed on schedule but then came ecclesiastical complications. The consecration of the burial areas could not proceed without a financial arrangement with the clergy and the vestries of all 108 parishes of the City on their claims under the Metropolitan Burials Act of 1852. The Bishop of London would not perform the consecration until all these matters were resolved. The delays, said Moss, were quite worthy of Trollope. When the first burials took place in June 1856 they were on unconsecrated ground. The first Church of England burial was in November 1957.

The cemetery quickly proved popular and by 1866 the annual total of burials had reached 7,604, at least half from outside the City.

Towards the end of the 19th century interest was developing in cremation and in 1902 the City's Burial Board proceeded with the construction of a crematorium at the cemetery, the first cremation taking place in March 1905.

Historian Moss concludes his account with praise for the high standards of maintenance of the lawns, gardens and woodland areas. Indeed the cemetery functions as a nature reserve, a haven for wildlife and a bird migration route. In 2001 it was named as "Cemetery of the Year" and received an award for its value as an open space, much used by local people.

*   *   *

Saving Epping Forest for London

Historian Arthur Osborn began his paper to the GHA in July 1951 by quoting from the preface of William Addison's book which tells the whole story in a few brilliant, short sentences:

"First it was the Forest of Essex, a stretch of waste and woodland covering the greater part of the County. Then it became the Royal Forest of Waltham, where Kings built their palaces and hunting lodges. Two great abbeys, one at Barking and one at Waltham, stood on its borders. Before the Dissolution most of it belonged to the monks, but when Waltham's fame declined and its energies were diverted from piety to gunpowder, Epping gave its name to what remained of the unfenced woodland. The splendour of the Royal Forest faded: its area was reduced and what was left became a haunt of deer stealers and highwaymen. Villagers who had formerly lived in dread of the law now lived in dread of those who broke the law. All who had to pass through it rode quickly so that they could be home by nightfall. In the nineteenth century it was threatened with complete destruction, but axes were swung for freedom and the Forest was saved. It became the People's Forest for ever, thanks to the Corporation of the City of London".

Historian Osborn goes on to give us fascinating details about this vast area which once had stretched from Stratford to Colchester. It was brought under forest law by William the Conqueror as a place for the royal hunt. Over the following centuries the forest shrank in size by deforestation and even more by continual encroachments – the enclosure for private use of what had once been common land – much of which took place chiefly as a means of raising revenue for the Crown.

The King's deer were all important. So, in Henry VIII's time enclosures were allowed provided the owners kept parts of their land sown with corn to which the deer could have access. Lopping, the rights of commoners to cut branches, had to be at least five feet from the ground to provide food and cover for the deer.

But enclosure of common land continued inexorably, first by the Crown and then by those Lords of the Manor who had found royal favour. Both Richard I and Edward I ceded land to the Abbey of Waltham, royal parks were enclosed. Wanstead Park remained untouched until the 16th century when the Manor of Wanstead was given to the Lord Chancellor.

The great shrinkage of the forest gathered pace at the beginning of the 19th century. Between 1821 and 1863 over £58,000 was collected by the Crown from the sale of forest rights. A House of Commons Committee reported in 1863 that of Waltham Forest's original 60,000 acres, 48,000 were by then enclosed private property and that, of the remainder, only Epping Forest with about 7,000 acres was still left to the commoners. And still the depredations continued. The Earl of Mornington, hereditary Lord Warden of the forest, was a particular offender, his actions a factor in the forest's diminution by 1871 to only 3,000 acres. This once magnificent open space was, indeed, threatened with extinction.

On 21 May 1871 the Common Council of the City of London unanimously resolved that it would take such steps as were in its power to save Epping Forest. It was the first and decisive step in a battle that would last for more than ten years.

Oddly enough, the City Corporation's involvement had begun nearly twenty years earlier through its purchase of land for its cemetery at Aldersbrook Farm (see the previous paper) which gave the City common rights over Wanstead Flats and, indeed, over the whole of Epping Forest. It was this purchase of one piece of enclosed land that served to stop the enclosure of so much more. The powerful City had a very strong weapon in its hand and used it to the full.

In 1874 the Master of the Rolls delivered judgement for the City against enclosure, the rights of commoners to graze their cattle over the whole of the forest with no manorial boundaries. The end of the story came with the passing of the Epping Forest Act in 1878 when Queen Victoria handed over the Forest to the people for all time, placing this vast open space in the City's keeping in May 1882.

Vested interests fought tooth and nail to preserve their ownership of enclosed land and the City spent some £250,000 on compensation payments to one manorial holding after another until it secured all 6,000 acres of the Forest. The legal fees alone amounted to £25,000.

Historian Osborn mentions some of the Forest's historical and literary associations. Dick Turpin used it for his smuggling and deer-stealing with a hideout in a cave near High Beach. Charles Dickens had the Forest as a setting for Barnaby Rudge while Anthony Trollope wrote many of his novels at Waltham House.

Perhaps the most interesting building now standing in Epping Forest is Queen Elizabeth's Hunting Lodge, one of her favourite retreats, now a museum.

Osborn concludes his story (this was in 1951) by saying that the Forest today is faced with almost as many dangers from enclosure and encroachment as it was in the "bad old days" of Lords of the Manor, the villains being the Minister for Town and Country Planning and neighbouring local authorities on the look-out for housing development possibilities.

Happily to say, 60 years after Osborn's paper, the Forest remains in the best of health under the watchful eyes of the City, its councilmen and four elected Verderers. On the ground there are uniformed Forest keepers who are all Special Constables. The Dukes of Gloucester are hereditary "Rangers" of the Forest.

*   *   *

How the City acquired
10,000 acres of open space

The City of London is not regarded as a particularly "green" place and yet from the gardens of the nobles and ecclesiastics of medieval England there has developed in more recent times a great holding of open space both beyond the City and much greenery within.

Historian Christine Cohen's paper of 2008, on the City's open spaces, begins with the little Bunhill Fields, just outside the City, an area associated with burials from Saxon times, which in the 17th century became a cemetery for dissenters and others whose religion was outside the Church of England. Among the famous people buried there were William Blake, Daniel Defoe and John Bunyan. The City took the site over in 1867 for use as a green space – a first small step in a long progress.

West Ham Park was the next to be acquired. The Park belonged in 1762 to John Fothergill (Quaker, physician and botanist), part of his Upton House Estate. There he developed a fine arboretum, his trees still giving pleasure to visitors more than 300 years later. After Fothergill came the Quaker Gurney family among whom was Elizabeth Fry, the great prison reformer. When they wished to sell the property in the 1860's, local residents worked with the family – and the City of London – to raise funds to purchase the 77-acre estate so as to preserve it as an open space. It was opened by Lord Mayor Andrew Lusk in July 1874. The Park, "to be maintained forever at its own expense" was declared open grounds and garden for the use of adults, children and youth. The present Committee of Managers includes members of the Gurney family together with members of the Parish alongside City aldermen and councilmen. It is home also to the nursery which provides the many thousands of plants for the City's own gardens.

In 1878 the Epping Forest Act of Parliament made the Corporation of London Conservators of the Forest (see previous paper); the same year saw the passing of the Open Spaces Act which empowered the City to acquire and safeguard land within a 25-mile radius to be kept for the recreation and enjoyment of the public. Christine Cohen remarks that these two advances were, in effect, the forerunner of the 20th century Green Belt policy.

(It is interesting also to recall that Herbert Morrison, once a vitriolic critic of the Corporation, later came strongly to regret that the City had not taken over the running of all London. He had come to believe that London would then have been kept to a more agreeable size and completely ringed by open space free of building development).

The Open Spaces Act enabled the City to acquire in 1880 Burnham Beeches, the 540 acres of magnificent beech pollards, many of which are more than 500 years old, in the county of Buckinghamshire.

An area of land known as the Kent and Surrey Commons, an outstanding area of chalk downland, is also under City ownership. These five sites – West Wickham, Kenley and Coulsdon Commons, Farthing Downs, Riddlesdown, and Spring Park also came into the City's care as a result of the 1878 legislation. They are sprinkled in a crescent within the old boundaries of Kent and Surrey, varying in size from 16 to 374 acres.

A considerable addition to the Common was made in 1990 when the City purchased Ashtead Common, a 500-acre of ancient woodland in Surrey with over 2,300 oak pollards, its history going back to before 1066 as part of the Manor of Ashtead.

Other than an occasional glimpse of its coat of arms, the City's part in the foundation of London's green belt is little known to the general public but its reputation made it the only possible custodian for Hampstead Heath following the demise of the GLC. There were however concerns of local people led by the redoubtable Peggy Jay, Chairman of the Heath and Old Hampstead Society. The City's fears were groundless and Hampstead quickly came to accept that the Heath had never before been so well cared for. (The author of this book who used always to sit next to Mrs Jay at the Hampstead Heath Committee sessions at Guildhall can vouch for her esteem of the City).

With Hampstead Heath's 800 acres came, too, Highgate Wood (70 acres) and Queen's Park with its 30 acres of urban recreation space in Willesden, northwest London.

Finally there are the City's own 150 gardens, churchyards (including Bunhill Fields just outside its borders), the much-loved miniature park of Finsbury Circus (now alas wrecked in the interests of 'Crossrail'), the Barbican lakes and gardens, Postman's Park – all providing welcome colour and refreshment for the large number of office workers coming into the City each day and its growing number of residents. Mrs Cohen rightly says in her paper that the post-war hero of this great urban gardening enterprise was Common Councilman Fred Cleary, most civilised of property developers, with a keen appreciation of the importance of open space and growing things within a modern city. As Chairman for many years of the City's Trees, Gardens and Open Spaces Committee, he would, on observing small patches of land on which nothing was happening, approach the owners with a request that it be handed over to the City (for a peppercorn rent) to be turned into a garden, however tiny. He is remembered in the Cleary Garden off Queen Victoria Street. Christine Cohen inherited his mantle, with great distinction.

* * *

Alive with the sound of music

"We meet within five days of Christmas and it seems right and proper that there should be a song in our hearts". It was with these happy words that a most civilised Historian, Alderman and for so many willing years the GHA Secretary, Alan Lamboll, opened the proceedings in December 1963, his paper going under the unassuming title of THE CITY WAITS.

He continued: I am not suggesting that the City's true love is to be found in music and song" (what an idea indeed!) "but there is no doubt that in past centuries the City did foster them with far more enthusiasm than has been apparent in modern times! Of course he was speaking long before the coming of the Barbican Centre and the splendid London Symphony Orchestra in its concert hall. And yet, even then, Lamboll reminded his fellow Historians there were Festivals, monthly BBC concerts in Guildhall and the existence of a City of London Choir. So it wasn't by any means just rebuilding and money-making in 1963.

But Lamboll's paper was back in far more distant times – to the City Waits who originated at the beginning of the 13th century as watchmen or guards who, on their rounds, were provided with horn and pipe to tell of their progress and raise an alarm if necessary. Their transition from watchmen to entertainers is recorded in a Common Council order requiring the Waits to walk each night along the streets with their instruments for the recreation of the citizens. The Marching Watch on Midsummer Day was the highlight of their year.

The first substantial record of the Waits of the City of London was a petition for official recognition in 1442. They asked Common Council to be allowed a livery and permission to wear the City Arms so that they could be identified. Nine leading Waits were granted these favours in return for which they took a suitable oath of office and undertook to be available to attend on the Mayor and Aldermen when summoned to do so.

In the 16th century as singers and instrumentalists they performed in the Lord Mayor's annual pageant and as the years went by their initial modest payments were regularly increased reaching £20 a year in 1605 – roughly equal to that of a carpenter or mason. By then they were required to play at the Royal Exchange every Sunday and on holidays. As they were offered engagements outside the Corporation service their pay was cut in 1650 to £13 6s 8d.

Success bred discord among the Waits "which perplexed and disabled them in performing their service to the City" and they were ordered by the Court of Aldermen to practise from 8 a.m. till noon, to "watch and walk" through the streets at the anciently accustomed times, to attend at the Royal Exchange, fines being imposed for absence and all their services to be performed in their gowns and chains – a strict regime to bring them back to the paths of righteousness!

What instruments did they play? In 1526 the Chamberlain had provided them with a sackbut (trumpet with a slide, a kind of trombone)' a drumslade is mentioned (but Lamboll does not elucidate), a set of recorders, six cornets and a flute, and of course there were drums. Some of the vocalists may have overstepped the decencies and in 1614 Lord Mayor Sir Thomas Hayes acted as a kind of Lord Chamberlain in censoring of blasphemous songs, the Court of Aldermen ordering that no songs in Latin, French or Italian should be sung until they had been read to him in English.

The busy Waits were there for all London's bit occasions – Thanksgiving Services at St. Paul's, the birthday celebrations of George II, at the (first) Proclamation of Peace in 1814, for all of which they were so well rewarded that new, aspiring Waits, paid for admission to their musical circle – the Lord Mayor receiving one-third of the purchase price. Later, the office of Wait was disposed of by public auction. The institution of the Waits was gradually allowed to run down by natural wastage. The very last Wait, Charles Seymour, who had been admitted in 1798 died in 1845.

Alan Lamboll regrets their passing. "Had the Waits survived the 19th century they might now be playing again on the steps of St. Paul's and in Finsbury Circus Garden – certainly taking part in the annual City of London Festival.

Lamboll reminds us, though, that the Waits were not the only musicians. In 1633 there were the City's seven Trumpeters, travelling with the Mayor to Richmond and Greenwich for a fee of 6s. each. They did not last long however. He tells us, too, that from an even earlier Society of Minstrels of the City of London, there evolved in 1350 the Company of Musicians, the fiftieth of the City's livery companies, makers as well as players of musical instruments.

*

"The Isle is full of noises; sounds and sweet airs, that give delight and hurt not": words that provided Alderman and Historian Sir Gilbert Inglefield with a title for a second paper on music in the City, SOUNDS THAT HURT NOT, delivered in November 1971.

Inglefield was one of the prime movers at Guildhall in the creation of the Barbican Arts Centre and, in particular, its magnificent concert hall, the home to be of the London Symphony Orchestra. But his paper to the GHA looked back to the origin and history of much earlier concert halls and how the City was involved in their evolution.

Until the middle of the 17th century, he wrote, it was an unheard of event that people should come together to hear music played to them and that they should have to pay for their entertainment. There was plenty of music around but it was official or ceremonial music – for the Church, the Court or the Lord Mayor. There had been earlier professional music makers – the City Minstrels, for example (one of whom was Rahere no less, the later monk and founder of St. Bartholomew's Hospital). There were, too, the City Waits although Inglefield quotes from a contemporary source, the "London Spy" which suggests their musicianship was not of the best: "We heard a Noise so dreadful that we thought the Devil was Riding through the City.... What was the meaning of this Infernal Outcry?" "Why", came the reply, "These are the City Waits". (See also the previous paper which takes a different view of the Waits).

Then, in the 17th century, wrote Inglefield, came the golden age of music in England – Bull, Gibbons and Byrd, Dowland, Attey and Ford, Ravenscroft and Lawes were in full song, many with a continental reputation, for English music and musicians were then an export to the countries of Europe.

Inglefield traces the history of music – making: first, through the playing and even composing by gifted amateurs; then with the patronage of musicians by noble families; finally with Royal support and appointment of The Master of the King's Musick – an office continuing unbroken over the years to Sir Arthur Bliss who held that appointment when Inglefield read his paper in 1971. (He digresses for a moment to tell us that Sir Arthur Bliss, three years before, composed a "Fanfare for a Lord Mayor" – indeed, for Inglefield himself!)

Music was not only heard at Court, though, but also in ordinary meeting places such as inns and taverns. And it was from tavern meetings that the modern concert has emerged, wrote Inglefield. It was here that the City started the musical ball rolling – from the pub to the Barbican.

Workmen and shopkeepers came to a tavern behind St. Paul's to listen to a chamber organ and to sing in concert. The inn was the pre-Fire Mitre and afterwards rebuilt as the Swan and Harp, better known to its clients as the Goose and Gridiron. Pepys used to frequent another Mitre in Fleet Street where there was music. Pepys also enjoyed music at the Black Swan in Bishopsgate.

After Charles II's return there came a new element, the Recital Hall with an impresario to organise the events. In 1672 the London Gazette announced "At Mr. Bannister's House called the Musick School will be Musick performed by excellent Masters beginning precisely at four of the clock and every afternoon at the same hour". The venue was "in Whyte Friars near the Temple Gate". For the shilling entrance you had a seat and small table and could order your refreshment. Inglefield says that Bannister's was the very first public concert hall in England. Bannister was sent by Charles II to study music in France, became a leader of the "King's Musick" and on his death was buried in Westminster Abbey.

While in the 18th century, when opera reigned supreme and Handel began to dominate the scene, music had moved to more fashionable parts of London, there still remained plenty of music inside the City. Performances now came to be given in the great livery halls, as well as in St. Paul's, often for charitable causes. Handel's operas were sung at Haberdashers' Hall in aid of the Lying-in Hospital in Aldersgate. The Stationers were, says Inglefield, the most enthusiastic with performances of Handel's "Acis and Galatea" and Purcell's "Dioclesian".

The concert hall as an architectural achievement was developed in the West End around the Soho area where the infant Mozart and his sister made their London debut, soon to be followed by Haydn. Music with fun and games was to be had in London's pleasure gardens – Vauxhall, Ranelagh and Sadlers Wells.

Inglefield observes, in his concluding words, how happy a coincidence it was that shortly after his address, in 1972, the foundation stone of the new Barbican concert hall would be laid, in the tercentenary year of Bannister's Musick Room in Whitefriars.

*

A third paper on MUSIC IN THE CITY, read by Wilfrid Dewhirst in September 1980, was devoted to musical education. Its first manifestation was a National Training School for Music in premises near the Albert Hall, the City's contribution (at the invitation of the then Duke of Edinburgh) to provide in 1876 ten scholarships of £40 each. That school in 1882 became the Royal College of Music.

The Corporation began to consider in 1879 whether a school of music should be established in the City and within a few months had decided that a demand indeed existed. In May 1880 the title Guildhall School of Music was adopted for this great City enterprise. Premises were found in three houses in Aldermanbury, almost adjoining the Guildhall. In September 216 pupils presented themselves for admission, the fee being one guinea per term. In 1886 a new purpose-built school was opened in John Carpenter Street.

The whole operation, from early inception to triumphant conclusion was carried through with quite incredible dispatch, the Common Councilmen and officers involved of rare enthusiasm, determination and dash. Even in those days the wheels of local authority, the City included, could move slowly. Dewhirst remarked "The Committee Minutes were terse beyond belief, almost as though opening a new school were an everyday event".

Dewhirst noted another City contributor to musical education – Sir Thomas Gresham – had founded his college in 1596 and of his seven professors the Corporation were to nominate four: Geometry, Astrology, Divinity and Music. Gresham College and its professors still continue to flourish, long since in the buildings of Barnard's Inn.

Dewhirst's conclusion: The Corporation's commitment to formal musical education began with ten scholarships of £40 and has now (in 1980) topped one and quarter million pounds. No other local authority in the country approaches this field without dipping heavily into the public purse – and the Corporation's achievement from its own private purse deserves more recognition than is generally accorded.

Since he wrote those words the Corporation budget for the Guildhall School has soared. And, of course, that budget pales in comparison with the City's truly vast expenditure on the Barbican Arts Centre – its "Gift to the Nation".

*

And finally, a paper the title alone of which would demand its inclusion in this history: APOLLO'S SWAN AND LYRE completes our musical quartet. Read in October 2006, it was presented by Dr. Andrew Parmley, Alderman and, unusually, a professor of music, teacher and himself a gifted player

He explained that the swan, as opposed to the peacock's material manifestation, stands for the ethereal, the presence of divine inspiration, symbol of the Muses. He reminded us, too, that in the 8th century BC the King of Rome, Numa, placed the Musicians' Guild first among Rome's eight city guilds. "So there you have it. The Musicians were number one!"

The guild to which Parmley devoted much of his paper was, however, the Company of Parish Clerks "whose claim to the title of number one in the City cannot be contradicted. After all, their identifying badge, the surplice, was in use long before livery was invented".

The Parish Clerks had long been associated with church music and were also pioneers of English drama, their miracle and mystery plays originating in the 9th century. According to Stow they played in 1390 at Skinners' Well for three days in the presence of Richard II. But they really made their mark in their association with church music from their original duties of chanting services in plainsong, to the establishment of thirty canons in the St. Paul's Cathedral, down to the time of Richard Whittington before whose election (for the second time) in 1406 they participated in a solemn mass.

Not all was praise, however. In 1613 a parish clerk, Thomas Milborne, was accused of singing the psalms like a gelded pig and was ordered to leave his church but could not be budged. Later the Master and Wardens approached James I for a new Charter and used their new powers to ensure that every clerk admitted to office could sing the psalms of David in proper tune. But with 97 churches within the City walls musical quality among the parish clerks remained patchy.

Parmley goes on to talk about the vast number of itinerant musicians, some little better than rogues, who were greatly resented by the competent musicians in the pay of the nobility or municipalities (such as the Waits). Again, it was in the reign of James I, in 1604, that a charter of incorporation was accorded to the City's Society of Minstrels from which grew the Worshipful Company of Musicians.

What instruments did these early musicians play? Parmley says they were either "loud" (and offensive) or "soft" (and inaudible). The loud group comprised strident shawns (akin to the later oboe) and sackbuts (ancestor of the trombone). It was probably a consort of shawns and sackbuts which preceded the new Lord Mayor in his annual procession. As accompaniment to a banquet soft instruments were required – lute, harp and recorders. The minstrels were first and foremost instrumentalists. The singers among them appear to have joined the Parish Clerks as their guild.

It was the ward of Cripplegate, said Parmley, which in the 17th century seems to have been the City's centre for music with many of the leading Parish Clerks living there and closely associated with its parish church of St. Giles and neighbouring churches. Whether parish clerks or minstrels they clearly liked to live close by one another for mutual support, ease of contact and business – and rehearsals. How appropriate it is that today St. Giles is home to an international organ school and that the Barbican teems with music from the Guildhall School and the Barbican Centre itself, observed Andrew Parmley.

He concluded his paper with these words:

"The City of London and its fringes provide one of the richest and most diverse concentrations of arts in the UK. The festivals and institutions in the City arts cluster contribute £325 million a year to GDP and support almost 7,900 jobs across the UK... The City is on the verge of owning the largest fully integrated arts complex in the World". Five years after his paper there seems to be no diminution in the City's progress towards this achievement.

* * *

The theatre and the City

In 1963 Alan Lamboll had written about the City Waits and their music (see Page 155). But five years earlier, in September 1958, it was the theatre that had taken his fancy and his paper began with a truly dramatic flourish: "Sad to relate the City Corporation did all in its power to suppress and stifle at birth the plays, players and playhouses".

Luckily, he went on, dramatic entertainment survived its unhappy infancy thanks to the enthusiasm of its creators and supporters, even if it was in the teeth of City opposition.

Lamboll's story begins in the 16th century when Puritanism was already well on its way. Here began the struggle between Church and stage, the Royal Court and the civic authority.

For the performers and their company the first problem was their status in the community. It was all too easy for them to be called "masterless men" or even vagabonds. So they sought the protection of some nobleman, wearing his livery and badge.

The Privy Council were responsible for regulation of amusements, their primary concern being the exclusion of heresy and sedition; control over the content of plays was largely in the hands of the City authorities. The Court of Aldermen in 1549 appointed two "Secondaries of the Comptors" to "peruse" plays and report on them to the Lord Mayor. The history of play-licensing in London really turns on an attempt by the Corporation – goaded by the preachers – to move from regulating plays to suppressing them altogether. The Privy Council felt that the City was exceeding its responsibilities and itself took over the licensing of plays with a Master of Revels appointed to perform the task.

There were frequent differences of opinion between City and Westminster, Mayor and Aldermen using the very real threat of plague during the 1560's and 1570's to banish plays out of London as a precautionary measure. However, the Earl of Leicester's men were given permission to play within or without the City walls, totally over-ruling the Corporation's edicts.

Then in 1574 came an Act of Common Council drawing attention to the disorders arising from players in the past – "unchaste and seditious speeches, interference with divine service, accidents arising from the collapse of wooden structures, the corruption of youth". Regulations were set out as to the content of plays – and, more particularly, to control all "playing places" and the persons in charge of them.

The playing places were the yards of galleried inns where a trestle stage would be set up at one end of the yard, the galleries providing space for the spectators. The best-known were the Bell in Gracious Street, the Boars Head at Aldgate and the Bull in Bishopsgate.

Following the City's new legislation it fell to one James Burbage, a joiner turned actor in the Earl of Leicester's company, to take up the cudgels on behalf of the players.

In 1576 he borrowed one thousand marks (£660) from his father-in-law and together they built a theatre in Shoreditch beyond the Lord Mayor's jurisdiction. Constructed of wood and thatch it was, appropriately enough, called "The Theatre". It was opened in 1576, making theatrical history, wrote Lamboll. To stand on the floor cost a penny, another penny for admission to the gallery, and a third penny for a stool.

Another theatre "The Curtain", was built nearby, its great claim to fame being that Shakespeare's Henry V probably had its first performance there.

On the dissolution of the monasteries, part of the old Blackfriars Monastery was granted to Sir Thomas Cawarden, Master of the Revels for Henry VIII while Richard Farrant, Master of the Children of Windsor Chapel, adapted part of the building as a theatre for performances by the Children of the Chapel Royal. Later James Burbage adapted another part of the monastery as a roofed theatre. Because it had a roof this made the Blackfriars a "private theatre" and so was spared the Lord Mayor's attentions. Burbage was up to every trick, said Lamboll. His company included William Shakespeare who played the Ghost in Hamlet and other small parts in his plays, most of which were performed at Blackfriars.

"The Rose" was the first theatre to be built across the river on Bankside, well away from interference by the City. There followed "The Swan", "The Globe" and "The Hope". There is remembrance today of this splendid theatrical quartet in the recreated Globe.

With the institution in 1880 of the Guildhall School of Music and Drama, Lamboll saw some measure of compensation by the City for its earlier prejudice and opposition to the theatre. By the time his paper was presented in 1958 he was able to welcome City support for Bernard Miles's splendid theatrical venture at his Mermaid Theatre in Puddle Dock.

There followed the City's total involvement with the arts in its creation of the Barbican Centre, not least the provision within that splendid complex of a custom-built theatre for the Royal Shakespeare Company. With the RSC's subsequent, ungrateful, rejection of the City's largesse the wheel had turned full circle; how the ghosts of Burbage and Shakespeare will have chuckled.

* * *

The creation of the Barbican Centre

This slice of modern history, the City's "Gift to the Nation" as the Barbican Centre has come to be described, can be said to have started in 1955, just nine years after the GHA itself came into being.

That year the architects Chamberlin, Powell & Bon, in the midst of what was still a vast bomb-site, were giving early thought to the creation of an Aldersgate/Cripplegate housing estate. In a feasibility study they touched on the desirability of "providing for mental recreation" the inclusion within the estate of a concert hall, theatre or a cinema.

At that stage Common Council were by no means unanimous in their enthusiasm for a residential estate in the City, let alone such fripperies as concert halls and theatres. But in 1956 Duncan Sands, the Minister of Housing, in a letter to Lord Mayor Sir Cuthbert Ackroyd, made clear his belief that the City should once again have a residential population – and that for these new City dwellers some artistic amenity should be part of the scheme. The following year Common Council accepted the Minister's recommendations and in 1959 Chamberlin, Powell & Bon were appointed to design the Barbican estate that would also have an arts element. A Barbican Committee was formed with Cripplegate Councilman John Henderson, who presented this paper in April 1991, as one of its leading lights.

The creation of the Barbican Arts Centre would become one of the great building sagas of the twentieth century, its modest initial budget of £11 million ending with a cost of £119 million. It was beset with difficulties almost from the start, the underground line from Moorgate to Barbican Station having first to be re-routed by London Transport, and the architects faced with a requirement that pedestrian movement throughout the new Barbican would be over high-level walkways. The arts aspect of the development would lead to some of the most bitter of debates within the Guildhall council chamber.

In 1963 there came a complete change to what had begun as a modest "amenity" concept. A noted authority on such matters, Anthony Besch, was invited to become the director of what was then

166

being called the Guildhall Arts Centre. He was not interested but came back with recommendations on its design, finance and administration.

His report, in 1964, dismissed any idea that the proposed theatre and concert hall could be part of the Guildhall School of Music and Drama and said that even later proposals for larger, independent facilities – concert hall seating 1,300 and theatre for 800 – were inadequate.

His proposals were for a concert hall seating at least 2,000 and having a resident orchestra, a 1,000 – 1,500 seat theatre as the home of a major theatrical company; a public lending library; art gallery; and first-class restaurant facilities.

A once sceptical Common Council, encouraged by speeches from a few enthusiasts, declared its support and the whole ambitious project moved forward with the Royal Shakespeare Company invited to become resident in the theatre and the London Symphony Orchestra resident in the concert hall. This was a totally new brief for the architects – a project on a truly grand scale. And somehow they had to meet the vastly increased space necessary for all these new requirements within pretty well the same ground area allocated for the earlier modest plans. It took them all of three years, their building of nine storeys being largely underground. A large "conservatory" was included to mask the underground theatre's fly-tower which rose sixty feet above stage level. The concert hall's large roof area was designated as a sculpture court. A world of its own it would comprise 560 halls, compartments and rooms.

Early residents of the Barbican Estate found at its centre when they started to arrive in 1969-1970 an enormous hole 400 feet by 250 feet and 80 feet deep – what was to be the future Barbican Arts Centre.

It became apparent when tenders were drawn up for its construction that the cost of this vast, highly complicated, scheme would be extremely high. Somewhat appalled Mayor, Aldermen and Councilmen agreed to think again and that an alternative use should be considered. The City Architect was instructed to prepare a scheme for an hotel and conference venue incorporating only the library and art gallery of the grand project. The scheme was presented to

Common Council in June 1970 but found little support. After this digression it was not until April 1971 that the original concept was given final approval – after a mammoth debate in Common Council. Work on the big hole in the ground began in October.

It was not long before changes were being made to the original plans, thousands of them, some from choice, some for reasons of economy, many to meet statutory requirements – "requirements that seemed to vary with every new inspector on the site, apparently an inexhaustible breed" observed John Henderson.

An early major change was to include "conference facilities" into the concert hall to bring in extra income. The conference idea grew in popularity with the addition of lecture theatres and cinemas, soon to be followed with exhibition halls. Shops and residential apartments were cannibalised to provide the additional office space needed to service the conference facilities. The many changes being made caused delays – and, of course, ever-mounting costs. To add to the Centre's problems there were lengthy strikes by the building workers – these years of the 1970's were notorious for strikes in almost every area of activity and the Barbican, both residential and arts centre, seemed to be particularly vulnerable.

The hoped-for opening of the Arts (and Conference) Centre in 1980 was in fact delayed two more years. The great night finally arrived and the Queen came on March 3rd 1982 for a great gala concert. The Barbican was at last in business.

It is amusing for the author of this history to recall that in its darkest days, with serious thought being given to scrapping the whole project, he and his wife were collecting signatures to a petition among the new residents urging the City Corporation not to give up!

In the outcome, with all its teething troubles, the Barbican Centre is something of a triumph for the City of London, a very jewel in its crown. John Henderson's paper to the GHA traces the steps to its achievement.

* * *

The City's pictures and Art Gallery

Looking today at the Guildhall Art Gallery (perhaps the most pleasing of post-war City buildings) and its considerable picture collection, it is odd to learn that it all began with twenty-two not particularly impressive portraits. Cuthbert Skilbeck told the story to his fellow historians in March 1965.

After the Great Fire of 1666 the City Corporation had appointed twenty-two of the nation's principal judges to devote themselves exclusively to the task of evolving order out of the chaos of vanished landmarks, lost boundaries and tenancy disputes. This great task was carried out to the entire satisfaction of all concerned and it was decreed by the Court of Aldermen in April 1670 that for their recompense "their pictures be taken in a skilful hand and kept in some public place of the city for a grateful memorial of this good office".

The King's Painter, Sir Peter Lely, accepted the commission but found to his dismay that the judges would not wait on him and expected him to attend on them at their various chambers. This was beneath a King's Painter's dignity, and the Corporation set its sights somewhat lower. Joseph Michael Wright got the job at the not too alarming price of £36 per portrait. The frames cost another £14 each. So, at £50 a head the pictures were painted of Sir Orlando Bridgeman, Lord Keeper of the Great Seal of England and his twenty-one distinguished colleagues.

The portraits were hung in Guildhall there being no other convenient place and so formed the nucleus for a collection. In 1682 the Corporation commissioned portraits of William and Mary, the first of its Royal pictures, to hang with the judges in Great Hall. There followed portraits of Queen Anne, George I, George II and his Queen, Caroline of Anspach, George III and Queen Charlotte.

Another judge, Sir Charles Pratt, earned the City's admiration when he, as Lord Chief Justice, ordered the release from prison of John Wilkes on the grounds that his arrest by the Government was a breach of Parliamentary privilege. The judge was given the Freedom of the City and Joshua Reynolds, no less, was commissioned to paint his portrait.

Perhaps the most famous of the City's commissions, and certainly the largest, 18 feet by 24 feet, was commissioned in the 1780's. It was John Singleton Copley's painting of the Relief of the Siege of Gibraltar by Lord Howe and the British Navy alongside the gallantry of General Eliott, the besieged Governor of the Rock and his soldiers. Copley, an American, was chosen because of his international reputation for depicting contemporary battle scenes. In storage throughout the last War and brilliantly restored in the Regents Park workrooms of English Heritage, it dominates the lower floor of the new Guildhall Art Gallery – indeed the gallery can be said to have been designed around it.

The Corporation was becoming known as a patron of the arts and, as such, a suitable recipient for bequests of paintings. Alderman John Boydell was the first large benefactor to the City's permanent collection – 24 pictures of distinguished soldiers and sailors including that of Nelson, and great ceremonial pictures including the famous mayoral procession by water of Lord Mayor William Pickett in 1789.

In the 1800's there came a succession of royal presentations to the City: As a reward for its loyalty to her in the face of the shabby treatment from her royal husband, Queen Caroline gave the Corporation portraits of herself and Princess Charlotte; Queen Victoria in 1839 presented a large portrait of herself on the throne; Louis Philippe's visit in 1844 was commemorated by a gift from the French monarch of a very large canvas showing the presentation of the City's address to him at Windsor Castle. This last picture was one of many casualties of the fire raids of December 1940.

In 1872 the Corporation received from Sir Davis Salomons (the first Jewish Lord Mayor) a collection of drawings depicting the demolition of old London Bridge and the building of its successor. The City's pictures were becoming more wide-ranging in their subject matter.

The Corporation committed itself to the idea of an art gallery to house its pictures in 1885 when, on a motion proposed by Councilman Henry Clarke, Common Council agreed to the creation of the Guildhall Art Gallery and, with the incredible dispatch that could be shown by the

Victorians if something took their fancy, it was opened the following year on the site of old court buildings adjacent to the Guildhall.

The size of the "Permanent Collection" was still very modest – a mere 288 pieces: paintings, sculpture, drawings and engravings. Its first Director was Alfred Temple, the son of a member of the Corporation staff who worked in the Town Clerk's office – a man with a passionate interest in art and a friend of at least two Royal Academicians. The salary offered was only half of what he had been paid in his previous job.

In 1890 Temple held his first loan exhibition of old and modern masters, dealers and owners co-operating magnificently to provide an immense success with 5,420 people attending on the final day. It was followed by other exhibitions, all equally successful, the sale of catalogues averaging 23,000 and with cash takings of nearly £600 per exhibition. Temple, with no assistance, would work until midnight to fulfil his numerous tasks.

Meanwhile, the permanent collection was growing steadily with bequests from Royal Academician Sir John Gilbert and Charles Gassiot whose complete collection of 107 pictures (including a Constable) came to Guildhall. Temple was given a modest sum to spend on acquiring pictures. The noted portrait painter, Sir Thomas Lawrence's depiction of John Kemble as Coriolanus was given to the Corporation. When Temple (who had been given a knighthood for his services) died the directorship was subsequently merged with the office of City Librarian when further purchases were made. One of the most important was William Logsdail's magnificent "Ninth of November" showing the Lord Mayor's Procession passing the Royal Exchange, a picture epitomising all the power and splendour of the City of London at the close of the nineteenth century.

The Guildhall Art Gallery was destroyed in the bombing of May 1941 but in 1944 a temporary replacement structure was put up within the shell of the old gallery. It was still there when Skilbeck gave his paper in 1965 and, indeed, would stay there for a good many years after.

*   *   *

171

Rebuilding of the Guildhall Art Gallery

Plans for a new art gallery were first conceived in 1951 with Giles Gilbert Scott the architect chosen by the Corporation to undertake the restoration of Guildhall as his first priority and then to enlarge Guildhall Yard and build an office block for Corporation staff. A small single-storey art gallery was included in the plans.

The office building was completed in 1958 and when Giles Gilbert Scott died in 1960 it was his son Richard who was given the task of designing a new Guildhall Yard, its size and the radical nature of his proposals prompting its referral to a public enquiry. Planning consent was finally granted in 1964.

But before work could be put in hand the Corporation now had other more pressing commitments. First would be a new West Wing to house the Guildhall Library, rooms to house Corporation committees and additional office space; after that an ambulatory running from the new West Wing along the front of Guildhall. Perhaps the art gallery could come next?

But no, there followed the discovery of a graveyard adjoining St. Lawrence Jewry church; it would take months to exhume the bodies and re-bury them elsewhere. At that point all further building came to a stop while the Corporation wrestled with the financial complexities and construction of the Barbican.

So it was not until 1986 that Richard Gilbert Scott received a call from the Town Clerk asking whether he was still alive and in practice. He was appointed, at last, to design the new Art Gallery while his partner in practice, the firm of D.Y. Davies, were to be the architects and project managers.

The brief was not just for a gallery. It was to include office space above and facilities within the gallery for receptions and other ceremonial occasions – and there had to be sufficient height for the Pikemen and Musketeers to do their drill! The gallery's main constraint was to allow for the hanging, conservation and storage of the City's now very large collection of pictures including the enormous painting, referred to above, "The Relief of the Floating Batteries". Gilbert Scott told the story of this considerable enterprise in a paper to the GHA in November 2004 when he said he believed the collection to be the largest in Britain after the National and Tate Galleries.

His first design was submitted in 1988. It was for a seven-storey building facing the Yard, five floors of offices above a double-storey art gallery. It went to another public enquiry where it was disliked by the Royal Fine Art Commission and English Heritage. A new design eventually emerged, much as it looks today, and described by English Heritage as "an arresting essay in eclectic expressionism" – whatever that may mean!

The Minister gave his consent and D.Y. Davies were instructed to proceed.

But... more unforeseen circumstances... a rare bird was discovered nesting in a bush that had grown up on the derelict site and had laid three eggs. This was England and English Nature ordered that the nest remain undisturbed until the birds had flown. Black Redstarts take their time and the demolition of the buildings on site was delayed once again for some months.

Came unforeseen circumstance No. 2. The remains of the entrance archway to a Roman amphitheatre were discovered and the site was soon beset with archaeologists and sightseers. The remains were declared to be a National Monument on a par with Stonehenge. Here were engineering and technical problems of great magnitude, the creation beneath an already complex building of an Amphitheatre Chamber. An enormous steel raft had to be built below the art gallery on to which would be transferred the weight of the whole superstructure above.

Then D.Y. Davies went bankrupt. W.S. Atkins were appointed in their place. The Lord Mayor laid the foundation stone in 1994 and the building was opened by the Queen in 1999. In the millennium year it received the City Heritage New Architecture Award. It is truly a building of the greatest quality.

It is worth recording the names of some of the artists whose pictures fill the walls of the Guildhall Art Gallery:

Sir Lawrence Alma-Tadema, William Shakespeare Burton, John Constable, William Holman Hunt, Sir John Lavery, Frederick Lord Leighton, Sir Peter Lely, Sir John Everett Millais, Balthazar Nebot, Sir Edward Poynter, Sir Matthew Smith, Sir James Thornhill, James Tissot, Henry Scott Tuke, Jan Vorsterman, George Frederick Watts, William Lionel Wyllie[*].

*

A final postscript: In 1987 the notable collection of eighty Dutch paintings built up by Sir Harold Samuel was, on his death, bequeathed to the City – with the explicit condition that they should be hung in their entirety in the Mansion House, in the Lord Mayor's keeping. The story of the bequest and some of the troubles it caused, particularly for the author of this volume when he was Chairman of the City's Libraries and Art Galleries Committee, and for the late and much lamented curator of the art collection, Vivien Knight, is told in "The Goings-on in Guildhall" (C. Douglas Woodward, Athena Press, 2008).

*   *   *

---

[*] "The City's pictures", a selection of paintings from the collection of the Corporation of London, was published in 1984 to accompany an exhibition at the Barbican Art Gallery.

From Guildhall Museum to Museum of London

Before the Museum of London there was the Guildhall Museum, its creation coming hard on the heels of a new Guildhall Library. The Library Committee was instructed by the Court of Common Council "to consider the propriety of providing a suitable place for the reception of such antiquities relating to the City of London and suburbs as may be procured or presented to this Corporation". The Museum came into being in January 1829, consisting of Roman and other antiquities found during excavations of the new Post Office in St. Martin le Grand.

Historian John Gapp, who presented this paper in April 1963, wrote that the idea of having the museum as a modest adjunct to the Library did not last for long, the museum soon outgrowing its humble beginnings, the soil of London abounding in the remains of its ancestors. By 1840 material had so accumulated to require one whole room of the Library. In 1841 came all the Roman material discovered in the re-building of the Royal Exchange. In 1872 the museum was given a whole floor to itself in the basement area under the Library. At the turn of the century a Museum Clerk was appointed: Frank Lambert, a distinguished museum official who later became Director of the Walker Art Gallery, Liverpool. His successor was Quintin Waddington whose articles in the "Evening News" became a popular feature of London journalism.

The story leaps to the post-War period when, from 1946, there came the vast programme of excavation opened up with the re-building of the City, its streets and buildings devastated by the War-time bombing. For the first time since 1666 large areas of the City had been cleared of buildings... a splendid time for archaeologists but with a museum that existed in a cramped space within the Library.

However, the collections grew and in 1950 a keeper of the Museum was appointed together with staff for cataloguing, overseeing excavations and cleaning and restoring archaeological finds. In 1955 the Keeper's suggestion that the Museum should move to the unoccupied Royal Exchange bore fruit. For the first time it became possible to display the Museum's many treasures, now much expanded as a result of the recent excavations. Some 120,000 visitors a year came to see the displays at the Royal Exchange.

When Gapp gave his paper in 1963 he wrote that the Museum's collections were particularly strong in the Roman and Medieval periods giving a detailed picture of everyday life of those times.

In 1959 came the great discovery at Bucklersbury of the Temple of Mithras with its group of marble heads of the gods once worshipped there, Mithras, Minerva, Serapis and Mercury. Other of the Museum's famous objects include the fine Roman tessellated pavement dug up, also in Bucklersbury, but this one in 1869. A more recent treasure was the sword presented to Nelson by the Court of Common Council after the Battle of the Nile.

In 1963 John Gapp could say that the Museum collection already enjoyed international importance with loan exhibitions being sent abroad. For example, a collection of medieval pottery on tour in Japan created something of a sensation. In 1958 a display was taken to Ghent as part of a European exhibition called "The Golden Age of the Great Cities". Though without the kind of resources of other exhibitors, who brought with them designers and architects, Guildhall managed to put on a splendid display supplementing materials from its own collections with artefacts from City churches and livery companies, a treasure was created that required insurance of a quarter of a million pounds.

Gapp looked to the future and reported that Common Council had agreed the Guildhall Museum should be amalgamated with the London Museum (then situated at Kensington Palace) to form the Museum of London which would be housed in a new building in the City. The project would be financed in equal parts by the Corporation, the Government and the London County Council.

The site eventually chosen was a rotunda on the highwalk at the western end of London Wall. The Greater London Council became the third partner in the enterprise when the LCC was abolished and when it, too, was disposed of the Corporation and Government remained to

176

finance it. The City provides six of its Governors while six others are nominated by the Prime Minister's office. In Gapp's concluding words the Museum of London provides for the telling not only the story of the Square Mile, but also that of the vast conurbation of Greater London which had sprung from the nucleus of London's small walled city.

* * *

No roads in the City but a great richness of street names

As Herbert Pike said in his paper for the GHA in February 1960, the street names of the City are full of interest. They reflect its ancient character, record the location of early trades, and recall the names of merchants and landowners. Some streets gave their names to wards, such as Bread Street, Broad Street and Coleman Street. Churches exerted a strong influence and there remain thirty-eight streets, lanes and alleys with the word "saint" in their names. The reason there are no "roads" in the City is because roads lead to and from a town.

A peculiarity of the City is the number of thoroughfares not being called street, alley, passage or any addition at all; from its gates City routes are simply called Aldgate, Bishopsgate and Moorgate. Together with London Wall, Houndsditch and Old Bailey they provide a link with the medieval defences. The City's streams have given us Holborn and Walbrook and ancient markets Cheapside, Poultry and Cloth Fair. Religious houses provide Austin Friars, Crutched Friars and Bevis Marks. Property areas have left Aldermanbury, Bucklersbury and Old Jewry.

Historian Pike in 1960 expressed the hope that new streets could similarly do without the suffix "street" and his suggestion was indeed followed with "The Postern" in the Barbican development still then to come.

Geography has played its part, the fall of the City towards the Thames being marked with Fish Street Hill, Dowgate Hill and Peters Hill while from the old Fleet River rose Ludgate Hill and Snow Hill. Marshland gave rise to Moorfields and fields to the north gave us Tenter Street where once cloth was stretched on frames called tenters.

It was, however, the legacy of old City trades that had so much to do with the naming of streets, some have long since disappeared but many remain: Bread Street and Milk Street, of course, and Poultry, Honey Lane and Beehive Passage, Hen and Chicken Court, Fish Street Hill, Vintners Place, Goldsmith Street, Fig Tree Court, Apothecary Street. The location of trades has resulted in Paternoster Row and

Square, Masons Avenue, Turners Alley, Dyers' Court and Salters Court. Then there are Shoe Lane, Leather Lane and Hosier Lane' Cloth Lane and Clothier Street, Threadneedle Street, Drapers Gardens and Taylors Gardens. Pike observes that for the future no congregation of traders is likely to give names to a Row unless it be Bankers or Brokers Row.

In medieval London streets acquired names from popular use by the citizens – the street by the river was naturally called Thames Street and the way leading down to the Fleet could only be Fleet Street. Love Lane and Bird in Hand Court acquired their names because of the amatory pursuits that took place in them.

Large property owners gave their name to streets traversing their buildings. The Basing family which produced four aldermen and six sheriffs created Basinghall Street. Philpot Lane is a memorial to Mayor Philpot who took on and subdued North Sea pirates, Suffolk Lane recalls the property owned by the Duke of Suffolk.

When streets bear the names of famous City people, those names were not given during their lifetimes or soon afterwards but very much later: Whittington Avenue in 1882; Tallis Street named after the Elizabethan composer 350 years after his death; Gresham Street came 300 years after Sir Thomas Gresham's passing. The reverse is true of Johnson's Court, home of Dr. Johnson, but named as such 200 years before the Doctor came to live there.

Royalty has scarcely left a trace of its passing through the City except for Queenhithe which took its name from Eleanor, wife of Henry II. Charles II's concern for the City after the Great Fire is commemorated in King Street (although not King Charles Street). An exception though is Queen Victoria who did have a street named after her.

And, finally, Herbert Pike tells of the many City ways named after inns and their signs: Every Monarch from Charles I is represented in King's Head Yard, court or alley; Lions red, white and black vied with horses, swans, bulls, bears, harts and cocks. The number three was ever popular – Three Cranes Lane, Three Nuns Court, Three Tun

Passage. Then there were Barleymow Passage and Bolt and Tun Court, Belle Savage Yard and Saracen's Head Yard.

The speaker said he was giving serious thought to moving to a new home, to Pike's Corner no less, hard by the Tower – a site beside the Watergate which looked most attractive and was clearly meant for him!

*   *   *

Cripplegate Without, Barbican of long ago

When Historian Eric Wilkins read this paper – "The Barbican in Retrospect" – in June 1959, the area lay desolate fourteen years after war had razed it to the ground. A fitting introduction, perhaps, to his look back in time to the desolation of this same area a thousand years before, largely uninhabited marshland. But changes were on the way.

In 1090 the earlier Saxon church of St. Giles was rebuilt and there began to spring up a small resident population. Entries in the rolls of the Court of Hustings show a steady increase in the number of people spilling over the wall and ditch from vastly overcrowded Cripplegate inside the wall to live and ply their trades in what had become Cripplegate Without: a varied enough mix – butcher and poulterer, girdler and weaver, brewer and carpenter. Later, after losing half of its by then more substantial population in the plague year of 1665, suffering numerous fires and being somewhat poverty-stricken in the 16th and 17th centuries, Cripplegate Without became the City's centre for textiles and clothing manufacture and warehousing.

Wilkins' paper devotes itself to the streets and buildings of the Ward and to some of its famous inhabitants.

Of the principal paths criss-crossing the area, two ran from west to east, first (marking the Ward's boundary) was the Barbican Street merging into Beech Lane. Its start was masked by the watch-tower, the burgh-kenning of the Saxons, (that is "Barbican") which gave the streets its name. As with other of its streets, Barbican became a place of large houses and extensive gardens, one of which was occupied by the Earl of Suffolk. Nicholas de la Beech, lieutenant of the Tower of London, who gave his name to Beech Lane, was a near neighbour.

The other main west-east path was Fore Street which lay close to the City wall and the church of St. Giles. It was here, at the top of Wood Street, some twenty-five yards south of Fore Street where stood the Cripplegate, oldest of the gates to the walled City, which gave the two wards, Within and Without, their name. Originally it was built by the Romans (long before their wall) as an exit from the fort at the north-west corner of Londinium. From this point ran the Roman road leading to Stevenage and the north. The site where Cripplegate once stood is today located at the junction of modern Wood Street with St. Alphage Gardens.

The principal of the south to north pathways was Redcross Street which began immediately opposite Cripplegate and stretched to a Benedictine house of the Abbey of Ramsey whose badge of a red cross was displayed there. Here, in the 16th century, as shown on the maps of that time and mentioned by Stow were numerous "fair houses", one being the mansion of Sir Roger Townsend, a hero of the Armada.

There was also the Redcross Street Chapel which, believed Wilkes, was the place Daniel Defoe (who lived nearby) had in mind when he wrote:

"Wherever God erects a house of prayer, the devil always builds a chapel there, and t'will be found, upon examination, the latter has the larger congregation".

East of Redcross Street was Whitecross Street, its name coming from the emblem of the Holy Trinity foundation situated there. In later times there were considerable warehouses, Whitbread's brewery and a debtor's prison.

The third of the south-north ways was Grub Street – "grub" meaning ditch indicated that at its southern end it joined the ditch adjoining the city wall. The street was once inhabited by bowyers and fletchers, then by keepers of bowling alleys and the houses of reputable authors – forerunners of the "Grub Street" community.

By 1650 it had become a place for poor authors lodging in the upper rooms of tumbledown tenements. Grub Street and its maze of dangerous courts and alleys deteriorated to such an extent that by the end of the 18th century this eastern part of the Ward had become known as the City's red light district, haunt of every vice and crime in the book. There remained some respectable if poor inhabitants who successfully petitioned Common Council for a change of name. Grub Street became Milton Street thus improving the street's reputation and also celebrating the great poet born nearby and burned in St. Giles Church.

Eric Wilkins concludes his paper with a roll-call of the great and the good who inhabited this corner of the City that would become the Barbican. "Can any ward boast a more distinguished company!" he asks – a truly generous tribute from a Deputy of the Ward of Cheap?

His list begins with Milton and Defoe and then moves to "Saintly Bishop Andrewes, Vicar of St. Giles and successively Bishop of Chichester, Ely and Winchester. Oliver Cromwell, married in St. Giles and his great enemy Prince Rupert. Two Lord Chancellors – Sir Thomas More born in Milk Street and the less saintly Judge Jeffreys who was practising at the Old Bailey aged 20 and on his death almost ruler of the City. John Speed, historian and map-maker. Two early Lord Mayors – Sir Christopher Packe 1654 and Sir Matthew Wood 1815 (a good many more in later times culminating in Sir Peter Studd 1970, Sir Allan Davis 1986, Sir Gavyn Arthur 2002). Lastly is William Shakespeare "towering above them all" one-time resident of Silver Street together with John Heminge and Henry Cordell, his partners and fellow actors who had the idea of printing 22 of his plays.

Not everyone at Guildhall was enthusiastic about the Barbican project. Wilkins certainly was, as the final words of his paper bear wholehearted testimony:

"Its history is rich indeed, for down the Barbican Queen Elizabeth the First rode in great state attended by Lord Mayor Sir Thomas Leigh, passing down Red Cross Street and through Cripplegate on her way to the Tower, just previous to her coronation". His hope was that in the not too distant future, the Barbican of tomorrow may receive her successor – as indeed was its good fortune.

* * *

The City and the Temples

The Temples – the Inner Temple and the Middle Temple – their wealth of 17th century red brick and stone, courts and winding passage-ways built around the church of the Knights Templars dating from the 12th century; their beautiful gardens; a place where lawyers have pursued their calling for nearly seven hundred years; an oasis of calm and peace just a stone's throw from the clamour of Fleet Street.

Here is, undoubtedly, the most beautiful part of the City of London – yet over the centuries it stubbornly maintained its separateness from the City and although now part of the City's largest Ward of Farringdon Without, the jurisdiction of the Temples still remains its own.

The quite fascinating history of the Temples was presented to the GHA by Historian James Keith in May 1978.

The Order of Knights Templars was founded in Jerusalem in 1118 and in England ten years later, their first house and church built in Holborn. They quickly outgrew these properties and being such a powerful and wealthy order were able to acquire the large area of land lying between Fleet Street and the River which became their new Temple, its church with the Templars' distinctive circular nave. Their occupation began in 1162 and there soon began a dispute as to who governed the area which would continue for the next eight centuries. At the time of the Templars the land was, of course, outside the City wall.

In 1308 Pope Clement V persuaded Edward II to assist him in abolishing the Order of Knights Templars. Their possessions escheated to the Crown, the City Sheriffs given the task of making an inventory of the buildings and goods to be taken into the King's ownership. The Sheriff's involvement would have made the City authorities believe the Temple to be under their jurisdiction.

Parliament took a different view in 1324 and decided that the land should be assigned to "other men of most holy religion and disposed to godly use". So they were delivered to the Hospital of St. John of

Jerusalem – "the Hospitallers". Shortly afterwards "Apprentices of the Law" came into the Temple and the two Societies of the Inner and Middle Temple became rent-paying tenants of the Hospitallers. In their turn, however, the Hospitallers were abolished in 1540 as part of the Reformation by Henry VIII and at that point the Temple was vested in the King, but with the tenancies of the two Inns being preserved. The Master who, then as now, governed the affairs of the Temple kept his position. Keith tells us that the Master at that time, one William Ermestede was an earlier Vicar of Bray who regularly changed his religion to suit the times – remaining Catholic under Henry VIII, becoming Protestant for Edward VI, Catholic again under Queen Mary and finishing as a Protestant for Queen Elizabeth.

James I was free with his charters – one for the Temple in 1608 and another, to add to its long collection, for the City a few weeks later. There being two charters hardly helped in deciding about jurisdiction and in an attempt to settle the matter the City and the Inner Temple petitioned the Privy Council presided over by Charles II soon after the Great Fire. There was no settlement for the City which continued to file claim after unsuccessful claim.

In 1669 Lord Mayor Sir William Peake had been invited to dine as a private guest at the Inner Temple. He let it be known he would arrive with his Swordbearer. The benchers had said he should leave his sword at home which he failed to do and he was firmly refused entry. Pepys in his diary describes the resultant fracas as a riot blamed by the City on the actions of the Gentlemen of the Temple.

The first thaw in relations between City and Temple came in 1839 with the establishment of the City of London Police when after some initial difficulties the two Inns agreed to participate. There followed the practice of residents and barristers in Inner and Middle Temples having their names added to the electoral roll of Farringdon Without which, geographically at least, embraced the Temples.

When the legality of this practice was challenged – as recently as 1959 – on the grounds that the Temples were not of the City but in its suburbs it led, not surprisingly, to much legal argument. It was decreed first by the Judge and then by Common Council that 1,584 who were on the Farringdon Without electoral register, a hundred-year-old practice, could not be disenfranchised and that the Temples were undoubtedly part of the City for municipal and county elections.

The Temples continue, and doubtless always will, to retain their separate independence. They continue also to provide a wide range of services for themselves such as paving, maintenance, cleaning, lighting of their streets but other functions are the responsibility of the Common Council – health and social services, police and libraries.

The Corporation's annual rating demand includes an additional and separate rate for the Temples which in 1978 when James Keith read his paper stood at some £31,000.

*

"Brilliantly the Temple Fountain sparkled in the sun and laughingly the liquid music played and merrily the idle drops of water danced and danced and peeping out in sport among the trees plunged lightly down to hide themselves".

I hope James Keith would approve this addition to his paper: the words of Dickens from "Martin Chuzzlewit" written beside the Temple fountain.

* * *

Bartholomew Close, the Rich Inheritance

Many parts of the City reflect their history in the layout of their streets and buildings and no part more so than Bartholomew Close. With three livery companies joining the Butchers in this Conservation Area of small properties, it was an appropriate moment to look at the origins of the close said Norman Hall in his GHA paper of 1987.

The site lay outside the Roman Wall adjacent to the Smoothfield where in Medieval times large crowds would assemble for jousting in Giltspur Street, rioting against the Government or for the sale of cattle driven from the fields of Hampstead down Cowcross Street.

The site itself was not involved in such diversions because the Monk Rahere had persuaded Henry I to grant him land on which to build a priory and hospital dedicated to St. Bartholomew. Around the priory a wall was erected with gates at regular intervals, marked today by the passages from Long Lane, Aldersgate Street, Smithfield and Little Britain. From 1123 until 1539 this large site was developed as a religious community with the Prior's house, cloisters, refectory, kitchens and infirmary all surrounding the Priory with its Lady Chapel, sanctuary, choir and nave. Within the priory wall was an open space "The Market of St. Bartholomew".

All this came to an end in 1539 with the suppression of the monasteries. The Prior and his canons were ejected and the whole property transferred to the King. It came into the possession of Sir Richard Rich, a close adviser of Henry VIII, for the sum of £1,064. 11s 3d. The Choir of the Priory was retained and converted into the area's parish church. Rich, now created a baron, had Catholic sympathies and gave up his investment to Queen Mary who installed the Black Friars there but bought the estate back from Queen Elizabeth for a mere £289. 9s 4d.

Back in business Baron Rich converted what had been the Priory transepts and Lady Chapel for secular use. Bartholomew Close remained a liberty outside the jurisdiction of the Lord Mayor and was not therefore described in Stow's Survey of London. The Close was inhabited by noble families – Walsingham, De Vere, Neville.

Rich's grandson, the third Baron, decided to develop the open space within the Priory walls, a clearly profitable move although Hall wondered if he took up the diversion because his wife Penelope, having given him six children, then began to live openly with Charles Blount, 8th Lord Mountjoy, another noble resident of the Close, giving him five children, a truly fecund lady.

Bartholomew Fair probably originated at the same time as the Priory and Hospital and within the Priory walls. As it grew it spilled out to West Smithfield, becoming England's great annual market place for the woollen and cloth trades. There came the attractions of the fairground, too, with the ill-behaviour provoking merchants to threaten to stay away. While historian William Fitzstephen wrote in 1173 "To this Fair the City merchants bring their wares from every nation under heaven", Ben Jonson expressed a different view around 1600: "this is the very womb and bed of enormity".

The Fair was closed during the Commonwealth but re-opened with ever greater licence at the Restoration. At Guildhall in 1760 the City Lands Committee considered its abolition but with a threatened demand for compensation from its owner the matter was allowed to drift. In 1854 the Fair ceased to exist and the new Smithfield meat market took its place.

Meanwhile, Bartholomew Close was being intensely developed, its vacant ground being covered with the narrow streets and small houses whose layout is exactly as positioned today. Cloth Fair, Kinghorn Street, Middle Street and Newbury Street are all still there with their courtyards and alleys. Many of the little houses and businesses are Victorian although there are 18th century survivals and even a pair in Cloth Fair dating from the early 1600's. The Fire of 1666 did not reach the Close at all. The church of St. Bartholomew the Great brings its special grandeur to this area but essentially the Bartholomew Close precinct remains one of the very few (and certainly the largest) of small-scale corners of the City and one where its history is apparent.

How appropriate that the very first of the City Heritage Awards, in 1978, was given for work on a derelict café, one-time bakery, on the corner of Newbury and Kinghorn Streets, restored with loving care to its original Georgian elegance" as the offices of Anstey Horne the surveyors.

Norman Hall remarks (somewhat wryly) that the area is now full of lawyers (he being one), architects and surveyors – and a betting shop!

*　*　*

New Court and the House of Rothschild

This paper, said Historian Chester Barratt in July 1967, is concerned with just one piece of Corporation property for which we are able to trace its history over the past 600 years during which time it has been in the continuous possession of the Corporation of London. When he delivered his paper the site had survived the winds that had swept so much away during and after the war as small buildings were lost in the development of big blocks: New Court in St. Swithin's Lane, headquarters of Rothschilds the merchant bankers, who have operated continuously on this site since 1809.

Some 630 years ago the site was owned by the Le Scrope family – Henry, Chief Justice of the King's Bench and Chief Baron of the Exchequer, and his brother Geoffrey, also a Chief Justice and later secretary to Edward III. In 1332 the City presented them with gifts for their work in Parliament – presumably on the City's behalf.

The property was sold to Roger de Depham (possibly related to the Scropes) who was a man of parts – Sheriff's Clerk, Town Clerk in 1335 doubling up as Alderman for the Ward of Candlewick and serving as Recorder of the City. He lived at New Court until his death. In his will he bequested all his City lands and property to the Mayor, Aldermen and Commonalty on condition that prayers were said for him and his family in the church of St. Swithin and Guildhall Chapel.

So it was that the City acquired the property in 1359 and from then on leased it to a succession of wealthy and prominent City people. John de Bures, draper, was a sheriff in 1358 and as a Common Councilman was entrusted with the keys of the City Seal from 1364 to 1377 and in that final year was wealthy enough to lend money to the Crown. In 1390 the mansion of New Court was leased to another draper, John Hende (the original hall of the Drapers' Company was nearby) who as Mayor the following year used the house for his mayoralty. He served as an alderman for Candlewick and Walbrook Wards for nearly 30 years. He was one of numerous aldermen who suffered the displeasure of monarchs – in his case Richard II, arrested, confined at Windsor Castle, released on bail of £2,000 (an enormous sum) and pardoned a year later.

Another unfortunate tenant was Mayor Sir Laurence Aylmer imprisoned and heavily fined by Henry VII's infamous extortioners Empson and Dudley. He was so impoverished that his great house in St. Swithin's Lane fell into decay and he was forced to petition the Court of Aldermen for financial aid.

The whole of the property was destroyed in the Great Fire of 1666 and its then tenant, Edward Bonham, was offered a new lease of 81 years with a covenant to rebuild. Since the cost of rebuilding did not appeal to him the City paid him £300 for surrender of the lease which was taken up by one Jeremy Mount who undertook the rebuilding, to good effect it would appear.

For in 1720 Strype, in his new version of Stow's Survey, described New Court as a "very handsome large place with an open passage into it for coach or cart. Here are very good buildings and at the upper end is a very good large house enclosed from the rest by a handsome pale".

When first occupied by the Rothschilds the building had been repaired to include a covered colonnade with steps up to the front door while within were marble chimneypieces, warehouse and country house wrote Chester Barratt. Nathan Mayer Rothschild, the founder of the English branch of the bank, moved into New Court in 1809 and a year later took a new lease of 21 years from the City to commence at Christmas 1815. Then, in 1813, Rothschilds purchased from the Commissioners for Bankruptcy the lease granted by the City for the house at 3 New Court and went on to acquire other parts of the estate.

When rebuilding was undertaken in 1880 the frontage of their property was 100 feet in length, the City then granting an 80-year lease for the extended site at a rent of £1,000 p.a. Eventually the whole site including further acquisitions by the bank, and transferred to the Corporation, was consolidated in the City's ownership and held by Rothschilds on a single lease of 80 years from Christmas 1962 at a rental of £42,800 p.a. At that time New Court's massive gateway, guarded by day, firmly closed at night (and on Jewish festivals), was dismantled to give way to an open courtyard.

Chester Barratt speaks of his paper as providing a "site pedigree" of this particularly interesting corner of the City and suggests that the history of other City Lands properties would be equally rewarding, particularly to the GHA.

Then as two postscripts to his paper: first, a total rebuilding of Rothschilds with the kind of modern building they required for their business in the new millennium; second, the sad decision by the City Corporation to destroy the City Lands Committee and its 400-year ownership and management of the City's property holdings.

*   *   *

College Hill where Whittington lived

College Hill, the narrow lane that runs from Cannon Street down to College Street, has a rich and ancient history but under a quite different name (or names). In its time this little street was one of the most important in London, wrote Historian Ralph Peacock in his GHA paper of December 1966. All the much larger streets which now surround it are modern.

In medieval days it was originally called La Riole, after a village near Bordeaux (which is still there). The wine from that district was brought in at Wine Wharf on Thames Street and carried up the hill to the hall of La Riole. It seems probable that merchants from the French village settled there, the better to market their produce. The Walbrook stream ran behind the back door of the hall.

It was here where Richard Whittington, the merchant prince who was four times mayor of London, chose to live. In a corner of his large property was the church of St. Michael which he rebuilt and which was generally known as Paternosterchurch in La Riole. Its name survives today as St. Michael Paternoster Royal, a Wren church rebuilt after the Great Fire.

Whittington had plans, also, for a College of Priests and almshouses but with time running out for him he left provisions in his will for the founding of both institutions. His livery, the Mercers, were appointed trustees of the two foundations which were erected in La Riole – or what in 1424 had come be called The Royal.

The College (which 250 years later would give College Hill its name) consisted of the Master, four secular chaplains, three clerks in holy orders and four choristers. There was an endowment of £63 p.a. In the almshouses with an endowment of £40 dwelt thirteen poor men. The College, dedicated to the Holy Spirit, continued until 1548 when it was dissolved on the suppression of monasteries, colleges and chantries. The almshouses were rebuilt after the Fire but gradually became dilapidated although they still accommodated thirteen pensioners, now all women. On the west side of the street was the large establishment of the second Duke of Buckingham.

College Hill remains one of the City's most attractive backwaters still full of historical memories: the church of St. Michael; the site of Whittington's house, marked with a blue plaque, and where later were his almshouses and college and, in the 19th century, the Mercers' School (the building there now, in sad need of restoration, looks derelict – a quite unexpected eyesore in this otherwise well cared for area). In total contrast are two spectacular late 17th century archways which take one through courtyards to a group of buildings, one of which is a three-storey brick house of 1688.

Opposite, around Newcastle Court where once was Buckingham House, is a solid three-storey red brick house of around 1730 through the windows of which can be seen its panelled interior and elegant staircase. Down towards College Street, to add to the College Hill's rich architectural variety are two mid-19th century warehouses.

At the top, northern, end of College Hill there once stood a small fortress known as Tower Royal which, according to Stow, was there in the time of Edward I and also known as "The Queen's Wardrobe". Historian Peacock tells us that during Wat Tyler's rebellion of 1381 when the Tower of London was stormed by the rebels, the Queen Mother, in residence there, fled for safety to Tower Royal until she was rescued by her son, Richard II.

This area of the City has long been a place for the halls of livery companies. In College Hill itself were once the Glaziers, Turners and Cutlers, though no more. In nearby Dowgate Hill there remain the Tallow Chandlers, Dyers and Skinners while in College Hill is Innholders' Hall.

* * *

Drapers' Gardens

When John Bennett delivered his paper in January 2011, Drapers' Gardens had undergone at least three revolutionary changes and were gardens only in name.

Between what is now Throgmorton Street and London Wall was a marshy area hardly built upon in medieval London but by the mid-1500's a good many houses were being built on what had been land once occupied by an Augustinian Friary. One of those houses had been bought by Thomas Cromwell.

Cromwell had been employed in his youth in Italy as a mercenary, then in a Florentine merchant bank and later handling ecclesiastical issues; he was fluent in Latin, Italian and French; well prepared when he arrived in England for anything and everything.

In 1523 he became a member of Parliament and in the later 1520's taken into the employ of Cardinal Wolsey, Lord Chancellor to Henry VIII. It was Cromwell who assisted in procuring the King's divorce from his first wife, Katherine of Aragon, and arranging his ill-fated marriage to Anne Boleyn.

After Wolsey's death he became ever more favoured by Henry – appointed Chancellor of the Exchequer, Master of the Rolls, Vicar General, Lord Privy Seal, Knight of the Garter, Baron and finally Earl of Essex. Cromwell was a prime mover in the suppression of the monasteries.

Cromwell became a very wealthy man and he had begun to acquire property, first in Old Broad Street and then in adjacent areas, including his Friary residence which was greatly expanded and surrounded by a great garden. This was the site of what we now know as Drapers' Gardens.

Cromwell's downfall in those unsafe times was swift and terrible. Accused of treason and heresy, he was beheaded on Tower Hill in July 1540.

On his death the house and garden passed to the King who had no use for them and in 1543 the large property was purchased by the

Drapers' Company who converted the house into their Hall, with its surrounding Drapers' Gardens. Drapers' Hall was burned to the ground in 1666 while ironically the gardens acted as a firebreak to further spread of the conflagration. The site has remained in the ownership of the Drapers' Company to this day, its magnificent Victorian hall fronting Throgmorton Street, quite close to the pre-Fire hall.

For three hundred years the "Great Garden", as it was called, continued to be developed as a garden, the Drapers' Company making improvements and allowing access to the public. Its climacteric came in 1874 with the City of London Flower Show, Princes Louise presenting the prizes. By then it was felt that the enormous value of the site could no longer be overlooked and the Drapers decided the gardens should be let on building leases. By the end of the century the Great Garden was no more, but covered in offices for stockbrokers, wine merchants and, strangely enough, the Persian Consulate General.

The next big change came in the 1960's when the small fry were swept away to make room for Richard Seifert's 29-storey office tower which Bennett describes as "a highly distinctive building in an otherwise unexceptional area". Seifert, we are told, regarded it as one of his proudest achievements. (The author of this volume thinks his later Nat. West tower greatly superior). It was not greatly loved and its demolition in 2006 was not mourned.

A new Drapers Gardens, completed in 2009, is architecturally a considerable improvement. Its highest, western, end is fifteen storeys, while it steps down to twelve in the middle and only five in the east. This stepped profile makes it something of a landmark astride the wards of Broad Street and Coleman Street. A pleasant feature is the little "park" inserted into Copthall Avenue with trees, flowers and nesting boxes for birds. On top of the building there are roof gardens as a reminder of the Drapers' Gardens long ago – alas not open to the public.

*　　*　　*

St. Martin-le-Grand:
Collegiate Church – and den of iniquity

Stow relates that from the time of Edward the Confessor there existed in Saint Martin's Lane a fair and large college of dean, canons and priests. It remained there for 500 years until in 1548 it was pulled down in the destruction of the monasteries. In its place a large wine tavern was built together with many houses for the wealthier citizens who continued to enjoy the exemptions from tax and other privileges of the previous religious occupants.

In his sparkling paper delivered in June 2010, Historian and Revd. Dr. Martin Dudley (Rector of St. Bartholomew the Great), tells us that "Stow had rather an idealised view of the college and its canons, making them more devout than history suggests they were".

In those days there was a plethora of priests, vicars, clerks and chaplains, one of whom, Richard Henney, was brought before the Mayor and Aldermen having been taken naked with Johanna, also naked, by the Constable and Beadle. Such behaviour among the chaplains was not unusual, wrote Dudley.

St. Martin's was a royal free establishment with its Dean appointed by the King. The canons were appointed by the dean and, like him, were clerks attached to the royal household. "It was more a corporation of officials rather than a religious house and the spiritual side of the college somewhat neglected". Some of the officers and ministers led dissolute lives elsewhere. Deans were held responsible and several were removed by the King's commissioners.

Deans were, however, favourites of kings. Edward I told the Mayor that no plea in the Husting of London would be permitted against "our beloved and trusty William de la Marche, Dean of St. Martin-le-Grand and our Treasurer in the Exchequer. Later deans held high office – Lord Privy Seal, Clerk of the Wardrobe; some went on to become Archbishops of both York and Canterbury.

Not surprisingly there was frequent conflict between such powerful men and the Mayor and Aldermen of the City. In the early 15th century the City, increasingly resentful of those who, within it, claimed exemption from its authority. The right of sanctuary enjoyed by St. Martin's was a particular cause of trouble since prisoners on their way from Newgate for trial at Guildhall were being seized en route and taken into the exempt precinct. In 1405 the City petitioned Henry IV to have this right annulled. He expressed sympathy but was unable to help.

Another area of much concern for the City was the fraudulent production in the precinct of articles such as brooches, rings, cups and spoons said to be of gold but were made of inferior metal, gilded or silvered over. Even when, in the reign of Edward IV, a statute against makers of such fraudulent work was enacted, St. Martin's was deliberately excluded.

A final case cited by Dudley was that of a goldsmith who had fabricated a Prior's seal for purposes of fraud and led to Dudley's closing words: "I guess the Mayor and Aldermen knew exactly who was skilled in fabricating seals and dwelt in the close at St. Martin-le-Grand; they also knew they couldn't easily go in and get him out of that den of iniquity".

*　　*　　*

From a street corner in Farringdon

A kaleidoscope of the City's history was unrolled in a novel way by Dudley Game in his paper of January 1961. He invited his fellow Historians to stand with him at the corner of Newgate Street and Old Bailey to meet in their imagination people who had in bygone days passed this way.

His first passer-by was a Roman soldier marching up Snow Hill and entering the walled City under New Gate – an entry way built subsequently to the wall itself. Here, Game reminds us, the wall turned south before reaching Lud Gate and at the turn was strengthened by a large bastion, the remains of which, in 1961, could still be seen beneath the courtyard of the General Post Office (they are still there but, alas, the Post Office is no more, having been well refurbished as part of the Merrill Lynch complex).

Game's second encounter – skipping a few centuries during which its Norman occupiers used the site as a dumping ground for rubbish and a place for hanging evildoers – was with an Augustinian brother; the monk would have been on his way to the great new Priory Church of St. Bartholomew hard by the Smoothfield.

Standing here on a day in 1240 we would have seen a crowd of battered Augustinians running away from the priory church following a fracas with followers of a visiting Archbishop of Canterbury, Normans to a man while their hosts were determinedly English clergy. Blood had been spilt and the whole city was in uproar.

Many were the wonderful processions which passed under New Gate. In 1375 when Dame Alice Perrers, Edward III's concubine no less, "Lady of the Sun", accompanied by many lords and ladies, every lady leading a lord by his horse bridle, came to West Smithfield to begin a great joust which endured seven days.

So much spectacular chivalry earned for the opposite street the name of Knight Rider Street, afterwards changed to Giltspur Street.

Six years after Dame Alice's glittering cavalcade there came a procession of a very different kind to the corner of Farringdon – Wat

Tyler and his peasant army. Strangely enough, Historian Game would it seems favour Charles Dickens' view of the encounter of King Richard II and Wat Tyler: "I think Tyler appears in history as beyond comparison the truer and more respectable man of the two".

In 1133 Henry I granted to the canons of St. Bartholomew a charter for an annual fair to be held within the precincts of the Priory. Later it spilled over into Smithfield and certainly in Stuart times was opened by the Lord Mayor whose procession from Guildhall would have passed by Newgate.

Mr Pepys was probably at this street corner on August 30th 1667 for he wrote in his diary: "I go to Bartholomew Fair to walk up and down there, among things find my Lady Castlemain at a puppet play and the street full of people expecting her coming out!" Then in December: "Back to Smithfield giving £50 for a fine pair of black horses for a coach – the first I ever was master of".

Something horrible on a chill February a hundred years earlier though, the smoke rising from the fire in Smithfield in which John Rogers, vicar of St. Sepulchre's Church at Newgate, was burnt to death – first of Mary's Protestant victims. The church itself narrowly escaped destruction in the Great Fire of 1666, the fire stopping at Pie Corner. Its saving is commemorated with a little gilt figure of a fat boy on which are the words: "This boy is in Memmory put up for the late FIRE OF LONDON occasioned by the sin of gluttony 1666".

On this very corner was Newgate Prison and after its poor condemned were no longer carted off to be hanged at Tyburn their unfortunate successors were publicly hanged outside Newgate, a spectacle that attracted the good citizens by the hundreds. James Boswell wrote of Tyburn in May 1763: "My curiosity to see the melancholy spectacle of the executions was so strong that I could not resist it although I was sensible that I should suffer much from it... I was most terribly shocked and thrown into a very deep melancholy". Thackery declared in 1847: "The sight of an execution (at Newgate) has left in my mind an extraordinary feeling of terror and shame and I pray God it may soon be out of the power of any man in England to witness such a hideous and degrading sight".

And then, passing our corner, came John Howard and Elizabeth Fry, first among those who sought to alleviate the sufferings of the poor wretches confined in Newgate.

On a happier note, Queen Victoria passed this way in 1869 to inaugurate on 6th November two brilliant engineering achievements – the creation of Holborn Viaduct and the building of Blackfriars Bridge. Dudley Game's concluding words were of regret that lack of time prevented him from introducing us to many more – not least Captain John Smith, explorer, trader and Governor of Virginia, who worshipped here in St. Sepulchre's; Oliver Goldsmith who lived and wrote in a room off Old Bailey: the great Dr. Johnson who came with other notables to investigate the mystery of the Cock Lane ghost; and that renowned Alderman of Farringdon Ward, John Wilkes. "But we have stood here long enough for one day!"

*   *   *

Fleet Street – Place and Concept

Joyce Nash, in this model of a paper delivered in May 1994, attributes her interest in Fleet Street to her contacts with the press as an educationist and the fact that she married a journalist. She presented the GHA with an impressively researched history.

Named after the Fleet River, this area in medieval times was ecclesiastical with the clergy living in their great houses of the White Friars and Black Friars. In the 18th century it was noted for the number of its taverns and as the home territory of Samuel Johnson and Mrs Salmon's Waxworks Museum.

It was in 1530 though that Wynkyn de Worde, a printer, brought from Alsace to London by Caxton, set up a printing office "at the sign of the Swan" on the south side of Fleet Street opposite Shoe Lane. Here was the beginning of book production and there followed news-sheets. As early as 1666 there was a two-page sheet of news and small advertisements.

Mrs. Nash thinks that it was Fleet Street's closeness to the City's trade and commercial activity and the gossip of its coffee-houses that helped bring about its role as a centre for the gathering and dissemination of news, chiefly from abroad.

The first of Fleet Street's newspapers appeared in the 18th century – the Daily Courant – the first issue being on 11th March 1702 its content entirely of foreign news. The first daily evening paper, The Star, appeared in 1788 (and, astonishingly, continuing into the 1970's).

Soon Fleet Street was bustling with newspapers – Morning Post, Morning Advertiser and Daily Telegraph. They swarmed across the street into adjoining courts and alleys. The Times had its offices and presses in Printing House Square, Blackfriars – not in Fleet Street but still of it and, in its early days, printed the worst of London's murder cases and sex crimes in Latin.

Already, in the early 1800's, John Walter, the owner of The Times was experiencing problems with his employees as he attempted to use steam power to operate his printing presses.

Towards the end of the 19th century Fleet Street entered a new era where the Harmsworth brothers, Alfred and Harold, acquired the decrepit Evening News and shortly afterwards published the first edition of their Daily Mail. Mrs Nash comments: "The Daily Mail represents the signpost that was to point Fleet Street into the heart of public affairs, politics and the national consciousness". Alfred Harmsworth became Lord Northcliffe, the first and most brilliant of the Fleet Street press barons, and a newly emerging literate society could afford his ha'penny a day Daily Mail and was able to understand its clear, simple language and air of excitement. Here was the beginning of high-circulation newspapers with a readership spread across the whole country. Lord Macaulay, the historian, observing the Press gallery at Westminster had coined the phrase "The Fourth Estate".

Having survived the two World Wars, Fleet Street began to demonstrate the unpleasant face of trades unionism, wrote Mrs Nash, with senior shop stewards – "Fathers of the Chapel" recruiting the work force and allocating the men to their duties in the foundry and on the presses.

The whole system operated on what were known as Old Spanish Customs. A foreman would engage three casual night workers where two would have been enough, the third man going home and taking his turn at work on a subsequent night. There were innumerable lightning strikes on the most trivial of grievances with thousands of newspapers lost on each occasion. Daily Mirror production stopped one night because the printers disliked the content of the editorial.

Up to the 1980's most newspapers were using techniques a hundred years old. Type was set by the antiquated "hot metal" system, time-wasting, dirty, labour-intensive and very expensive. All newspapers operated on a financial knife-edge. Two of them, the News Chronicle and The Star were forced to close down. In an effort to challenge the unions' stranglehold, The Times under Lord Thompson was shut down for a year.

It was Rupert Murdoch, the following owner of the newspaper, who almost single-handedly devised the operating plan that would change the nature of Fleet Street. In the first instance he smuggled new computer-age equipment into a site he had acquired in Wapping. Coaches with obscured windows carried technicians and journalists into the new plant.

His problem would be to persuade the unions to abandon the hot metal process and adopt the new technology (knowing full well they would not). He moved the negotiations in a manner to encourage them to use their favourite weapon – the strike. But this time it was for them a fatal move. There was not the traditional response of capitulation. He dismissed all the union members for breach of contract.

The immediate aftermath was unpleasant with pitched battles outside "Fortress Wapping" between hundreds if not thousands of protesters and the police who sought to provide a path for workers through the gates; the vans taking Murdoch papers for distribution outside were attacked.

Murdoch won and Fleet Street as an industry was changed for ever. Other newspapers brought in the new technology and they, in their turn, faced down the now diminishing power of the unions. Suddenly newspaper publishing became a profitable business.

Alas the Murdoch revolution had one grievous result for the City as the proprietors, one after another, forsook their Fleet Street printing presses for cheaper and more easily serviced premises in Canary Wharf and elsewhere.

It was truly the end of a famous era, the "Street of Adventure" with all those famous newspaper signs – Express and Telegraph, Bolton Evening News and Kentish Gazette, Reuters and Press Association – giving way to a new and much less romantic culture of banking houses. Happily the barristers from the Temples are still there as are El Vino and The Cheshire Cheese.

*

Another view of Fleet Street's history came in October 2001 from Christopher Mitchell who with his brother owned and ran the famous El Vino Wine establishment, a business set up by his grandfather in 1915.

His paper touched on Sweeney Todd's famous barber's shop whose tilting chair conveyed his unfortunate clients to the cellarage below on their way to becoming the meat pies sold in the shop opposite. And Mitchell told how he looked across the street to Peales Hotel at the corner of Fetter Lane where, indelibly inscribed on its wall, was a sign: "Peales Hotel – Rooms by the Hour" (Peales was a place where the author of this volume had the occasional liquid lunch in his days as a journalist).

Fleet Street's golden era lasted a hundred years from the end of the 1800's. It was a time when people wanted to know what was going on in the world, to read about the rich and famous and to enjoy the latest scandals. The arrival of a daily newspaper on the breakfast table or its collection from news vendors became a must and Fleet Street was there to fill that need.

It was the introduction of the Koenig steam press in 1814 that made possible the mass circulation of daily papers, turning out 4,000 sheets per hour. There followed the Hoe rotary press and linotype machines. The great days of the press Barons were well and truly founded.

The Observer, founded in 1791, passed to the Harmsworths and then to the Astors and eventually to Tiny Rowland; the Telegraph, launched in 1885 went from Lord Camrose to the Berry family and then to Conrad Black; The Mirror launched by Harmsworth passed to Cecil King, then to the Cudlips and on to Maxwell. The Express owned by Beaverbrook passed to his son Sir Max Aitkin and then to Trafalgar House.

*

While the City's giants, Gog and Magog, high up in the Guildhall, are so well known there are two others which are not so familiar. These are the Wooden Giants of Fleet Street which provided Lt. Col. William Dove with the subject for his paper to the GHA in June 1964. These are the giants which strike the clock bells every quarter of an hour at the Fleet Street church of St. Dunstan in the West.

The church was associated with acts of penance in the 14th century and Historian Dove cites the case of a citizen who had insulted (or perhaps assaulted) an alderman, the culprit ordered by the Mayor to walk from Guildhall through Chepe and Fleet Street carrying a lighted candle three pounds in weight and to deposit it on the high altar at St. Dunstan's. The penitential journey had to be made with head, legs and feet bare.

There had been a clock on the church which survived the Great Fire but in 1671 a clockmaker named Thomas Harrys offered to build a new clock for £80 and the old one. He was, indeed, given the old clock but was paid only £35 – a rather low remuneration for the splendid new clock he provided that same year.

It was the first clock to show the minutes as well as the hours. But its greatest feature was to incorporate figures of two men each holding a pole-axe who would strike the chiming bells at each of the quarter hours. The clock became one of London's marvels, attracting crowds of sightseers. This part of Fleet Street became a happy hunting ground for pickpockets.

In 1830 when Fleet Street was widened to cope with increasing traffic, the old church was demolished – there were few conservationists around in those days – and the Marquis of Hertford purchased the clock and had it re-erected in the garden of his Regent's Park house, achievement of a lifelong ambition. He named his house St. Dunstan's, that house later becoming the headquarters of the world-renowned organisation for blind ex-servicemen.

Happily the church was rebuilt in 1839 on the site it still occupies today but the clock remained in the Regent's Park garden. A hundred years later in 1935 Lord Rothermere, the new owner of St. Dunstan's and the clock, with his Fleet Street connections, offered to have it taken down, repaired, and re-erected at St. Dunstan's Church as a gift to Fleet Street to commemorate the Silver Jubilee of King George V's reign. The architect was Albert Richardson (later President of the Royal Academy) and Col. Dove's family firm was entrusted with the work of removal and re-erection of the clock at the church.

So it was that 264 years after the wooden giants first struck the bells of St. Dunstan's Church on 28th October 1671, they did so again on 24th October 1935, to become once more one of the great sights of Fleet Street.

*   *   *

The London Charterhouse

The Charterhouse, that treasure of early medieval London, which has occupied its site just north of the City for 640 years, served first as a burial ground for victims of the Black Death in 1349. A piece of waste ground belonging to the Hospital of St. Bartholomew, it was bought for the purpose by Sir Walter de Manny, a nobleman of Norman descent, a soldier who fought at Crécy, one of the first Knights of the Garter and associate of Edward III and his family.

Some twenty years later, perhaps foreseeing his own death, it was de Manny who founded on this same site a priory of the Carthusian Order of monks with instructions that he should be buried in its church at the foot of the high altar steps. A Carthusian monastery was a "Chartreuse" which, rendered into English, became a Charterhouse.

Part of the fascinating history of the London Charterhouse was told in January 1955 by Historian Paul Paget who certainly possessed the right credentials.

He was one of the two partners of the Seeley and Paget architectural practice who were invited to undertake the reconstruction of the Charterhouse after the destruction it had suffered from war-time bombing (John Seeley had by then become Lord Mottistone).

Carthusian monasteries followed a set pattern taking as their model La Grande Chartreuse near Grenoble in France: the monks' 'cells' quite sizeable two-floor cottages each with its own garden set round three sides of a large cloister; refectory, chapter house and, above all, the church. Much remained, incorporated in later developments, at the outbreak of war in 1939.

In their researches, however, Mottistone and Paget came to the conclusion that the church had, in fact, already been destroyed much earlier, at the time of the Dissolution and that what actually remained of the great priory was only the chapterhouse. Much detective work disclosed a brick-built tomb within which was a leaden coffin containing the remains of Sir Walter de Manny.

Wrote Paget: "Thus in locating the last resting place of the monastery's founder, we had in fact rediscovered the forgotten ground plan of the church in which he was known to have been buried. This led to a complete reassessment of the whole layout of the monastic buildings".

The remains were to be re-interred in their original tomb but, in order that all might be reverently conducted, Mottistone and Paget were anxious to obtain some suitable material to act as a pall over the somewhat mutilated coffin, a difficulty at that time because of clothes rationing and coupons required for everything. Happily, in 1944, next door to the architects' office their next-door neighbour was the one surviving cloth merchant – in Cloth Fair, where else! The good neighbour had just the thing, some stuff he used to supply to monks in Ireland for their habits.

In 1545 Henry VIII granted the whole of the property to Lord North who proceeded to demolish much of the monastic buildings and to build himself a palace out of the ruins. A monk who had fled from the Charterhouse said that among his other iniquities Lord North was using the church as his dining hall. Paul Paget, as a result of his researches, was able to tell us that in reality the church had been almost totally destroyed soon after the Dissolution and that Lord North was not using the church as his dining hall but was using its stonework as a quarry for the building of a new dining hall which, indeed, survives to this day.

In 1611 the great house was up for sale and was purchased by Thomas Sutton (said to then be the richest commoner in England) to establish his joint foundation of a school for 44 poor boys and a hospital for 80 poor gentlemen. At its peak in 1825 there were 480 pupils most of whom were fee-paying and eventually, in 1872, the school moved to Godalming. Part of the premises were sold to the Merchant Taylors Company for their school but, in due course, that school, too moved to the country.

After the extensive damage from bombing in 1941 and the Mottistone/Paget restoration, part of the former cloister was given over to a new Medical School for St. Bartholomew's Hospital. Within the surviving and restored buildings the pensioners of Sutton's Hospital continue to dwell, as did their predecessors 400 years ago, in the tranquil and beautiful surroundings of the London Charterhouse. Above the 17th century Library is the Great Chamber described as the finest Elizabethan room in England before the destruction of 1941. The Chapel where the pensioners worship was once the Chapterhouse. Thomas Sutton is buried there. [*]

* * *

---

[*] I am indebted for these final paragraphs to "The London Encylopaedia" third edition published 2008 by Macmillan – C.D.W.

St. Mary-le-Bow Church

Members of the Guildhall Historical Association have been surprisingly neglectful of the City churches as subjects for their papers. So, from its still early days, it is particularly welcome to have Col. Charles Whiteley's discourse on the church of St. Mary-le-Bow, "one of the chief monuments of the City" as he described it in September 1950.

Its site is as historic as London itself with Roman bricks still visible in the arches and walls of the crypt. Almost certainly there was a Saxon church here. It is known that the Normans built a church on this site in 1080, the groined vaults of the present crypt belonging to the late 11th century (what is today's crypt would have then been some twenty feet higher, at ground level). Stow relates that during a violent storm in 1191 the church steeple fell into Cheapside.

Whiteley tells us that the name "le Bow" was derived from its being the first of the City's churches to have been built with bows – as arches were then called. The church was one of the thirteen Peculiars of the Archbishop of Canterbury and therefore outside the diocese and jurisdiction of the Bishop of London. It was the place where the ancient Court of Arches was held to adjudicate on ecclesiastical cases – as it still does today. The Peculiars were abolished by Act of Parliament in 1847.

In 1666 Bow Church was destroyed to ground level. Sir Christopher Wren's restoration gave the City what must be the most beautiful of all his spires and towers – as befitting what Whiteley called the principal of the City's parish churches. (Floodlit as it is these days on winter evenings it is an enchanting sight). Rebuilding was accomplished quickly in just three years from 1671 to 1674 except for the steeple which was completed in 1680. At that time the parishes of All Hallowes Honey Lane and St. Pancras Soper Lane (whose churches were not rebuilt after the Fire) were united with St. Mary-le-Bow.

There is a City Dragon on the summit of Wren's spire which was celebrated in a verse of 1690:

"Look how the country hobbs with wonder flock
To see the City crest turned weather cock
Which with each shifting gale verses to and fro
London has now got two strings to her Bow".

Until the early 1500's there was only one Bow Bell, then came three more and finally a fifth, largest of them all. But much earlier the one bell sounded the curfew. In 1334 an order was made that no-one should be on the streets "after the hour of curfew had rung at the Church of our Lady at Bow". To be born within the sound of the curfew, rather than Bow Bells, was said in olden time to distinguish a "cockney" – that word derived from "cockernay", a cock's or misshapen egg, a contemptuous term for a milksop or townsman. (Most of us will be content with the more up-to-date version).

Wren built his steeple to carry a peal of twelve bells but only eight were hung – the big tenor and seven others. In 1723 the big tenor cracked, its replacement cast in the Whitechapel bell foundry. In 1743 the other seven were recast in Whitechapel and two more added to provide, as Col. Whiteley said, one of the finest peals in the World.

In the 1930's the whole of the exterior of the church and most of the bells were in urgent need of attention. A public appeal was successful in raising funds for structural repairs and Gordon Selfridge of the Oxford Street store paid the entire cost of re-casting and re-hanging the bells. The new peal rang out on 7th July 1933, dedicated by the Archbishop of Canterbury.

Bow Church was partly destroyed in the heavy bombing of May 1941. Happily it has been beautifully restored as one of the City's great treasures.

It also possesses its own treasures, its collection of old silver being one of the finest and most valuable in England. Two silver chalices and two plates are Elizabethan, dated 1568. Two alms dishes are dated 1635 and 1660. Two flagons are from 1630.

*

Recent history centres around two of the Church's colourful rectors – Joseph McCulloch and Victor Stock.

Joseph McCulloch, described in his obituary as the enfant terrible of the Church of England who, in books and broadcasts advocated among other things the disestablishment of the Church and the ordination of women priests, came to St. Mary-le-Bow in 1959 and was almost wholly responsible for its rebuilding after War-time destruction.

He remained its Rector for twenty years during which he instituted his famous 'Dialogues' using the church's twin pulpits every Tuesday lunchtime to converse with well-known figures – writers, broadcasters, actors and politicians – about issues of the day. He is affectionately remembered for smoking cigarettes in a small pipe which he used as a cigarette-holder.

Victor Stock who followed him as Rector continued the Tuesday lunchtime Dialogues and created an award-winning vegetarian restaurant in the crypt of the church. An ardent conservationist, he was in the forefront of the fight to prevent the destruction of Mappin and Webb and the other listed buildings around it to make way for No. 1 Poultry.

A fellow City priest, Peter Mullen, reviewing Victor Stock's book entitled "Taking Stock" described him as "colourful, dazzlingly witty, multi-talented, much in demand not only for his preaching and pastoral skills, but as counsellor to the great and the good, entertaining broadcaster and hilarious after-dinner speaker... Now he has published these scintillating memoirs... But why the relentless name-dropping? 'The Queen Mother half turned around and winked... Prime Minister Tony Blair came up and shook hands with me'. And so on every page".

Victor Stock was appointed Dean of Guildford in 2002 and has now retired.

*   *   *

216

The Whitbread Story: The history of the Chiswell Street Brewery

In the year 1734 the widow of a Bedfordshire farmer sent one of her young sons, aged fourteen, to be apprenticed to a brewer. Samuel Whitbread, was his name. Thus Historian Cuthbert Skilbeck began his paper of December 1968 which traced the fascinating story of the City's most famous brewery.

Young Samuel was apprenticed to John Wightman, owner of the Gilport (later Giltspur) Street brewery at Pye Corner. Mrs Whitbread was required to pay £300 for her son's indentures. A few months before completion of his eight-year apprenticeship the 22-year-old set up in business on his own in modest premises on the corner of Old Street and Whitecross Street, a quarter of a mile north of Chiswell Street, where, in 1750, he bought the small Kings Head Brewery, the start of his famous enterprise.

The Chiswell Street area was popular with brewers being supplied with good water and wood for their fires, cheaper and more plentiful in these parishes of St. Luke and St. Giles outside the City wall. In the 1740's and 1750's there were no fewer than eight breweries close to Chiswell Street.

His partner retired in 1761 and Samuel Whitbread was left as sole proprietor. His capital was not large for as seventh child he had come to London with a comparatively modest patrimony. John Howard (the prison reformer), a relative and friend, helped him and Whitbread himself worked tirelessly to develop his business.

The brewery grew much larger and Whitbread introduced innovations of the most modern kind. James Watt's Steam Engine was one of the wonders of London. It replaced the six horses previously required to turn the wheel of the malt-grinding process. The great Porter Tun Room, the unsupported roof-span of which is exceeded in its majestic size only by that of Westminster Hall was completed in 1784. The Porter Tun Room withstood the bombs of 1940 and when the brewery closed at the end of the 1970's became the central feature of an impressive entertainment facility, the recipient of the City Heritage Award of 1979.

Skilbeck told his fellow Historians that throughout his life Whitbread did all in his power to better the lot of the poor. He instituted an early profit-sharing scheme with his employees and gave generously to hospitals and churches. He was a member first of St. Luke's Church, Old Street, and then of St. Giles, Fore Street. As a Member of Parliament for 22 years from 1768 he was among the first to oppose the slave trade.

His son, Samuel the second, was less well-known for his business acumen but famous for his political activities as a member of the Whig opposition under Charles James Fox and following in his father's footsteps in his hatred of injustice and oppression. His patronage of the arts included the rebuilding of the Drury Lane Theatre.

The business of the brewery continued to flourish under the control of successive members of the Whitbread family who remained the controlling element when the partnership was converted into a company.

While the brewery still existed – and even afterwards – it served the City in a very particular way by providing each year the great white shire horses and their harness to draw the Lord Mayor's coach in the annual November show through the City streets.

While the brewery has been gone for 30 years its buildings remain in Chiswell Street, their latest manifestation as an hotel and restaurants, still something of a City institution – although, oddly enough, always just outside the City's boundaries.

*   *   *

The Ward of Bread Street

As Alderman Murray Fox remarked when he read his paper in April 1974: "looking back through the GHA records, I cannot see that we have had a paper on a Ward, and I think it is about time we did". Had he been with us today he might have added that his offering still remains the only ward to have been so distinguished!*

Bread Street as a ward existed from the early 13th century, in its early days taking its name from its presiding Alderman. Some ten acres in area. In the time of John Stow it had five churches (two in Bread Street itself and three in Friday Street) and a population of 1,700, comprising 292 families. That was at the end of the 16th century. "Today" declared Murray Fox "We are a godless lot without a single church. The last was St. Mildred's, burnt down in 1940 in spite of the fact that it adjoined the fire station – the fire station almost the only building in the ward to escape destruction.

This part of the City, as its name implies, was famous for its bread market, the Assize of Bread strictly controlling quality and price. 'Foreign' bakers (i.e. anyone not a freeman of the City) were not allowed to enter Bread Street and any baker convicted of dishonesty would be drawn through the streets on a hurdle with the offending loaf round his neck. Near the boundary with Queenhithe was the fish market (before Billingsgate) to keep the smell in one place.

At the end of the 15th century came Goldsmiths' Row, ten fair dwelling houses and fourteen shops each four storeys high, built along the south side of the City's prime shopping street, Cheapside. For 130 years this was the centre for silverware, the trade controlled by the Goldsmiths Company.

Then in the 1600's, the eastern part of the ward became famous for its inns which served as clearing houses for rumour and news and meeting places. It was at a dining club in one such inn in Friday Street

---

* Oddly enough until today, Monday 31st October 2011, as I am working on his paper, having at lunchtime listened to an account of Queenhithe (see page 221 – C.D.W.

that discussions took place leading to the founding in 1698 of the Bank of England. Ben Jonson, Shakespeare, Milton and Addison all at various times, came to dine in the Friday Street inns.

Two livery companies had their halls in Bread Street – the Salters, just off Watling Street from 1640 to 1650 (they may have had a business connection with the fish market) and the Cordwainers, whose hall was in Distaff Lane, right up to 1940 when it was burnt down and never rebuilt.

With the gradual demise, from the late 1770's, of the City's craft and merchant guilds and their replacement with banking, insurance and broking, the character of Bread Street Ward was changing too. Not being a banking area it turned largely to the textile trade and it remained the mainstay of activity of the ward and its business in 1940.

It was fifteen years before a serious start was made on rebuilding. In 1974 when Murray Fox read his paper not a single textile firm remained. The Bank of England occupied a very large site bounded by Cheapside, New Change, Watling Street and Bread Street (alas its handsome brick buildings now lost to No. 1 New Change) in addition there were the Financial Times in Bracken House (the buildings still there but now a Japanese bank), Spillers, Brooke Bond and Wiggins Teape (all gone now) but with the promised coming of the Credit Lyonnais where once stood the ward's famous fire station. The elegant French bank is still there.

* * *

Ripa Regina: The Soke and Stews of Queenhithe

In October 2011 Historian Gordon Haines, the Alderman for Queenhithe, came up with a worthy rival to his Bread Street neighbour and certainly one worth waiting for!

He named his paper 'Ripa Regina: Soke and Stew' – Ripa Regina being the Queen's Bank (or Hithe) of the River; Soke the Saxon district of the city which later became the ward; Stew we come to later.

The harbour was there in Roman times and is seen today as the only remaining Saxon dock in the world. Its name of Queenhithe derives from Queen Matilda, the riverbank being the Queen's hithe or quay with all the dues and profits from river trade being given to the unpopular and arrogant Matilda. Its first mention as a Ward was in 1265. A few years later John Stow wrote that Ripa Regina may be accounted the very chief and principal water gate of this Citie. It provided perfect mooring for vessels of all shapes and sizes. Its queenly owners, first Matilda and then Eleanor wife of Henry II grew wealthy from ownership of the dock and possession of the tolls and taxes from its trade.

Not only was the Thames the source of London's wealth, beauty and dignity, it also brought squalor, misery and suffering to those who dwelt along its towpaths and within Queenhithe's labyrinth of mean streets. By the Middle Ages, wrote Haines, the river was associated with licence, smuggling and theft, mortality and filth. Inevitably prostitutes joined the flotsam and jetsam of the riverbank – and it was easier to get to them than their sisters over the water in Southwark. Here they worked in the stews of Broken Wharf and St. Michael Queenhithe. For the City authorities the desire to collect "putage" – a tax on prostitutes – had to be balanced with the need for public hygiene. In the year 1427 John Tanner, scrivener and stewmaster, proclaimed that his stew for women of Barkerisland in Queenhithe was but a good and honest hot bath. It appears that stews could be baths as well as brothels. (See also the rival claims of Southwark, page 250.

Queenhithe in Tudor times was already the centre of London's fur trade and a proclamation was issued that: "whereas the common and lewd women of this city have assumed the fashion of being clad in the manner of good and noble damsels... it is ordered by the Mayor, Aldermen and Commons that no such lewd women shall be so attired (in furs) but go attired openly with a hood of cloth and with vestments untrimmed with fur... so that all may have knowledge of what rank they are". (Poor little things on those cold Queenhithe streets!)

Plague, fire and the construction of ships too large to dock at the hithe achieved what ordinance and statute could not and by the late 17th century Queenhithe's reputation as the hub of the City's sex trade had all be disappeared.

*   *   *

The Bishopsgate Institute

It was, appropriately enough, the Bishopsgate Alderman, Historian Michael Oliver, who delivered this paper in November 1992 (ten years before he became Lord Mayor) on one of the ward's great architectural and social achievements.

The Bishopsgate Institute was one of three educational foundations of the 1890's (the others being the St. Bride's Institute and the Cripplegate Institute) created from the proceeds of moribund City charities.

One such charitable endowment had been for the provision of old women's flannel petticoats which the rector of St. Botolph, Bishopsgate, William Rogers, believed would be better spent on the provision of a spacious library. He was the prime mover in the creation of the Bishopsgate Institute, the foundation stone of which was laid in May 1893 with speeches from Rogers, Prime Minister Lord Rosebery and the Governor of the Bank of England. Before that a luncheon was given at the Mansion House so that although not mentioned by Michael Oliver, Lord Mayor Stuart Knill must have been there too!

The opening received enormous and largely eulogistic publicity – but the petticoats still cast a shadow. The renowned Blackwoods magazine proclaimed:

"It is almost incredible that so golden an age can have come to Bishopsgate that flannel petticoats for poor women are no longer required there. Books may come and books may go but flannel is a perennial need. And to think that we have done away with that in order that a number of louts may have a nice warm room in which to read the worst novels and the sporting news in the papers and neglect their natural work".

The library in the new Institute was an instant success. Long queues were waiting for it to open on New Year's Day 1895. Some 8,000 people visited the library that day and 4,500 application forms issued to intending borrowers. By the end of the week 10,000 had been registered. Rogers' hopes were confirmed a dozen times over; Blackwoods totally confounded.

The Bishopsgate Institute encompassed a multitude of roles: educational, cultural, recreational and charitable, roles which have grown and developed over the years. A variety of languages are taught in classes there, musicians and their audiences flock to the Great Hall for recitals and the Institute cherishes its long-established links with the City Music Society.

Oliver's paper included the curious history of the Minute Book of the "First International Working Men's Association" – a volume that was part of the collection of books in the library about the labour movement. The minute book was celebrated because it contained details of the inaugural meeting of what was to become the "Comintern" – the Communist International. One of the delegates, perhaps the most important, was none other than Highgate Cemetery's most famous occupant, Karl Marx.

Its value as an historical document was unquestionable but one of the Institute's governors, David Romain, saw it as something far more sinister – nothing less than a blueprint for Red Revolution. He insisted that it be banned from readers' eyes and locked away in the strongroom. The result was that users of the library clamoured to read something so shocking and when Romain was on holiday in 1933 the Institute offered it to the British Museum where it was gratefully accepted. Romain on his return was furious and withdrew the offer and deposited the book in a safe deposit at a local bank.

It took Ivan Maisky, the Soviet Ambassador in London in 1941 to request a sight of the book so as to make a transcript for the Lenin Library in Moscow. The governors initially refused the request (Romain was still there) but a letter from Winston Churchill led to a swift change of heart.

In 1992 when Michael Oliver read his paper plans were in hand for a programme of improvements to the Institute and now in 2011, as these words are written, a major restoration project has just been completed. The Bishopsgate Institute more than holds its own among the Heron and Broadgate towers.

* * *

Whittington's Longhouse

Well, here's a thing, the story of a late 14th century edifice and social benefaction, one of many given to the citizens of London by its four-times Mayor, Richard Whittington.

Historian Alan Lamboll said in his paper of April 1975 that the Longhouse established on Thames-side in the Ward of Vintry, with almshouses above, was unostentatious and could never have become a public monument but it achieved a certain degree of affection among Vintry inhabitants who, in the 17th century, were moved to make a protest against their destruction.

The Longhouse was a public convenience, a privy, otherwise known as a house of easement. The structure was indeed long, consisting as it did of two rows each of 64 seats, one side for men and the other for women. "Longhouse" became a popular name to denote a privy, almost certainly the result of the Whittington edifice.

The oft-times Mayor had a practical appreciation of public health, the seats overhanging a long, narrow gulley that discharged into the Thames and was flushed by the river with each incoming tide. He saw nothing unhygienic in people living above the privies; after all, in his more traditional almshouses – and, indeed in houses generally – there was at that time a cesspit below them. So over the Longhouse were six rooms for the almsfolk of St. Martin Vintry. In 1632 when the parish no longer wished to house their poor above the privies the rooms were let at 20 shillings a year.

Even after the Great Fire there remained a need for the Longhouse although only twelve seats were provided in the new edifice, the greater part of the site being leased for other uses. In 1675 Vintry Ward were complaining to the Lord Mayor and Aldermen that the City was not maintaining the house of easement properly, nor were they providing candles and a lanthorn, a complaint made year after year since 1607.

In 1685 the lessee of the lodgings over the privies complained they were a great annoyance and very little used and petitioned that the

Longhouse be closed and it was, indeed, locked up. Five years later the local inhabitants discovered that its closure had caused them hardship, that the Longhouse be reopened so that they could once again enjoy the benefit of Whittington's noble gift.

An investigation was ordered by the Court of Aldermen and it was then found that the owner of the property, George Peck, had so altered the building and the dock beneath that "the tide cannot have sufficient ingresse and regresse to purge away the soyle". Mr. Peck was ordered forthwith to open the common houses of easement and take care that all impediments to the water flowing be removed.

Over the years new leases were granted to various members of the Peck family, then to an extended line of Pettiwards, one of whom was called on to convert the houses of easement – which were not only useless but a great nuisance to the neighbourhood – into some useful building for the improvement of the City's estate. However, the next lease, in 1772, specifically demanded their retention – as shown on a plan submitted by George Dance, no less.

Even into the mid-1800's when an 80-year lease was granted for the Mines Royal and Battery Works including a frontage on the Thames and a jetty into the river, it still reserved the common house of easement under the premises (but now with a cistern above so that tidal cleansing was no longer necessary).

But while the privies remained they were probably never in use and the insistence on their retention faded away. Certainly no mention of them occurs in the next lease of 1935. Perhaps it is appropriate that today's City Cleansing Depot in Bell Wharf Lane is adjacent to the site for so long occupied by Whittington's celebrated Longhouse.

Note: This paper was written originally by Historian Philip Jones and published in the "London Topographical Record".

* * *

A Gift in Fenchurch Street

In 1391 in the reign of Richard II the remarkable William of Wykeham – Bishop of Winchester, Lord High Chancellor of England, founder of Winchester School and New College, Oxford – acquired the site on which now stands 84 Fenchurch Street. Thus Richard Saunders introduced this paper in March 1983.

At the time of Wykeham's purchase the property was known as "Mountjoy's Inn". The purchase price was a handsome one, 4,000 English marks plus 500 French gold francs. Although England and France were, as usual, at war, the property was at least partly owned by a religious order in Savoy and it was to the Savoyards that the 500 French francs went.

From 1391 right up to the present "Mountjoy's Inn" (and other houses on the site) appear regularly in the records of New College Estate. Clearly it was a gift to the college Wykeham had founded just a few years earlier.

One of the college's tenants in the 16th century was the notorious Doctor Roderigo Lopez who was accused of a plot against the life of Queen Elizabeth to whom he had been appointed chief physician. A New College account roll of 1592 shows that Lopez was paying rent for "Mountjoy's Inn" as a sub-tenant of two other doctors, both of them alumni of the college. Portuguese and a Jew, his fate was sealed and he was executed in 1595.

In the Great Fire of 1666 the eastern end of Fenchurch Street including the area owned by New College escaped its ravages so that a survey of 1732 referred to medieval buildings. The name "Mountjoy's Inn" was no longer being used. Of its various parts the surveyor said "the Mansion House was very old, out of repair, uninhabited for some years... the Coach House and stables are in good repair... seven other houses in the street may stand 30 or 40 years longer". The total rent at the time of the survey was £478 – the tenants being two apothecaries, a pawnbroker, baker, carpenter and an attorney.

Up to the 19th century the site continued as an Inn with surrounding houses and gardens. But a plan of 1873 showed the whole property as having been developed as a single residence, coffee roasting shop, stables, a dairy and printing works. The old Inn had been converted into a warehouse.

In the 1890's the College granted leases for further development. One was to the Charing Cross and Strand Electricity Company who proposed to build an electricity sub-station there. All the 19th century and early 20th century buildings on the site were demolished to make way for the granite-clad office block erected in 1980.

Richard Saunders' story is by no means unique in City property ownership but a continuity of 600 years is no mean record for a slice of real estate to have remained in the same hands since its 14th century endowment.

*   *   *

Outdoor Monuments in the City of London

It all began with a question in the Court of Common Council addressed to the Chairman of the Special Committee: what was to be the fate of the Wilkes Memorial, alleged to be sinking perceptibly into the gentlemen's lavatory in Ludgate Circus.

For Historians that question was the starting point of a quite fascinating paper read in August 1949 by no other than Sir Cuthbert Whitaker, founding father of the Guildhall Historical Association five years earlier who, on that August day, was 76 years of age and had served on Common Council for 44 years. A great veteran of the GHA.

Whitaker tells us that the Chairman of the Special Committee* assured the questioner that not only would he look into the sinking Wilkes Memorial but would obtain a report on all of the other City outdoor monuments. He overlooked the fact that Guildhall – as with all Government or Municipal Offices – worked in watertight compartments, the Special Committee officers not really communicating with their opposite numbers in City Lands and Corporation Records.

So, even when a report emerged from the Special Committee, Whitaker and one or two other knowledgeable Councilmen soon observed that there were some glaring omissions – the most glaring of all being the exclusion of the Monument.

Whitaker's paper describes eleven of the forgotten monuments:

The Monument was designed by Christopher Wren to commemorate the Great Fire but constructed under the direction of the City Surveyor (and was ever in the keeping of the City Lands Committee until that committee's destruction in 2011). Sir Cuthbert quotes the lines of Alexander Pope – "Where London's column pointing at the skies, Like a tall bully, lifts the head and the lies".

---

* The "Special Committee" was set up in the 1880's to oppose Government plans to "reform" the Corporation and was re-established in 1904 to combat attacks by the London County Council. It stayed in being until the early 1950's to be replaced by the Policy and Parliamentary Committee.

Pope, a Catholic, objected to the inscription on the base of the Monument attributing the Fire of London to Papist incendiarism. The inscription was removed in the reign of Catholic James II and restored in that of Protestant William and Mary and stayed until 1830.

Whitaker, for no very good reason, gives us a bonus here, the Clerihew –

"Sir Christopher Wren
Said: "I am dining with some men.
If anyone calls
Say I am designing St Paul's.

Aldgate Pump There was an Aldgate Well in the reign of King John, and a pump was erected in place of the winch and bucket around 1600. In 1871 because of street widening it was moved ten feet to the junction of Leadenhall Street and Fenchurch Street. The quality of the water was dubious in the extreme (the well was believed to have been responsible for cholera deaths) and the handle of the pump chained up. The pump is still there and has recently been restored as an ancient monument.

Aldersgate Boundary Marks Obelisks associated with drinking fountains were set up in Aldersgate under the will of Alderman Robert Besley in 1877. Their removal to Postmen's Park in 1932 was opposed by members of the ward but their removal was carried out two years later (presumably as an aid to traffic flow) and a plaque placed on the wall of 107 Aldersgate Street to mark the boundary.

Bunhill Fields Burial Ground was situated in the borough of Finsbury (now subsumed in Islington alas) but maintained by the City Corporation. It contains the graves, all of which are intact, of Susannah Wesley (the mother of John), Dr. John Owen, John Bunyan, Daniel Defoe, Dr. Isaac Watts and William Blake, all members of the Free Churches. Restored after the war-time damage it has always attracted visitors, many of the Americans seeking forebears of the Pilgrim Fathers.

Whitaker reminds us that an Act for the preservation of the ground as the very first of the City's open spaces was passed in 1867 since when the Corporation made itself responsible for its upkeep. He tells us that when he was Chairman of the City Lands Committee in 1923, he was called upon to renew John Bunyan's nose which had been broken off either by a mischievous urchin or, more probably, by an American souvenir hunter. He believed that the Corporation Works Department kept a supply of Bunyan's noses.

Cornhill Pump Another well, another pump. The Cornhill well was built in 1282 but there is silence surrounding it until rediscovery of the spring in 1799 when the pavement began to sink. That year a pump was erected by subscription from the Bank of England, the East India Company and the fire offices (insurers) banks and businesses in the ward. Water quality deteriorated and in 1875 the pump handle was removed.

The newly-appointed Medical Officer of Health advocated the closure of all City pumps and provided statistics of impurities found in water from 35 of them. At the end of the 19th century the Corporation took over all responsibility for maintaining fountains and troughs from the Metropolitan Fountain and Cattle Trough Association.

Holborn Bars Stone obelisks about seven feet high bearing the City Arms mark the site of the western entry to the City.

Paul's Cross (see the paper on Page 119). Oddly enough the preaching cross was labelled "Fountain" on the Ordnance Survey map at the time of the reconstruction of the City after War-time destruction.

Royal Exchange All around are statues: on the north wall of Hugh Myddelton who brought New River water to the City and Richard Whittington; at the east end a statue of Thomas Gresham, founder of the Exchange; inside is a statue of Charles II by Grinling Gibbins and in an opposite corner Queen Elizabeth. Statues of Queen Victoria and Prince Albert and where they should eventually be located have resulted in long debates by the Gresham Committee which manages the Exchange for the City Corporation and the Mercers' Company. Some of the statues were removed to the Central Criminal Court (the Old Bailey).

St Brides and Bridewell Schools A boy and girl charity children of 1711 over the entry from New Bridge Street. There are similar figures over the doorway of the church hall in Bishopsgate Churchyard. (They have recently been taken inside the hall for safekeeping to protect them from being stolen).

Smithfield Garden and Fountain Above the fountain is a life size figure of a naked woman and the Chairman of the Central Markets Committee after conferring with the Smithfield Superintendent and the Medical Officer of Health decided that the lady was quite definitely "in an interesting condition". In order to preserve her virtue the Chairman provided a wedding ring which, according to Whitaker in 1949 "may now be seen on the third finger of her left hand... would-be thieves should know it is only of 9 carat gold".

Note: The complete list of outdoor monuments in the City, updated, can be seen in the Guildhall Library.

*   *   *

The Guildhall Crypts

In 1411 Mayor and Aldermen took the momentous decision to rebuild the Guildhall. That work, which took fourteen years to complete, was fostered and supported by Richard Whittington as one of his benefactions to London. That the Hall has proved adequate to the needs of the citizens for 550 years bears witness to his and other mayors' foresight. It bears witness also to the skill of the craftsmen of the day and the materials they used. With these words the admirable Philip Jones, Deputy Keeper of the Records, opened a memorable paper on the particular history of the Guildhall crypts in October 1961. At that time the eastern of the crypts had recently been restored.

The present Guildhall was by no means the first, for a Guildhall is mentioned as early as 1135. More than likely, believed Jones, it is the third. We read in the City's records that the Common Council met in the Outer Chamber of Guildhall in 1352 and in the Upper Chamber around 1400. Before 1411 the Guildhall was a substantial building full of activity.

In his paper Philip Jones suggested that what happened in 1411 was that Guildhall was enlarged in 1411 and that the new larger hall was built around and as an extension of the older building in an easterly direction. He further suggested that the present (i.e. in 1961) ruined western crypt is the crypt of the Guildhall prior to 1411 and the oldest part of the present building.

We know that this western crypt stood till 1666 and collapsed at the time of the Great Fire. Its construction was less elaborate and less sturdy than the later eastern crypt. It had been used as a market place for cloth for a century before the fire. In view of its importance for trade it was in fact rebuilt quite quickly by 1670.

Jones provided detailed evidence to show that the western crypt was built before the eastern one and argued that if, indeed, it contained the last surviving ruins of the Guildhall prior to 1411, its importance and significance could not be over-stressed.

The paper must have helped in the decision of the Guildhall Restoration Committee to recommend that the west crypt should be restored and eight years later the Court of Common Council gave their approval. Now both east and west crypts play their brilliant part in the ceremonial and entertainment for which Guildhall is renowned.

* * *

The City's Rivers – the Walbrook and the Fleet

While Alderman Clive Martin's paper (May 1989) is about the Walbrook and Fleet he first acknowledges that London owes its existence to the Thames, the subject of the following paper.

On the north bank of the Thames are the two hills of Ludgate and Cornhill from which flowed the Fleet and the Walbrook, both of them of great importance to the life of London. From Roman times they provided fresh water and continued doing so into the 12th century. With the City's commercial growth they supplied the power for the waterwheels of millers, tanners and leatherworkers.

Two tributaries joined to form the Walbrook under what is now Drapers' Hall and going from there under the Bank of England, Poultry and along the line of the street called Walbrook and so into the Thames at Dowgate Dock.

On the banks of the Walbrook where once stood a Roman palace and the Temple of Mithras there continued through the centuries to be important and splendid buildings – numerous livery halls and the churches of St. Margaret Lothbury, St. Mildred Poultry and St. Stephen Walbrook.

But as early as the 14th century Walbrook River was causing problems. In a Court of Common Council in May 1383 it was said: "the watercourse is stopped up by divers filth and dung thrown therein by persons who have houses along the course. The Aldermen of the wards of Coleman Street, Broad Street, Cheap, Walbrook, Vintry and Dowgate are to let the Chamberlain know of those throwing filth or rubbish into the watercourse, how many latrines there are and to whom they belong". Latrines over the river were permissible on payment of two shillings to the Chamberlain.

Alderman Martin says in his paper that a glance at the river wall from Blackfriars Bridge reveals a cavernous opening, now all that remains of the Fleet.

Its one-time tributaries, the Holbourne and the Turnmill, rose in Hampstead and Highgate joining together at what is now Camden Town and flowing to King's Cross, Clerkenwell and Farringdon. It formed the City's western boundary, part of London's defences against the Royalists in 1643 when thousands of men, women and children went out with pickaxes and shovels to erect enormous earthworks along its length.

As with the Walbrook the banks of the Fleet had their waterwheels for grinding, in addition to grain, powder for dressing the hair and liquorish. The river's journey through the slaughterhouses of Smithfield turned the water red.

The Fleet was a tidal inlet with ships carrying corn, wine and firewood up as far as Holborn Bridge. It was also the means of transporting stone from Kent for building old St. Paul's. It provided water for the moat around the Fleet Prison near Ludgate.

After the Great Fire which destroyed all the dwellings and warehouses along its banks the river was given a new lease of life, much deepened from Thames to Holborn and with new banks of brick and stone. The enormous cost of the project was funded from tolls which discouraged ships from using it and trade dwindled. In 1733 the Fleet was arched over, the wharves becoming streets. Twenty years later, to save money, sand from the dirty Fleet instead of the much cleaner Thames, was used to lag the paving stones which became dangerously slippery to walk on. The river had become a sewer.

At the end of his paper, Alderman Martin expressed his regret at the gradual destruction of "what must have been two delightful streams. We will never see them again, but perhaps the Barbican Lake will serve as a tribute to their memory – and a reminder that there was once a natural pool by the church of St. Giles, Cripplegate".

* * *

Two Views of the Thames

From London's own modest but important little rivers to the mightier Thames which gripped the attention of two other Historians.

We were reminded by William Sykes in March 1952 that the Thames was one of England's "Royal Rivers" owned and managed under the King's prerogative. In 1197, however, Richard I in some need of money after his return from the Crusades (and subsequent imprisonment) sold the royal rights to London for 1,500 marks, a considerable fortune at the time. A face-saving formula was devised in a Charter that made it plain that the change in ownership was chiefly in the interests of the city.

"Know ye all that we, for the health of our soul, our father's soul, and all our ancestors' souls, and for the common weal of our city of London, have granted that all weirs that are in the Thames be removed. Also we have quitclaimed all that which the keeper of our Tower of London was wont to receive of the said weirs. For it is manifest to us that great detriment and inconvenience hath grown to our said city of London by occasion of such weirs".

The Charter was confirmed by King John (who was also, to some extent, dependent on the City's coffers). So it was that from the 13th century the Mayor and Aldermen were responsible for the Thames from Staines down to the river's mouth at Yantlet Creek opposite the later Southend.

It was a responsibility not without its problems. With the river becoming the receptacle of sewage and anything else which people living nearby (not least from the Walbrook and the Fleet) chose to dispose of, complaints were constant. An Act of Henry VIII prohibited the casting of filth and rubbish into the river. Little improvement was seen. The City bestirred itself in 1770 by setting up a Navigation Committee – it was more the interference with shipping than pollution that concerned Guildhall – and the committee's first step was to acquire a 132 foot-long barge to remove obstructions.

Rather more effective was the building of a series of locks up-river at Chertsey, Shepperton, Sunbury and Teddington in the early 1800's. The project was carried through, in the teeth of opposition from His Majesty's government but eventually Parliament gave its permission. Tolls were imposed on craft using the river to help keep it navigable. With competition from the new railways river traffic declined and income from the tolls dwindled.

Ownership of the river became increasingly less viable as the cost of maintaining its navigability grew. The City Corporation refused further to be the sole contributor and relinquished all claims to the bed and soil of the Thames. In 1857 a new Board of Conservancy was set up consisting, originally, of the Lord Mayor, two Aldermen, four representatives of the livery companies, the Deputy Master of Trinity House and three Crown nominees. Just 600 years after the Crusader's grant the City ceased to control the waters of the Thames. The final chapter in this story came in 1908 when responsibility for the river east of Teddington passed into the hands of a newly formed Port of London Authority. The Corporation did retain some little say in the Thames Conservancy, having a seat on the 37-man board along with, in those days, the Port of London Authority, London County Council and other riparian authorities. At the time he presented his paper William Sykes was the Corporation man on the Thames Conservancy.

*

"The Lord Mayor's View of the Thames" presented by Alderman Sir Hugh Wontner in January 1979 was a celebration of those splendid processions periodically undertaken by Lord Mayor and Aldermen – "a sort of nautical beating of the bounds" as he put it.

But first he told Historians of the four stones or pillars bearing the City arms which stood on the north bank of the Thames: just beyond Staines Bridge, on the Essex foreshore a mile beyond Leigh at Yantlet Creek, on the Isle of Grain and at Upnor on the Medway in Kent. These were the boundary stones marking the limits of the

Corporation's former conservancy rights over the Thames as well as parts of the Rivers Lea and Medway.

By virtue of several royal charters and an act of Parliament of 1394 which appointed the Mayor as conservator, the City exercised this jurisdiction for more than six-and-a-half centuries.

We do not know when stones were first erected but owing to the effects of weather and tides they had been renewed periodically. In 1755 when the stone near Leigh, the Crowstone, had been missing for several years, Lord Mayor Stephen Janssen personally supervised the digging of a hole and a replacement pillar being sunk within it on the exact spot where the ancient mark was fixed.

In the earlier centuries of the City's jurisdiction the principal concern was fishery preservation, fish being enormously important in the diet of medieval and Tudor times. Later the emphasis moved to improvement of navigation requiring the appointment at Guildhall of a Navigation Committee which stayed in being from 1770 to 1857.

A Waterbailiff who, like the Swordbearer and Common Cryer, was one of the esquires of the mayoral household, was sub-conservator of the Thames and under the Mayor patrolled the river looking out for offences and encroachments. The Lord Mayor himself held conservancy courts each year with juries empanelled to inquire into all offences committed on the river and to proceed on the verdict of such juries to the punishment of offenders. The courts were held not in the City but at various places near the riverside in the riparian counties of Middlesex, Surrey, Essex and Kent: Westminster Hall, the Southwark Courthouse, a house in Deptford, the Anchor Inn at Stratford.

About every seven years these courts of conservancy were combined with the "view" of the jurisdiction, the grand progress on the river mentioned at the beginning of this paper.

One such view took place in August 1633. The Essex jury was summoned to attend at the blockhouse, Tilbury on Wednesday 14th August, when Lord Mayor Sir John Robinson was greeted with a gun salute, he and the Aldermen having travelled there in the Mercers' Company barge (the Mayor's barge being out of commission). From

Tilbury they crossed to Gravesend to the Kent jury where the captain of the blockhouse there similarly greeted them by "shooting off divers pieces of ordinance" and the court sitting at the Town House. After dinner at the Angel Inn the mayoral party set forth for Rochester, the Lord Mayor and Aldermen going by coach, the rest of the party on horseback. En route a poor woman whose husband "was hurt with a horse" was given 20 s. and another poor woman whose horse was hurt was also given 10 s. Clearly the London riders were a boisterous party.

Supper and lodging were taken at the Crown in Rochester and next day the Lord Mayor and Aldermen went by water to Queenborough and back to Gravesend. They travelled from Chatham in one of the royal pinnaces (lest the weather be stormy) buying oysters on the way from a poor fisherman in the Medway. Another night's supper and lodging were at Gravesend, together with dinner the following day. The party were back in the City for Saturday and Sunday and then on Monday 19th they set forth for the western part of the view, the Middlesex jury having been summoned to the Bush Inn at Staines. The markstone was inspected and Mayor and Aldermen entertained at Mr. Benjamin Stone's house on Hounslow Heath. For supper and lodging they moved to the Saracen's Head at Kingston where the Surrey jury met the next day, 20th August, at the Town House.

The great expedition comprising four courts, various inspections and some ten dinners and suppers came to a triumphant end at the Saracen's Head. Expenses included payments to the City Waits and their trumpeters and to the "Common Hunt" for his attendance with the hounds (see page xx). Clearly an enjoyable time was had by all wrote Wontner.

The views continued through the late 18th and well into the 19th centuries, with occasional upsets – such as the time Lord Mayor Brass Crosby and a small group of supporters descended from their Admiralty yacht into two small boats to visit the Leigh Stone. Wind and tide were rough and the boat carrying the Mayor ran aground and had to be hauled off by twelve sturdy men across the mud to the beach.

A most splendid view took place in 1796 when it coincided with a visit by the Imperial Russian Navy. Mayor and Aldermen in their Trinity House yacht having attended a conservancy court at Gravesend, they sailed to the Nore where the mayoral party were cheered by the British and Russian men-of-war and the Lord Mayor went aboard the Russian flagship with a salve of eleven guns.

Later, viewing the stone at Upnor he and his party processed along with Mayor and Aldermen of Rochester, preceded by the band of the Royal Marines from Chatham. There followed a grand dinner at The Crown in Rochester, where the Russian Vice-Admiral, Mayor of Rochester, Major-General of Marines and the High Sheriff of Kent were among the Lord Mayor's distinguished guests. Those were certainly the days!

*　　*　　*

Swan Marking and Swan Upping

Long ago the King's swans – they were ever royal birds – were at least as much esteemed for their flavour as for their beauty. In the 1200's Henry III would send requisitions to his sheriffs to lay in stocks in readiness for visits he planned to make: a mere 40 for Christmas at Winchester, more than 100 for longer tours around the country.

Although swans were in the ownership of the monarch there were others who had a fancy for them and towards the end of the 15th century "certain persons had stolen cygnets and hence yeomen and husbandmen, and persons of little reputation became possessed of swans".

The story of swans was told to Historians in November 1983 by that indefatigable and ever-welcome speaker, Cuthbert Skilbeck.

An act of Parliament was passed in 1483 prohibiting any but the King and his sons having a "game" of swans or a swan-mark unless they received a grant from the Crown. The Abbot of Abbotsbury enjoyed such a right and had his game of swans as did the City of Oxford. Indeed, a good many individuals and institutions owned swan-marks during the 16th and 17th centuries. The marks were on the birds' upper beak, some incorporating elements of their owners' arms. Ownership was at its highest level in Elizabethan times, the royal treasury being a considerable beneficiary.

Swan keeping was also a source of profit from the buying and selling of birds for food and the sale of cygnets to add to owners' stock. In 1274 the price of a swan for food was fixed by the City's Statuta Poletrice at 3s. while the best capon sold at 2½ d., a pheasant for 4 d. and a goose for 5d. No banquet was complete without a swan.

Two livery companies with halls near the river, the Dyers and the Vintners, share with the reigning monarch, ownership of swans on the Thames above the tideway. Every July the three Swan Masters and their crews take part in the Swan Upping Voyage*1 lasting a week during which the various broods are rounded up, and the swans and cygnets counted. While the royal birds are no longer marked (Queen Alexandra objected to the practice in 1910 as being crude) the Dyers maintain a single nick in the beak and the Vintners two small nicks*2 originally the beaks of the royal swans had five nicks) – so then and now all three Games of swans are clearly differentiated. There are some 500 royal swans and cygnets on the river and 65 belonging to the Dyers and 45 to the Vintners, all of them well cared for.

*　　*　　*

---

*1 Until recent times the voyage started at London Bridge and ended at Henley. Now it begins at Walton and ends at Whitchurch.

*2 The sign of the famous coaching inn, the "Swan with two necks" changed over the centuries, at one time showing a swan with two necks, then two swans swimming side by side and finally a swan with one neck and its beak marked with two nicks.

Parish and Ward Boundary Marks

Even in June 1948 when noted Historian Sir Frederick Tidbury-Beer read his paper, the City's boundary marks, once so plentiful, were rapidly disappearing and since then, with so much of the City rebuilt, many more have vanished.

As their name implies Parish boundary marks were to establish the limits of each of the City parishes, a matter of some importance both to the church authorities (in the collection of tithes, for example) and to the people living there. They were usually fixed on the face of buildings at first floor level.

Their origin was in the "parish perambulations", a custom going back to Anglo-Saxon days. These perambulations took place during Rogation Week or on Ascension Day because of their religious connection, with the accompanying priest beseeching divine blessing on the parish lands for the harvest to come.

The procession would consist of priest, church-wardens and parish officers at the head followed by boys armed with wands or boughs with which to beat the stones (and sometimes themselves being given a whipping for good measure). The perambulations were lengthy and strenuous with even in some of the smaller parishes as many as a hundred boundary marks to be inspected. The proceedings invariably finished with a substantial dinner. The accounts at St. Mary Woolchurch Haw for 1664 showed a cost of £5 12 s., which in 1681 had risen to £8 10 s. – goodly sums in those days.

The ceremony in later days – still occasionally practised in one or two parishes became a triennial event simply known as "Beating the Bounds" with choirboys wielding the wands.

In his paper Tidbury-Beer had identified twenty-five parish boundary marks and five ward boundary marks. The parish marks identify the church, the year in which it was installed and, in some cases, a number indicating its position around the boundary. Some examples (drawn by him) are illustrated in these pages.

Some marks were attached to the interior walls of buildings. In Guildhall is one of St. Michael Bassishaw dated 1784 and an even earlier, 1680, Cheap ward mark. The parishes of St. Michael and St. Lawrence Jewry and the wards of Cheap and Bassishaw met within Guildhall. Granite stone marks were built into roadways such as two in London Wall near its junction with Blomfield Street which identify the boundaries between St. Stephen and All Hallows parishes and the wards of Broad and Coleman Streets. There were pavement marks, too, usually of brass or iron. A group of five were located close together to the north of Royal Exchange Buildings – a place where the parishes of St. Bartholomew by the Exchange, St. Michael Cornhill and St. Benet Fink meet, together with the wards of Cornhill and Broad Street.

Tidbury-Beer's paper is more than an account of boundary marks. His enthusiasm for aspects of City history shines through in a dozen-and-one details about these ancient parishes. St. Bartholomew by the Exchange was there in 1225 on the south-east corner of Bartholomew Lane. Close by was Sir William Capel's mansion, his residence as Lord Mayor in 1503. The church had been rebuilt in 1438 and Sir William added a chapel a few years after his mayoralty. The site of his mansion was later occupied by the first Stock Exchange. That Stock Exchange was in a house in Sweeting's Rents, the stock jobbers moving there from Jonathan's Coffee House in 1773. It was because of their original association with Jonathan's that the more recent Exchange was always referred to as "The House" and the attendants as "Waiters".

Long before the Honourable Artillery Company had its headquarters in City Road there was an Old Artillery Ground stretching from Spital Square to Artillery Passage (where, in another curious by-way of history, dwelt the grandparents of the author of this book who had fled Berlin around 1890!).

The Old Artillery Ground was a "spacious field" planted with teazles for the use of woolworkers, the teazle sufficiently important to London's trade to be incorporated in the arms of the Clothworkers' Company. The field was leased in 1537 to the "Masters, Rulers and Commonalty of the Fraternity or Guild of Artillery of Longbows,

Crossbows and Handguns". The guild had various names before eventually becoming the HAC, the word "Honourable" first used as a courtesy title in 1685, only to be officially confirmed by Queen Victoria. The HAC shares a mark with the parish of St. Botolph Without Bishopsgate which in Tidbury-Beer's day was displayed inside the Bishopsgate Institute.

There must once have been hundreds of boundary marks defining the limits of wards and in particular parishes within the wards. A few remain. Perhaps a latter-day Historian could be prevailed upon to tell us how many, if any, still remain and where they can be found.

*　　*　　*

Deptford and its historic
links with the City

Deptford, unlike neighbouring Southwark, was never part of the City but in its colourful history there were so many links that it fully deserves a place in this section of the GHA book, not least because it made a splendid subject for a GHA paper by Historian Dudley Game in January 1973.

Deptford derives its name from the deep ford and bridge over the Ravensbourne stream which here meets the Thames; it once used to operate five silk mills. The bridge has carried a countless multitude of pilgrims, merchants, soldiers and players as well as English and foreign royalties, since it was part of the main highway from Dover and Canterbury to London. It was also the route taken by rebels on their way to attack London – Wat Tyler, Jack Cade and Sir Thomas Wyatt.

Deptford became particularly important in Tudor times, Henry VIII using money from the dissolution of the monasteries to found two hospitals there. They were given what must be the longest name of an institution before or since: "The Master Wardens and Assistants of the Guild Fraternity of the most glorious and undivided Trinity and of St. Clement in the Parish of Depeford Strond in the County of Kent". (Out of these hospitals with such a lengthy name was born Trinity House of the pilots of London).

Each year a grand procession came from London to visit the hospitals. There were banners and music and the firing of cannon; the celebration was kept up until 1852.

The great change in Deptford's role from fishing village to Navy dockyard had come in 1513, a year before the hospitals, and the real reason for their creation by Henry. It was here that his ships of war – Hannibal, Termagent and Terrible – were built and launched. It was to Deptford that Francis Drake returned in the treasure-laden Golden Hind after his three-year navigation of the globe. Queen Elizabeth dined on his ship and bestowed upon him the honour of knighthood. It took twenty wagons to carry the treasures back to London.

Peter the Great, Czar of all the Russias, came to Deptford in 1698 to learn about shipbuilding – and rented the near-by house of Sayes Court from John Evelyn, the diarist.

Deptford remained a shipyard well into the 19th century, a Royal Victualling Yard established there in the 1740's and continuing to meet the demands of an increasing Navy throughout the Napoleonic wars. The yard was sold in 1869 for £70,000, the new owner selling part of it to the City Corporation for £94,640 as a market for live cattle being shipped from America.

Historian Game tells us that Evelyn's house of Sayes Court was a place where Christopher Wren came to dine together with another Deptford man, Samuel Pepys. Not far from Sayes Court in a humble thatched cottage they met Grinling Gibbons whose carved frame for a Tintoretto Crucifixion was considered to be a greater wonder than the painting! It was the beginning of a famous partnership between Wren and Gibbons.

Pepys was a frequent visitor to Deptford, his duties at the Navy Office taking him from his work in Seething Lane to be rowed from Tower Stairs to inspect the dockyard. There were, it was true, other attractions for Pepys at Deptford. At the dockyard he sought out one Bagwell, a carpenter, to strike up an acquaintance with him. Bagwell's wife, a pretty woman, had called at the Navy Office one day on some small errand. Bagwell was found a better ship to work on. Mrs Bagwell, the diarist observed, was a virtuous, modest woman. Before long Pepys had cured her of that.

Dudley Game goes on in his paper to speak of one other special link between Deptford and the City which was through the building by Peter de Colechurch of the first stone London Bridge and the creation of the Bridge House Estates (see also page xx).

For medieval man, bridges were regarded as a pious undertaking before God, to be supported by the giving of alms – how much more so in the case of London Bridge, a wondrous architectural and engineering achievement, the only crossing of the Thames for many miles, a vital part of the City's defences.

Gifts and bequests for "God and the Bridge", particularly gifts of land and property, poured in over the centuries, to create the great wealth of the Bridge House Estates. The gifts came from lands in Southwark, Bermondsey, Greenwich – and Deptford.

One of the most interesting of the Deptford properties, and one which was still owned by Bridge House in 1973, was an inn called "Le Christopher on le Hoop" which came under the will of John Clifford who was the chief mason of London Bridge. In his will of 1411 he left all his lands in Deptford and neighbouring areas to his wife Lettuce for life but thereafter to pass to the bridge wardens on condition there were annual prayers of remembrance for the souls of John and Lettuce. The Christopher inn was renamed in 1757 The Dover Castle and when Game delivered his paper in 1973 was still standing in Deptford High Street.

*   *   *

Southwark: London's Second City

While Deptford was never actually part of the City, its much larger neighbour, Southwark, most certainly was, the young king, Edward VI, first presenting Guildhall with royal charters giving the City manorial rights over the land to the south of London Bridge and then in 1550 disposing of all his Southwark property to the City in return for £647 2s 1d.

However, the links between the City and Southwark, began far earlier and with Southwark's own chequered history provided Robin Sherlock with an abundance of material for his entertaining paper delivered to the GHA in June 2009.

Sherlock writes that people lived in this area south of the river in pre-Roman times and that Southwark derived its name from the eventual building of a river wall – the south work – to match its Londinium counterpart across the river.

As the years passed there was increasing trade between London and the manors of Southwark, particularly after the building of Peter Colechurch's stone bridge across the Thames.

Nor was Southwark's trade restricted to materials and commodities. Its nearness to the City and its all-too loose system of government soon made it a sanctuary for criminals and others fleeing the more rigorous City authorities. Moreover the citizens of London found that crossing the river could provide them with pursuits outlawed on the north bank.

The stews of Southwark became notorious with the Bankside prostitutes affectionately known as "Winchester Geese" since they plied their trade within the Liberty or estate of the Bishop of Winchester whose see stretched from his palace at Winchester to the Thames. Wherrymen hired to row the citizens to their pleasures of Southwark were ordered to moor up their boats at night to stop the practice. To deal with continuing riot and disorder the "Clink" and six other prisons were built in Southwark.

There were, of course, many other attractions of a more admirable kind in the borough: the taverns and two of the most famous coaching inns, the George (still there in a reduced form) and the White Hart (where Mr. Pickwick made the acquaintance of Sam Weller). Above all, there were the theatres – the Globe, the Rose and the Swan, the players having been driven from London by surprisingly puritanical Lord Mayors and Aldermen, even Queen Elizabeth supporting their banishment.

Difficulties faced by the King's tax collectors in collecting tolls and rents led the guardians of Edward III (over 200 years before Edward VI's sale of Southwark) to grant the City rights over "the said town of Southwark" in return for a payment of £11 a month. The City enlarged its holdings by acquiring two more manors. The scene was thus set for Guildhall to take over the governance of all Southwark in 1550, the Lord Mayor riding around the precincts in a great procession to the sound of trumpets.

The money paid to Edward VI came from the Bridge House Estate which, through the gifts and bequests made in celebration of London Bridge (not least from the people of Southwark), now had extensive holdings of land and property there, such holdings bearing the Bridge House mark. So even before Edward VI's Charter Southwark and the City were closely attached.

In 1550 this borough of Southwark covering a large area and a substantial population and with its own particular problems was given the status of a ward of the City, its 26th, with the title of Bridge Ward Without. It was not only larger than most of the existing 25 wards but differed also in that while it had its own Alderman, it had no Common Councilmen. The Alderman was not elected by the citizens but imposed by Guildhall. There were no wardmoots. Southwark's population could not feel they had any stake in its governance. Historian Sherlock writes that the creation of a ward, while bestowing a new dignity did not provide a co-ordinating authority for an area that was in practice governed as if it were a loose collection of villages.

(Successive Aldermen did their best to promote Southwark's interests within the City but as the years went by the office became something of a sinecure in which a past Lord Mayor could spend a few years assisted in his duties by Surrey Justices of the Peace. And yet Bridge Without continued in being for all of 350 years, so must at least have satisfied some of Southwark's needs for settled government, these arrangements continuing until 1899 with the creation of the London County Council and the metropolitan boroughs of Southwark and Bermondsey – "A Miraculous Survival", C. Douglas Woodward, Phillimore 2011).

*

In his concluding paragraphs Robin Sherlock mentioned Southwark's ancient "Courts Leet". Forty years earlier, in June 1969, another GHA Historian read a paper – "The Courts Leet in Southwark" – and it is Ralph Peacock's history to which we now turn*.

Maintenance of the peace was a prime function of town administration and Southwark, sitting at the City's main gate, was a convenient bolt hole for thieves and those who desired to evade trade regulations, a refuge for the bawdy, gamblers and the drunk. For such reasons the City sought to exercise control over its suburb across the Bridge, wrote Peacock. The "Court Leet" was the chosen means.

There were three separate manors, or estates, within Southwark. The City had owned one of these known as Guildable Manor since 1444. Two others, the King's Manor and Great Liberty Manor came to the City in 1550. For each of them a Court Leet was established, the first being in 1444, the others set up in 1552. Their annual gatherings were presided over by the Lord Mayor, Aldermen and Sheriffs.

While throughout the year the Courts Leet could issue ordinances aimed at maintenance of the peace and punishment of miscreants – tradesmen who sold bad meat, underweight loaves or beer of poor quality – they were in effect the chief organ of local government.

---

* The Leet was a yearly court held by lords of certain manors; it also meant a selected list of candidates.

Indeed, they were the counterpart of the wardmoots held in the City's original 25 wards.

The official in overall charge of the three Courts, Leet was the Bailiff or Steward until, in 1804, responsibility for Southwark was given to the City's senior judge, the Recorder of London.

Peacock tells us of the proceedings of a Court Leet held on 14th October 1549 when it was recorded that 32 freeholders and some 100 residents were absent, the former each fined 12d and the latter 2d. There follows the names of defaulting bakers and brewers, those whose pavements needed mending, those who had made affrays or been responsible for nuisances. The Court then made 18 ordinances and instructed the Bailiff to see that they were executed.

The matters and cases before the Court were brought before the Leet jury numbering up to 24 persons who acted as prosecutors. The Court also appointed ale tasters and flesh tasters to assist the jurymen in their presentation of offences and defaults. The Court Leet was not too bothered about procedures, rather did it reflect the wishes and complaints of the manor's inhabitants. It was all very democratic we might say.

Despite the passage of years and great political changes the Leet has continued to be held and Leet juries appointed to this very day, if only to serve as a reminder of past times.

Their greatest triumph perhaps was to draw attention in the late 1800's to the appalling lack of sanitation in the borough, particularly in the market and St. George's Fields and latterly about a proposed amalgamation of the Southwark parishes with the City. All the impetus came from Southwark, with only lukewarm support from Guildhall and in the teeth of bitter opposition from the London County Council. In evidence it was said that the only bond then binding the City to Southwark was that "once a year the Steward of Southwark holds a Court Leet, the principal business in connection with which appears to be that of holding a dinner".

The upshot was that the ancient borough was dismembered with the Guildable Manor and the Great Liberty Manor becoming part of the Borough of Bermondsey and the King's Manor part of the new Borough of Southwark.

However, the historic links between Southwark and the City do in fact remain: the Recorder is still Steward of Southwark; the Secondary (who manages the Old Bailey, the Central Criminal Court) remains the High Bailiff of Southwark; jurors are still summoned to the Courts Leet (Robin Sherlock who wrote the earlier part of this paper is one of them) and the Court Leet still meets each year (albeit chiefly for Dinner) with invitations to the Lord Mayor-Elect, the Sheriffs and the Chief Commoner of the day (in which capacity the author of this volume has enjoyed his own participation in the famous Courts Leet of Southwark).

*

In this, the last part of our Southwark history, Wallis Hunt's paper of July 1971 on the Southwark Compter painted a grim picture of the penal conditions that prevailed in London, as elsewhere, over the centuries.

Before 1550 Southwark was not without places of detention such as the Marshalsea and the Clink. But when the Bridge House Estates became responsible for all the City's lands and liberties after that date it was felt they needed a gaol of their own.

For over a hundred years they used part of St. Margaret's Church as courthouse and compter, extending the prison around 1600. That first compter was destroyed in a fire that raged along Borough High Street in 1676. It was rebuilt a few years later and then in 1717 a new prison was built in Tooley Street, this one destroyed in the Gordon Riots of 1780, probably a rehearsal for the rioters before they poured across London Bridge to bring havoc into the City. The building of the fourth – and last – compter was completed in 1795.

Hunt remarks that it could not have been very well built for almost the whole of its duration successive Keepers were petitioning the Common Council for "such relief as their wisdom and humanity shall deem meet" on account of its "very ruinous and dangerous state". A floor had collapsed, the leadwork of the windows was too decayed to hold glass and the prisoners with nothing but bare boards to sleep on and scarcely one blanket between two of them were "exposed to inclemency of the weather". It seems that even the Keeper's house was not a lot better although presumably he had blankets enough.

Promises of improvement came but save for a few rugs and more blankets little was done to improve the lot of the inmates. Almost the only change was a large increase in the number of prisoners. "Your Petitioner's prisoners" said another letter to Guildhall "have for allowance a two penny loaf each per day". These were poor debtors. In the Marshalsea, according to Dickens, some of the debtors had access to somewhat better fare. Although in 1817 the High Bailiff still felt it necessary to refer to the compter as "this public grievance" it was largely because of overcrowding. Commitments for debt had risen from 53 in 1809 to 730 in 1818 and the compter's share of these unfortunates peaked at 80 men and 80 women. At that time the City issued detailed rules and regulations which, said Hunt, would even today seem enlightened for a prison regime with the prisoners allowed to "amuse themselves by way of exercise at any games approved by the Keeper" and some improvement in cleanliness and sanitation. "Tea, coffee, milk, beer and victuals" could be brought in and visitors allowed twice a day.

By this time most of the indictments were for stealing but there were also a good many sentenced for assault. By the late 1830's the City authorities were beginning to worry about the costs of administering justice in Southwark. The compter was adapted for use by female prisoners only, some being moved there from the City's own compter in Giltspur Street (which was even more overcrowded). By 1852 application was made to the Home Secretary to move any remaining prisoners back to Giltspur Street and by the end of the year all the prisoners had gone. In 1855 Common Council ordered that the compter should be demolished. The City's long vigil as a gaoler outside its own boundaries had finally come to an end – and with it a particularly black page in the GHA history.

* * *

PART FIVE

INTERLUDE: TO PRAISE GREAT MEN

Many among the City's great and good – and the not so good – have made their entrances and their exits in the preceding parts of this history. In this short section there feature a handful of men whose stories were felt by GHA speakers to merit special attention: Shakespeare, Pepys, Dickens, Horace Jones and John Wilkes.

William Shakespeare – Citizen and Player

William Shakespeare – Citizen and Player was chosen as the subject for his paper in April 1962 by Historian Roland Champness. His purpose would be to sketch a picture of William Shakespeare during the time he lived in London. His theme was to stress the fact that our greatest poet and dramatist was not only a son of Stratford-on-Avon but also a citizen of London where he passed the most productive years of his life and gave to the early theatre the fruits of his genius. In this sense, wrote Champness, we can truly claim him as a Londoner.

Among the many gaps in our knowledge of Shakespeare's personal history we do at least know of his baptism on the 26th April 1564 and that whatever happened to him in the intervening years he was most certainly in London, at the age of 28, with his first part of Henry VI being performed at the Rose on Bankside. It has been surmised by many historians that Shakespeare left Stratford for London some five years earlier, aged 23. The next few years most likely saw him finding employment of sorts with James Burbage's company of players at the Theatre (as it was simply called) in Shoreditch and the Cross Keys in Gracious (later Gracechurch) Street.

Champness suggests he graduated to playing small parts and that Burbage might have given him some old plays to rewrite and discovered he had a potential playwright in his company. By the autumn of 1594 the "Chamberlain's men" under Burbage were grateful to have Shakespeare writing exclusively for them.

A year later came positive evidence of his position as a provider of entertainment for the Court with a record of payment of £20 "To William Kempe, William Shakespeare and Richard Burbage servantes to the Lord Chambleyne for twoe several comedies or enterludes shewed by them befor her Matie in Xmas tyme laste paste" at Greenwich Palace. From City records we know that Shakespeare was from 1596 to 1599 living in the parish of St. Helen's Bishopsgate.

These years were a period of great creativity with Two Gentlemen of Verona, A Comedy of Errors, Love's Labour's Lost, A Midsummer Night's Dream, The Merchant of Venice, Richard II, Richard III,

Henry IV, King John and Romeo and Juliet – all having been written by the middle of 1598. He was also playing in Ben Jonson's "Every Man in his Humour" with Burbage, Condell, Kempe and others at the Curtain in Shoreditch.

When in 1599 the Burbage brothers, to avoid persecution by the Mayor and Aldermen, removed the Shoreditch theatre to Bankside, using its old timbers to build the Globe, Shakespeare contributed to the cost. He was clearly well established and had bought for £60 New Place, a "pretty house of brick and timber" considered to be one of the best houses in Stratford – but still living in London for most of the year. In 1599 he moved into new lodgings in the Liberty of the Clink on the Surrey Bankside.

Hamlet, written exactly in the middle of Shakespeare's career, was a landmark in his dramatic output, its success bringing crowded houses to the Globe throughout 1602. That same year Twelfth Night was performed as an entertainment in Middle Temple Hall.

Upon the death of Queen Elizabeth and the accession of James I the new King speedily appointed the Lord Chamberlain's Men his own servants: Shakespeare, Burbage, Heminges, Condell and the others of the company. They were sworn in as Grooms of the Chamber, ranking between gentlemen and yeomen, and the Master of the Great Wardrobe supplied each with 4½ yards of scarlet cloth for their royal liveries (players even one so renowned as William Shakespeare had their place in the 17th century – and far beyond!).

About this time Shakespeare moved from Southwark to the far more fashionable parish of St. Olave in the Ward of Cripplegate. Here he lodged with Christopher Mountjoy, a French Huguenot, at the corner of Silver Street and Monkwell Street, who supplied the queen with head-dresses of golden net. Some years later he was called to make a deposition in favour of Mountjoy in a family squabble heard at the Court of Requests at Westminster.

In March 1613 Shakespeare bought the gatehouse of the old Blackfriars priory as a property investment and the conveyance bearing his signature was acquired by the Corporation in 1843, now one of the Guildhall Library's cherished treasures.

About that time he probably departed London for the last time. He died on 23rd April 1616 on his 52nd birthday and was buried within the chancel of Holy Trinity Church, Stratford-on-Avon.

In the City Shakespeare is honoured in the quiet little garden where once stood the bombed church of St. Mary Aldermary (the church that was re-erected in Fulton, Missouri). Here is the pedestal bust of the playwright placed there in 1896. It is a memorial to John Heminge and Henry Condell, fellow actors and friends of Shakespeare, both of whom lived in this parish and are buried there.

To them, who published the First Folio of 1623 the world owes an incalculable debt, wrote Champness. Their dedicatory epistle to the Earls of Pembroke and Montgomery reads: "We have but collected them (the plays) and done an office to the dead; without ambition either of selfe-profit or fame, onely to keep the memory of so worthy a Friend and Fellow alive as was our Shakespeare".

The inscription says: "The fame of Shakespeare rests on his incomparable dramas. There is no evidence he intended to publish them and his premature death made this the interest of no-one else. Heminge and Condell, co-partners with him at the Globe, from the accumulated plays there of thirty-five years with great labour selected them. No men were so competent, having acted with him in them for many years and well knowing his manuscripts. What they did was priceless, for the whole of his manuscripts with almost all those of the dramas of the period have perished".

* * *

Samuel Pepys: The Unequalled Self

We who are privileged to be members of the Guildhall Historical Association are proud to call ourselves Historians but we are of course only amateur historians. Very occasionally a paper is read to us by a real, professional, historian. One such visit, in March 2003, was made by Claire Tomalin whose paper for the GHA reflects all the brilliance of her splendid biography "Samuel Pepys: The Unequalled Self".*

Unusually her talk was given in the Old Library at Guildhall and was introduced by Lionel Altman, the Chairman of the City's Libraries Committee as a celebration of Pepys' tercentenary.

*

Pepys is remembered for many things and most famously as a diarist: for 9½ years from 1660 to 1669. He wrote an unparalleled account of the great events he witnessed, the restoration, the plague, the fire and war, and of his own professional and private life for which he is probably remembered even better. He had no model when he started to write and effectively invented his own form. He produced an extraordinary 1¼ million words and maintained a candour that no diarist has ever matched. He saw the greatness of the world and recorded it, but he knew that the small things in life mattered as much. From the very first page he balances the great, General Monk in Scotland, and the small, his wife Elizabeth's periods when she was expecting to be pregnant and then she found she wasn't.

Pepys is remembered also as an administrator and reformer in relation to the navy and the organisation of Christ's Hospital... at 50 he was so powerful a civil servant that he persuaded the authorities to allow him to run a government office from his own home.

We remember him too as a man with a strongly developed interest in the arts, music, theatre, painting and poetry. He thought himself, in

---

* Published Viking (hardback) 2002 and Penguin (paperback) 2003

his own phrase, "a liberal genius". A liberal genius in the 17th Century meant someone who cared for gentlemanly pursuits and studies and for whom the arts were important. I think that if Pepys had not needed to earn his living as he did, he would surely have devoted his life entirely to the arts. We know he wrote music; his first written work was a novel he wrote at Cambridge called "love a cheat" something one would dearly love to see.

We remember him as a brilliant reporter. Even before the diary starts, Pepys was writing letters for his cousin and employer, Edward Montague, who became the Earl of Sandwich. A few marvellous letters have survived in which he describes riots in London, for instance, this is still in the 1650's. There is one where he talks about the apprentice boys attacking the soldiers who were trying to maintain order in London.

We remember him also as a keen committee man, hardworking, clubbable, effective and with a wide range of interests, including his membership of the Royal Society of which he became president in the 1680's.

We remember him as a lover of books who collected a fine library of 3,000 books. He had very particular views about his library: he didn't want to have two copies of the same work, so he disposed of one Shakespeare folio, after acquiring a second one. He also arranged his books by height: some of the books in the Pepys library stand on a sort of shoe to bring them up to the height of the ones next to them. Pepys had very definite ideas about how his library should be arranged: he had special presses, special bookcases, made by a navy joiner.

These are the various ways in which he was remembered: but what I want to concentrate on today is Pepys the Londoner. He was known by his friends to prefer London to all other places and since here we are at the Guildhall it seemed a good idea for us to concentrate on Pepys and London. Pepys was born in London, he was educated in London, he was married in London, he worked here, he sat in Parliament, he was imprisoned in London and he was buried in London. Quite a claim to be a real Londoner!

He was born in 1633 when London was still effectively a medieval place with timber and plaster houses. He was born on the western edge of the city, in Salisbury Court, just off Fleet Street. His first world was Fleet Street, the south facing slope going down to the river with crowded alleys and wharves. The Thames itself was the main thoroughfare through London: if you wanted to get round London quickly then you went by the river, there were terrible traffic problems already on land. His father had come to London from East Anglia, an ignorant 14 year old boy and apprenticed himself to a tailor. He served his apprenticeship and became a not very successful tailor himself. Pepys' mother was a north London washmaid. They had no intellectual interests though the father was musical.

The family lived above the shop, the house backed onto St. Bride's churchyard, where many of the Pepys children who died young were buried. Samuel Pepys was the 5th of 11 children, 7 of whom died leaving him the eldest survivor and aware of the precariousness of life. His own health was poor. Looking back he said he didn't remember a day he didn't suffer pain from the stone in his kidney. Around those tightly packed courts and alleys off Fleet Street there were frequent outbreaks of plague. Sometimes Pepys and his brother Tom were sent out to board in the country at Hackney Fields.

London, in the time of Pepys' birth and childhood was still rural. In 1630, St. Martin's Fields were still used for pasture and drying clothes. The parishioners petitioned against building over the fields, but the Earl of Leicester built his house in 1631 and 50 years later (this was all in the course of Pepys' lifetime) the whole square, Leicester Square, had been built around. There were open fields to the west of the Haymarket during Pepys' childhood and the Haymarket was not paved until 1697 when he was an old man. Lincoln Inns Fields were enclosed by fashionable houses from 1638, when Pepys was 5, so a lot of the country was disappearing. Moorfields was the first civic park: it was levelled and planted with 300 trees before Pepys was born in 1605. It was described as 'a garden of the city' and a pleasure 'place of sweet airs' for citizens to walk in. The area was well known to Pepys of course: perhaps the thing we remember best is his visit to the plague pit in Moorfields, but he did go to Moorfields in salubrious times also.

His childhood coincided with the run up to the civil war and what he saw, I think, as a child, was the theatre of the street: puritan preachers in the streets, all sorts of sects including women preachers; public executions and Charles I greeted by the citizens with branches of bay and trumpets in the windows; and great rejoicing as the City geared itself up to oppose Charles I. The most spectacular moment which Pepys witnessed as a boy of 9 was when Charles I attempted to pursue 5 members of parliament into the city and was mobbed by city crowds shouting "privilege of parliament, privilege of parliament". Charles I was not back in London until 1649 when he was executed in front of the banqueting house, with Pepys as a schoolboy watching and approving.

At St. Paul's where he went to school the high master, John Langley was a strict puritan, probably why Pepys was so strongly on that side of the argument. The education at St. Paul's in those days involved compositions which were delivered orally in Latin, so the boys really learned to stand up and speak. Pepys was proud all his life of being able to stand up and speak in public and he was very scornful of those who couldn't. From St. Paul's he then went on to Cambridge where again there were public disputations instead of handing in weekly essays, so he continued this tradition!

When he came to marry, he was married in a secular ceremony because he had a private religious ceremony a littler earlier. His wife Elizabeth was a penniless girl who was then only 14 years old. She was just 15 years old when they had the secular ceremony which took place in St. Margaret's, Westminster. At that time, he had no money and was working as a servant for Edward Montague. They lived in a little turret room in Whitehall Place thanks to Edward Montague, one of Cromwell's advisors and statesmen, who had rooms in Whitehall Place.

Later, as he suffered more and more from the stone, he decided to have surgery and asked Thomas Hollier of St. Thomas's and St. Bartholomew's to perform the operation. It was not done in hospital, but privately in his cousin's house in Salisbury Court off Fleet Street.

His father lined up members of the family to pray for Pepys' recovery. The operation worked: it was a great moment in Pepys' life as it restored him to his energies and capacities.

We can see from all these London touches, how much the city was the element in which Pepys felt at home. It nurtured him; he knew every street; he knew the open spaces; he knew the riverbank. It was the place where he witnessed so many public events and also lived through his own private crisis and it is where the impulse to take up his pen to become a diarist was developed. This familiarity with London feeds into almost every page of the diary. Pepys is the first writer to give a detailed account of what daily life in London was actually like: its domestic routines; its office routines. It gives us a sense of its rhythms. For instance, each year you notice he gets up earlier and earlier as spring advances and when midsummer arrives, he sometimes expresses his sadness that the best of the year is now over. We see him riding in the park; we see him having a difficult time trying getting a cab after the theatre; we see him gawping at court events and state occasions; we see him shopping with his wife; we see him shopping with a girlfriend at the exchange at the angle of Cornhill and Threadneedle Street. We can follow him along the Strand and we can follow him on the river. In winter he shows us boys playing football in the icy street where the horse traffic can no longer move. On a hot summer day he shows us how he takes the afternoon off of work to drive a lady he has his eye on in a hired coach up to Highgate where they have a sweaty fumble. On another more decorous day in April he goes with his wife, the maids, the boy and the dog for a picnic along the riverside path of the South Bank and they gather cowslips and enjoy their slices of cold meat. Pepys' familiarity with walking along the South Bank, (he would walk to Greenwich, he would walk to Deptford and to Rotherhithe), is very touching. He would buy cherries at what is still called Cherry Garden Pier: there were cherry orchards there. It is worth following his steps: changed as it all is, you still have some sense of familiarity.

Pepys loved hanging around the dressing rooms to meet the actresses, although he was a very bad theatre critic. I don't think he had a good word for any of Shakespeare's plays at all except perhaps

Hamlet! You can learn from Pepys how to conduct an illicit love affair, how to take a boat over to the South Bank. You learn a lot about life at Court: Pepys loved the soap opera aspect of life at Court. He did not have a very high opinion of the king, but was always pleased to go along and have a look at what was happening at court. You can learn a lot about life below stairs. Pepys' record with women was not good, but he tells us probably more about women in the 17th century than anyone else because he was interested in them. He observed them, and he observed all classes of them; maids, shop girls, countesses, actresses. It is a great richness of the diary that you can find out so much about women from it. He was always as interested in servants as in courtiers. Pepys was a great expert on house improvement. It was one of the things I adored in the diary: he was the original knocker through. Hardly a month goes by without some account of how he's improving his house in Seething Lane and changing things.

I said he was a great reporter and I want to say a little bit about one piece of reporting in the diary which is his account of coming here to the Guildhall on 11 February 1660. General Monk had arrived in London and made his headquarters here. The state of London was really anarchic. The people were exhausted. They were terrified that a new civil war was going to break out. Cromwell had died in 1658 and Richard Cromwell had been in power for a very short time. Monk, although he had marched his army down from Scotland, had not made at all clear what his intentions were, so neither Pepys nor anyone else had any idea what was going to happen. On 11 February 1660, Monk made it clear that he would exert his authority and tell the corrupt Rump Parliament to reform itself. Everyone in London saw that this strong action was a sign that matters were going to be taken in hand. On that day, Pepys first goes to Parliament, sees what is happening there, sees a Quaker saying to one of the Rump members, Arthur Hazlerigg, "thou must fall" and this puritan member of parliament looking quite nervous, as indeed he should. Then you see Pepys walking with a friend, deciding to come to the Guildhall: they walk through London stopping to talk, stopping to send off letters to his patron in the country, stopping to pick up a bit of fast food, they find it very difficult finding anything to eat but they get hold of a chicken somewhere. When they get to the Guildhall, Pepys characteristically finds Monk's secretary, takes him to a tavern and gets him to tell him the chief points of Monk's letter to Parliament which Pepys then writes down in his diary. Pepys reports on how the populace suddenly realise that Monk's soldiers are good people, "bless you, bless you" and give them money. Pepys' description of this long day ends with a marvellous account of the rejoicing that breaks out in London.

This is what Pepys wrote:

"in Cheapside there was a great many bonfires, and Bow bells and all the bells in all the churches as we went home were ringing; the common joy that was everywhere to be seen; the number of bonfires there being 14 between St. Dunstan's and Temple Bar and at the Strand I could at one view see 31 bonfires; indeed it was past imagination both the greatness and the suddenness of it".

It is just the beginning of the account of the political events of 1660 which Pepys gives all through the first year of the diary: a truly extraordinary document about regime change which is what it was, as it was lived from day to day.

I have tried to just touch on some of the riches to be found in the diary. I have only scraped the surface, missing out many things including Pepys' attendance at the Lord Mayor's dinner here in October 1663. It was the first time Pepys had been asked and the invitation signalled a big social step up for him. He was obviously determined not to be impressed when he came so he complained: he complained about the lack of napkins and knives; he complained about almost everything except the food and the wine which was superb. He returned many times to Guildhall, the last visit in 1695 when he attended the wedding of two Christ's Hospital children, a blue coat boy and blue coat girl, both inheritors of fortunes from wealthy London citizens. They were led by boys and girls of the school through Cheapside to Guildhall chapel where they were married by the dean of St. Paul's and she given away by my lord mayor.

It is a cheerful Pepysian note to end on.

*   *   *

Charles Dickens

This portrait of Dickens, GHA Historians were told in July 1961 by Major Stanley Wells, was based on that definitive biography of three volumes, each of some 500 pages by Dickens' great friend John Forster. Major Wells's reading research was something of an achievement in itself.

A child first of Portsmouth Dockyard where his father was a clerk in the Navy pay office and then of Chatham to which the family moved when he was four, Dickens revelled in the environment of Chatham and Rochester with all their maritime and historic associations. He had schooling with a Baptist minister, giving him an early foundation of knowledge and use of the English Language.

When he was nine his father fell on hard times, the family having to move to mean lodgings in London. The father was arrested for debt and confined to the Marshalsea prison. Dickens was placed in a boot-blacking factory at Hungerford, Charing Cross. Happily, after two years the family fortunes improved, the father released from the Marshalsea and Charles sent to school in Hampstead. After leaving school he worked for two years in a solicitor's office: all these early experiences used to the full later in his career.

Although his ambitions then were for the stage he saw journalism as a more promising road, taught himself shorthand and at the age of seventeen became a reporter at Doctors' Commons and two years later was reporting from the gallery at the House of Commons. Then, aged 23 came the important move as a reporter on the Morning Chronicle newspaper. Besides his reporting he became a prolific contributor to the Old Monthly Magazine where began the "Sketches by Boz".

Then in March 1836 came the advertisement in The Times which, as Major Wells wrote, was the foundation of all Dickens' future success:

"The Pickwick Papers. On 31st March will be published the first number of The Posthumous Papers of the Pickwick Club containing a faithful record of the perambulations, perils, travels and adventures, and sporting transactions of the Members, edited by Boz, to be continued monthly, each monthly part embellished with four illustrations, price 1/- of all book-sellers".

The first return on this publication brought him in no less than £2,500.

From then on Dickens used his pen to create his great and splendid gallery of portraits, the whole of London life, the life of the streets, of the City being depicted in his pages. On an almost annual basis his novels were written and published, practically all of them in monthly numbers:

1837 Oliver Twist, 1839 Nicholas Nickleby, 1840 The Old Curiosity Shop, 1841 Barnaby Rudge, 1843 A Christmas Carol, 1844 Martin Chuzzlewit, 1845 The Chimes and the Cricket on the Hearth, 1846 Dombey & Son, 1849 David Copperfield, 1852 Bleak House, 1854 Hard Times, 1855 Little Dorritt, 1859 A Tale of Two Cities, 1860 Great Expectations, 1864 Our Mutual Friend, 1870 The History of Edwin Drood (unfinished).

At the age of 24 Dickens had married the 21-year-old Catherine Hogarth. Her father was editor of the Evening Chronicle and their simple marriage was conducted at St. Luke's Church, Chelsea by the Rev. Charles Kingsley, father of the author of "Westward Ho!".

In 1842, taking his wife with him he paid his first visit to the United States travelling to New York and many other cities being welcomed everywhere with the greatest of warmth. From 41 of New York's leading citizens he was invited to attend a Public Dinner "In testimony of our respect and high regard and as a thankful tribute to your genius and the rich intellectual feasts you have so often spread before us".

Clearly he was loved in America to which he returned for a six-months visit in 1867 for the purpose of giving a series of readings from his works. He went to all the great cities and always the places where he read were filled to overflowing.

He had begun his public readings in this country in 1858, developing a quite new art, selecting episodes from his novels, dramatising them, and making himself word perfect of their content so that he could apply his full histrionic talent to audiences throughout the land, Belfast and Dublin, Edinburgh and Glasgow as well as London's biggest halls. It is estimated that he gave 423 readings at home and abroad (not counting those given for charitable purposes) and earned the enormous sum from them of £45,000. It was however, as Wells wrote, enormously demanding of his health and undoubtedly curtailed his life.

Other than when he was editing a newspaper in Fleet Street it appears that his contacts with the City were infrequent. He did take the chair on at least three occasions to raise money for charities and at one of them – for the Newsvendors Benevolent Institution ("Old Ben") – in his toast to the Corporation of the City of London he told the guests he had "never witnessed a Lord Mayor's Show except from the point of view obtained by all the other vagabonds on the pavement".

Perhaps that remark led to his being invited by the Lord Mayor, Sir James Duke, to attend a Mansion House Dinner in celebration of "Literature and Art". Wells does not tell us if he had been asked to speak – probably not and what a missed opportunity if that were so.

In March 1870, when he was entertaining the Clerk of the Privy Council at dinner, Dickens showed him a collection of photographs depicting scenes on the battlefields in the American Civil War, which had been given to him in Washington. The Clerk mentioned these photographs to Queen Victoria, who expressed a wish to examine them. Dickens at once forwarded the collection for her Majesty's inspection. The Queen then desired an opportunity of thanking him in person and in obedience to the Royal Command, he went to Buckingham Palace where he was received most graciously; the interview was prolonged for an hour and a half and he ever remembered the Queen's kindness on that day. Her Majesty begged his acceptance of a copy of her "Leaves from the Journal of Our Life in the Highlands", in which she had written his name and said: "The humblest of writers would be ashamed to offer it to one of the greatest", but that it had been suggested that she should give it with her own hands. Her Majesty then spoke of her desire to possess a complete set of his works, and a specially bound set was forwarded to Windsor and placed in the Queen's private library.

Dickens worked through to the finish and died on Thursday, 9th June, 1870, at his home, Gads Hill Place, Rochester. In his Will, which was proved at £93,000, he expressed the desire for an exceedingly modest burial, and that he might rest in the churchyard in the shades of Rochester Cathedral, but The Times on the following morning in its leader wrote:

"Statesmen, Men of Science, Philanthropists, and other Benefactors of their race, might pass away and yet not leave a void which will be caused by the death of Dickens. They may have earned the esteem of mankind, their days may have been passed in power, honour and prosperity; they may have been surrounded by troops of friends, but, however pre-eminent in station, ability or public service, they will not have been like our great and genial novelist, the intimate of every household. Indeed such a position is attained not even by one man in an age, it needs an extraordinary combination of intellectual and moral qualities before the World will thus consent to enthrone a man as an insuperable and enduring favourite. This is the position which Dickens has occupied with the English and also with the American public for a third of a century.

Westminster Abbey is the peculiar resting place of English literary geniuses, and among whose sacred dust lies there, or whose names are recorded on the wall, very few are more worthy than Charles Dickens of such a home. Fewer still, we believe, will be recorded with more honour as time passes and his greatness grows upon us".

So it was that the Nation claimed its own, and on Tuesday, 14th June, 1870, at 9 o'clock in the morning, in the presence of only his family and a few friends, Dickens was laid to rest in Westminster Abbey.

*   *   *

Sir Horace Jones, Architect of the Victorian City

Could readers feel that Horace Jones is somewhat an odd bedfellow with such national treasures as Shakespeare, Dickens and Pepys? And yet... he was certainly a great man of the City and like Wren, albeit on a less elevated level, his legacy is all around us still to see.

The paper describing his achievements was read in October 1995 by Keith Knowles who began on a high note:

- On Friday 30 July 1886 the train pulled out from Victoria Station. Horace Jones settled comfortably in his seat and reflected that this was to be the journey of his lifetime and tomorrow the summit of all his ambitions and achievements. Accompanied by his wife, he was travelling to Southampton, thence by ferry to Cowes to be in good time for his attendance at Osborne House the following day.

Knowles tells us - almost as an aside - that another traveller that day to Osborne House was William Gladstone who had just resigned as Prime Minister (over the Irish Question, what else?) to hand over the Seals of Office to the Queen. He would shortly be replaced by the Marquess of Salisbury, leader of the Unionists.

On Saturday 31 July Mr. and Mrs Horace Jones travelled by coach from Cowes to Osborne House for the investiture. There they met the other six men to be honoured that day – four medical men, one naval man and the Mayor of Weymouth. Jones was the last to be touched by the royal sword and rose as Sir Horace. After the investiture the six men were entertained by the Prince of Wales aboard the Royal Yacht "Osborne" lying in Cowes Roads.

From his portrait painted as President of the Royal Institute of British Architects two years earlier, Jones was a well-built handsome man, bearded as was then the custom, with the overall impression of a strong personality. He was known to be very hard working, outspoken on occasion, even brusque. At the time of his investiture he was 67.

Jones was very much a product of the City having been born at the family home in Sise Lane where his father and brother practised as solicitors. After he had qualified as an architect in 1842 he was employed as a quantity surveyor which gave him a grasp of the cost of buildings and assisted also in the design of cloth warehouses in Gresham Street and Wood Street. He travelled and studied in France, Italy and Greece.

From the 1840's to the 1860's he was engaged in the design of a great variety of buildings – Cardiff Town Hall, a great house at Caversham Park near Reading, a music hall in Walworth (a galleried building with cast-iron frame – a material he enjoyed using), the Metropolitan (later Royal Free) hospital in Grays Inn Road, stores and shops in the West End including Marshall and Snelgrove.

However, aged 45, the joys of private practice had receded and when, with the death of James Bunstone Bunning, the Corporation sought a new City Architect and Surveyor Jones was one of the six applicants who were invited to sit on Guildhall dais with the Lord Mayor each delivering a short presentation to the Common Council assembly of 177 Councilmen and Aldermen.

It was a long and demanding voting procedure, the six first being reduced to four and then to the final two: Richard Bell and Horace Jones. In that final vote Bell received 82 votes, Jones 95, whereupon the Lord Mayor declared Horace Jones Esq., Citizen and Fishmonger (all six candidates were members of a livery company) to have been elected the City's new Architect and Surveyor.

The voting had been remarkably close. The salary was, for the time, generous at £1,500 p.a. Keith Knowles points out that in 1864 a skilled craftsman such as a carpenter or stonemason received six shillings a day.

There was a vast programme of work waiting for Jones. The City markets were, according to the RIBA Journal, a particular disgrace, all seven of them. Apart from designing new ones Jones had to negotiate the purchase of the ground, settle claims for compensation, and design such extras as wharves and jetties.

Unlike the buildings of today (with the exception of the Barbican complex and the Guildhall Art Gallery) those of Horace Jones in his twenty-two years of creativity were intended to last and, indeed, most are still there today between, 125 and 150 years later, still highly functional and six of the eighteen among the best examples of high Victorian architecture, one of them, Tower Bridge, famed as an icon of London's skyline.

First, though, the market buildings and first among them the Central Meat Market at Smithfield, an enormous project stretching 631 feet east to west and 246 feet north to south, completed in 1864. Described as Italianate in design it introduced such innovatory concepts as a roof with two thicknesses of glass to keep the interior both cool and light. When in the mid 1990's it was necessary to refurbish the 130-year-old market to bring it into line with modern hygiene requirements the essential elements of Horace Jones's design – its red brick façade, Portland stone pilasters, cast iron gates and screens required little more than cleaning and repainting.

Jones's s second market project was the conversion of the former Deptford dockyard into the Foreign Cattle Market the interiors of which, wrote Knowles, with their great spans of iron and timber, bore comparison with the best examples of 19th century industrial architecture.

Within the City, in 1877, the meat market at Smithfield was complemented with the fish market at Billingsgate, another splendid piece of Victoriana with a deep vaulted basement providing an enormous deep-freeze. It was still there in the early 1980's until the traffic congestion of Lower Thames Street necessitated the building of a new market in Canary Wharf. Happily calls for the demolition of Billingsgate were overridden; its restoration was effectively achieved (as a place for exhibitions and other special events) by a perhaps unexpected hand, that of Richard Rogers.

Jones's other market triumph was the creation of Leadenhall as a covered collection of shops and eating places which has maintained its special character from 1882 to the present day.

He was much involved, too, in works within Guildhall itself – notably the building of a handsome new library and museum. That "new" library has since become the Old Library as impressive as ever but given over to receptions for visiting heads of state and dinners (following the building of a new Guildhall Library in the west wing of the Guildhall).

It is only since the Second World War that Common Council has held its meetings in Guildhall itself. Before that the Lord Mayor would preside over aldermen and councilmen in a separate council chamber, the third and last being Horace Jones's most elegant twelve-sided Gothic-style chamber of 1884, destroyed, alas, in the bombing of 1940.

His most famous structure of all was Tower Bridge, a project in which he was the architectural genius, while Sir John Wolfe Barry was the engineer. The great bascule bridge providing an urgently needed additional vehicle crossing of the Thames while allowing access for shipping into the Pool of London, celebrated its centenary in 1994. It remains one of the nation's international landmarks.

*

Before and after Horace Jones

We have celebrated the renown of the City's great Victorian architect, Horace Jones (page 273), but he did have predecessors and successors, a line of men stretching back to the year 1478 when Edward Stone was chosen by Common Council as Master of the Works of the City. His main task – with advice from three aldermen and three commoners – was the repair of the City walls and cleansing of its ditches.

Clerks of the Works in the early days were journeymen rather than specialists. Nicholas Duncombe (1662 – 1676) was temporarily suspended pending an investigation of the death of a passer-by who fell into a hole in Fleet Street which Duncombe had left insufficiently protected at night.

All changed with the appointment of George Dance, senior, followed by his son George Dance, junior, who between them served the City as Clerk of the Works for a period of eighty years. George Dance senior's appointment from 1734 to 1768 gave him a virtual monopoly of the City's architectural work and it was this official position rather than any other qualifications which led in 1737 to acceptance of his design for the Mansion House.

"The result" (wrote Historian Richard Beck in October 1979) "in spite of its Palladian portico and Egyptian Hall displayed neither scholarship nor sensibility. He was better at less pretentious municipal buildings and churches".

Beck was far more generous in his praise of the 27-year-old Dance junior who was appointed to succeed his father in 1768. He had been trained as a surveyor and had studied architecture in Italy. In his 48 years' service with the City his early promise was more than fulfilled, his achievements ranging from designs for All Hallows church, London Wall to the new Newgate prison. It was his work that persuaded the Corporation to change the title of his successors from Clerk of Works to Architect or Surveyor; Common Council remained averse to the separation of these two offices for many years. However, when James Bunstone Bunning was appointed in 1843 it was accepted that an architect of eminence should hold the post. Bunning's work included the famous Coal Exchange (see page 97), Holloway Prison, the Metropolitan Cattle Market at Islington and the rebuilding of Billingsgate.

And then came Horace Jones – but still designated Architect and Surveyor. It was only in 1961 that George Chandler was elected by Common Council as City Architect; four years later the post was redesignated City Architect and Planning Officer.

*　*　*

John Wilkes: A Friend of Liberty

Sir Edward Howard confessed to his fellow Historians that for him the attractions of history lay not in institutions or ancient offices but the lives of remarkable men. His paper in March 1969 was, indeed, devoted to a most remarkable man who, all his life, was consistent to one cause and in his Will asked that his epitaph should be "A Friend of Liberty".

It was a most appropriate moment for a remembrance of John Wilkes since it was, as Howard pointed out, the 200th anniversary of Wilkes's expulsion from Parliament – the most important year of his life!

He married young, aged 21, to Mary Meade, 32, and wealthy. It was a rather loveless marriage which soon broke up but it gave him a daughter he adored and the Manor of Aylesbury. There he sat on the local bench as the Squire and met powerful friends including George Grenville and William Pitt. With Grenville's support he became High Sheriff of Buckingham in 1754.

His first attempt to enter Parliament at the age of 27 was for Berwick-on-Tweed. He lost that election but with Pitt's support (and at a cost of £7,000) he was returned for Aylesbury in 1755, retaining the seat five years later.

Pitt was succeeded as Prime Minister by the unpopular Earl of Bute who ran a paper called "The Briton" for propaganda purposes. Wilkes started a periodical called "The North Briton" in which he ridiculed Bute's government and its favouring of Scottish interests. His paper was vastly amusing to some and aroused anger in others. At least two members of Parliament challenged him to duels. Wilkes fought them both, being quite badly wounded in one of them.

Bute's government resigned in 1763 and it seemed that the purpose of "The North Briton" had been accomplished. However, the King's speech heralding the new administration of George Grenville goaded Wilkes to fury. So appeared on 23 April 1763 the famous No. 45 that would set London by the ears.

Edward Howard wrote that reading it today there seemed nothing in it to warrant the charge of seditious libel but it did seem to many – not least George III himself – that the King was accused of being a liar. The printer, Balfe, and Kearsley the publisher were arrested immediately as eventually was Wilkes despite being a Member of Parliament. He was imprisoned at the Tower.

When the case came before Lord Chief Justice Pratt the latter ruled that as a Member of Parliament he was privileged and to the special delight of the City of London he was released. The cry went up "Wilkes and Liberty" and the mob escorted him home.

Before the Government could take further action Wilkes instituted proceedings against the Secretary of State for theft of his papers (his house had been ransacked in search of evidence against him) and wrongful imprisonment. He obtained £1,000 damages and both printer and publisher were freed.

Wilkes, though, was now broke (a condition in which he found himself for most of his life) and had the famous No. 45 of "The North Briton" reprinted to sell as souvenirs. He also published a somewhat scandalous parody of Pope's "Essay of Man" entitled "Essay on Woman". A copy was acquired by Wilkes's old adversary* Lord Sandwich, and read with some relish by him to a scandalised House of Lords. The Commons ordered the Sheriffs to have the reprinted No. 45 burned by the Public Executioner on the steps of the Royal Exchange but the City mob rescued the pamphlets from the fire.

Wilkes was expelled from Parliament in January 1764 and a new writ for seditious libel issued against him. He was in Paris recovering from the wound he had received in his second duel and when he did not turn up in court was declared an outlaw.

Wilkes returned four years later and announced his candidature as an M.P. for the City of London, no less. In those days the City returned four M.P.'s but it was four aldermen headed by Lord Mayor Sir Thomas Harley who were elected. Wilkes immediately stood for

---

* Lord Sandwich, addressing Wilkes, told him he was sure to end up on the scaffold, unless he died first of the pox. Wilkes replied: "That depends, my Lord, on whether I embrace your Lordship's politics or your Lordship's mistress!"

the constituency of Middlesex which he won with a large majority. The unpopular Lord Mayor Harley had every window in the Mansion House smashed.

But how could an outlaw be elected to Parliament? The Government's dilemma was solved when Wilkes with his usual daring impudence announced his surrender to the charge of outlawry. Crowds of well-wishers went with him to court where he was fined £1,000 and given a sentence of 22 months. The mob prevented the Sheriffs taking him to the Kings Bench Prison in Southwark so Wilkes went there in his own good time and was lodged in some comfort. The crowds grew, the Riot Act was read and the army called out. Eleven people were killed in what became known as the Massacre of St. George's Fields.

In the two elections which followed he remained top of the Middlesex poll but the Commons declared him unfit to be a member.

Then came the great turning point in Wilkes's life. While still in prison he was, in 1769, elected Alderman for the Ward of Farringdon Without. Having served his full term Wilkes was released in 1770 and took his seat in the Court of Aldermen. Almost immediately he became engaged in another battle with Parliament.

Journalists writing in the newly emerging newspapers were not permitted to report debates in the Lords or Commons and recorded them in a disguised form. An M.P. protested against one such report and raised the question of privilege. The House of Commons had the printers arrested but one of them was taken in the City and came before Alderman Wilkes sitting as a magistrate in the Guildhall Justice Room. Wilkes set the printer free.

The printer was ordered to appear at the Commons but, encouraged by Wilkes, refused and when a Commons messenger came to arrest him Wilkes charged the man with wrongful arrest. This time the case came before Lord Mayor Brass Crosby, and Aldermen Oliver and Wilkes at the Mansion House; they placed the messenger in the Wood Street Compter.

An angry House of Commons committed the Lord Mayor and Alderman Oliver to the Tower but, inexplicably, not Wilkes. Eventually the Commons realising, wrote Edward Howard, they had bitten off more than they could chew, gave way; and never again refused to allow parliamentary debates to be reported.

Within Guildhall, unlike Parliament, Wilkes's stock was rising. He was elected a sheriff in 1771 and Master of his livery company the same year. In 1774 he was chosen as Lord Mayor. King George was not pleased but did not withhold his consent. With his City prestige he was also elected yet again as M.P. for Middlesex and this time was allowed to take his seat (although with a busy mayoralty he could not have found much time for Parliament).

Lord Mayor's Day 1774 was a memorable occasion, the crowds exceeding 200,000 it was believed. The main procession was by water with the livery companies' barges accompanied by hundreds of small craft. The event was called Wilkes's Naval Review with gun salutes from both banks of the river.

Howard, Lord Mayor himself soon after delivering this paper, wrote that Wilkes proved quite a remarkable Mayor with his daughter Polly a worthy Lady Mayoress. Among the guests at his Mansion House banquets were the Archbishop of Canterbury, Warren Hastings (before his problems in India), Sir Joshua Reynolds and James Boswell.

At the end of his mayoralty, Wilkes was greatly in debt and described himself as an extinct volcano. Friends helped him to survive and when, in 1779, the office of Chamberlain (a remunerative post) fell vacant Wilkes applied and was elected by the Court of Common Council. Howard tells us that he proved most efficient, welcoming many notable people to the Freedom of the City – William Pitt, Lord Cornwallis, Lord Howe and Lord Nelson. He always started off his Freedom speeches with the words "I give you joy". There could be no doubt that this half of the Chamberlain's work would have greatly appealed to John Wilkes. As to the oversight of the City's finances one can but marvel that a man so troubled by debt in his private life was able to cope, for a good many years, with the complexities of the Guildhall finances.

In Parliament his theme was ever Freedom. He supported the American colonists, spoke for religious tolerance and against the traffic in slaves. He mellowed in his old age and became reconciled to his old enemy, George III. It was said that only the King and Wilkes kept their heads in the Gordon Riots. He died at the age of 72 in December 1797.

PART SIX:

FROM SILKS AND PORCELAIN TO BANKING AND INFORMATION TECHNOLOGY: THE CHANGING FACE OF CITY ENTERPRISE

From the time that Tacitus described Londinium as a town of high repute and a busy emporium for traders – even through the dark years of Saxon and Viking depredations – London's power and independence has been based on its trading expertise and commercial enterprise. From the 12th century the Guilds – grocers, fishmongers, salters, bakers and vintners, mercers, haberdashers, skinners and clothworkers – were not only controlling and expanding their members' businesses and trades but were seen by citizens, mayor, the king himself, as providing the basis of London's social order.

In this section of our history are recorded aspects of London's commercial activity as described in papers presented by GHA members over the past sixty years.

The Silk Industry

Sam Walker in his paper of April 1956 sets the true starting date for the silk industry as the year 2,640 B.C. when the Chinese Empress Hsi Ling Shi encouraged the cultivation of the mulberry tree, the rearing of the silkworms (to which she personally devoted herself) and the reeling of silk.

Walker tells us that in England the silk industry was closely bound up with the history of weaving, one of the most ancient of crafts, the Weavers being the oldest of the City's livery companies dating from the early 12th century. However it was not until the reign of Edward III that the first official reference to silk appeared in the Statute Book of 1363. Silk was then used for embroidery and in the making of threads, cords, ribbons and braids. The first silk fabrics were probably brought to England from Genoa. It is recorded, though, that gold, silver and silk were being woven in London in 1473.

Silk stockings were presented in 1560 by Sir Thomas Gresham to Sir William Cecil to whom he wrote: "I have sent you herewith two payre of blacke silke hosen, and a payre for my lady your wife". In the same year Queen Elizabeth received from her "silk woman" a New Year's gift of silk stockings and declared that thence forward she would wear no other.

Earlier the silk women were complaining to the Mayor and Aldermen about a Lombard merchant who, they said, was buying up all London's raw silk, raising its price, and damaging their livelihood. He was convicted, not for attempting to corner the silk market but of a customs offence. In the 16th century the Court of Aldermen were badgered into negotiations with Mistress Trotte and other silk women but eventually it was Master Silkmen who took over the trade, the women becoming their employees.

The Revocation of the Edict of Nantes in 1685 resulted in the flight to this country of large numbers of Huguenot refugees. Many were weavers who settled in Spittalfields (one among them being Augustine Courtauld) – and it was the arrival of these craftsmen from Tours and Lyons (whose skills had raised silk manufacture in France to heights of prosperity) that made the weaving of silk in England one of our most flourishing trades. In the 18th century there were some 18,000 silk looms being operated in Spittalfields, each of them giving employment to a family of three or four.

The culture of raw silk and the planting of mulberry trees, for example in the gardens of the Drapers' and Grocers' Companies, had been established well before the coming of the Huguenots. In 1631 the Court of Aldermen allowed the setting up of twelve silk mills. In the early 1800's introduction of the Jacquard weaving process opened new possibilities for design of colourful silks.

The City's involvement with the silk trade was declining in the late 18th century as weaving firms moved out of London into the provinces. The industry as a whole suffered badly from the free trade principles of the 19th century, with imports of silk fabrics five times greater than home production. All rather odd, is it not, that in a period of England's greatest industrial expansion this particular industry fared so badly.

* * *

London's Role in the History of English Porcelain

The majority of the population, if asked, would probably associate the English porcelain or china industry with its natural home in Staffordshire and the city of Stoke-on-Trent where Minton, Spode and Wedgwood and many others were based. Elsewhere they would have heard of the great factories of Royal Crown Derby and Royal Worcester. They would know little of the factories at Bow, Isleworth, Limehouse and Vauxhall, although some might be aware that china was once made in Chelsea. Yet it is in London that the English porcelain industry has its roots. Thus did Historian James Sewell open his paper to the GHA in October 2007.

While London lacked Staffordshire's natural resources of clay and coal to fire the ovens it had advantages of its own. It was far and away the largest city in England and the centre of fashionable society. It had craftsmen in the jewellery and metalworking trades whose skills could be applied to other materials. A most important port for international trade it also had access to a substantial wholesale network and a large number of retail outlets. Moreover it had a long-established pottery industry of its own, well known for the tin-glazed earthenware known as English delftware. These had been made in the Aldgate area in the late 16th and early 17th centuries and later in Southwark, Lambeth and Vauxhall.

The secrets of porcelain manufacture were known to the Chinese for centuries and a few pieces found their way to Europe from the 14th century onwards. Chinese porcelain began to be imported by the Dutch, its quality attracting the attention of Europe's rulers and the wealthy.

The introduction of tea drinking in the second half of the 17th century and its vast popularity was followed by the importation of vessels in which the tea could be prepared and served. By 1720 some two million tea pots, dishes and small cups and saucers were being imported into England each year by the East India Company.

The Company's trade was entirely centred in the City of London. Goods were landed at its wharf at London Bridge, stored in warehouses near Bishopsgate and sold from East India House in Leadenhall Street. The sales there were by auction in large lots and the porcelain was bought by a group of merchants known as the London Chinamen.

The first manufacture of porcelain in Europe was at Meissen near Dresden in Saxony in the early 1700's, soon spreading to factories in Vienna and Venice. Experiments elsewhere resulted in the discovery of "soft-paste" porcelain (as opposed to the Chinese and Meissen hard-paste formula) and it is with this that most of the English factories were concerned.

The Bow Factory was established in the 1740's, the prime mover being a linen draper in Cheapside and liveryman of the Haberdashers, Alderman George Arnold. One of his partners was John Crowther who had a wholesale china and pottery business near the Tower. Bow secured a new patent specifying the use of "Virgin Earth" or bone ash – a vital breakthrough for English manufacture leading eventually to the formula we know today as English bone china. Bow had become an important producer, advertising its wares: "A great variety of useful and ornamental china is available for sale at a toyshop in Cornhill near the Royal Exchange". In February 1753 Bow opened its own warehouse in the same area. Bow was one of the largest factories of the day employing some 300 workers including 90 painters. Not only did its products sell well in England and Ireland but it was exporting to America.

The most famous of the early English factories was, however, that of Chelsea. The business was started by a Belgian silversmith named Nicholas Sprimont who moved from Soho to Chelsea where his wares were reported in the "Daily Advertiser" in 1745: "We hear that the China made at Chelsea is arrived to such Perfection as to equal if not surpass the finest old Japan". The earliest surviving dated pieces bear the triangle mark and the words "Chelsea" and 1745 on the base.

The factory became very successful and moved to larger premises in Lawrence Street with its own showroom. It also had showrooms in the Mall and Piccadilly. Sprimont was also able to copy some Meissen pieces which were said to be of finer quality than the originals.

Chelsea specialised in the production of desert wares, figures and vases for the wealthy and was also known for its "toys" – elaborate scent bottles and very small seals in the form of tiny figures and animals. Sprimont's declining health led to the factory's decline. About 1783 the buildings were sold.

With so much porcelain being imported and being produced in 18th century London the china trade flourished. "Chinamen" listed in London directories rose from 18 in 1753 to 52 in 1774. The majority were in the City and formed an association called the China Club in 1785 which operated an auction ring to control wholesale prices. The ring fell foul of the East India Company, its members involved in lawsuits and the club was disbanded. Some of the Chinamen continued in business, the splendid shop of Thomas Goode in South Audley Street in Mayfair a surviving example.

James Sewell ends his paper with the ballad which recorded a famous incident in a London china shop of 1773:

On Holborn Hill the first of May
The Trust I do declare Sir,
A furious Bull did run away
Which made the folks to stare Sir,
This Bull was stout, this Bull was strong.
He ran and made no stop, Sir,
Till horns and all he rush'd headlong
Into a China Shop Sir!...
The cups and platters there he dish'd
And knock'd the Mugs about, Sir!
The china-men they swore and fish'd
But could not get him out, Sir.
An such a clatter made he then,
And such a great uproar, Sir,
With Sheriffs, Mayor and Aldermen,
Was never heard before, Sir.

*   *   *

The City's Textile Industry

Some form of trading in textiles has always existed in the City and in the 18th century it began to take larger shape. By then, in addition to wools from Bradford and cottons from Manchester, such specialised products as lace from Nottingham and hosiery and knitwear from Leicester had become available. Also, as trade with the new world developed imports and exports moved through the western ports. From north and west great horse-drawn wagons came through the Cripplegate and thence to the coaching inns around Guildhall. They were huge establishments with stabling for the horses and accommodation for the waggoners surrounding a large courtyard which provided space for the waggons. The "Swan With Two Necks" in Aldermanbury became the first centre of the trade, business being conducted in the inn, which became an early form of textile warehouse.

It was Historian John Henderson, Cripplegate Councilman and himself engaged in the textile business who recounted this fascinating story in February 1988.

As the volume of trade grew, supplemented by large imports from the East through the Port of London, and as London's increasing population spread further and further from the centre, the bulk handlers or wholesalers began to separate themselves from the stalls and shops that served the public and their need for warehouse space became insatiable. First, the gardens of the large houses in and around Aldermanbury and Wood Street were sold and then the houses themselves. By 1820 this area of Cripplegate had become established as the principal wholesale textile market for London and the south of England.

The coming of the railways would put the great coaching inns out of business and the space they occupied could be used to build yet more warehouses. Workpeople no longer had to live within walking distance. A devastating fire in 1884 destroying much of the northern part of Wood Street opened the door for yet further building of big new warehouses.

Cripplegate and its neighbouring areas – Bread Street, Watling Street, Little Britain and St. Paul's Churchyard were now the home for wholesaling middlemen together with manufacturers and retailers in a vast complex of the City's textile industry. From the 1840's the industry grew and flourished and by the turn of the century the stage was set for what Henderson called "the halcyon days" that would continue right the way through to the 1939 war.

The trade was headed by large multi-department warehouses, about ten in number, each carrying an astonishing variety of textile products from all over Britain and abroad, the customers being small shopkeepers who visited their suppliers weekly to replenish their stock.

Then there were the "specialist houses" established by provincial manufacturers such as Morley and Wolsey whose warm winter underwear and hosiery was in great demand as protection against the cold. Millinery firms from Luton were there too, with others selling menswear, children's' clothing, baby linen and haberdashery.

There were "smallwares", firms selling ladies' collars and blouses, scarves and handkerchiefs. And up the rickety stairs of buildings no-one else wanted were an army of agents representing manufacturers around the country, all part of this vast and complex network of activity that was the City's thriving textile industry. It was essentially a warehousing operation but there was a quite sizeable manufacturing element as well, some of the processes being parcelled out to home-workers: men's ties, women's clothing, artificial flowers, hat and cap makers. Some of the clothing sweat-shops were situated in Fore Street.

These trades survived the restrictions and shortages of the First World War and thrived again through the 1920's. The most serious setback came with the slump of the early thirties but business again picked up right until the disastrous night of 29th December 1940 when in what was one of the most intense incendiary raids of the war almost the whole of the City's textile area – along with so much else of course, the Guildhall, churches and livery halls, Cripplegate was laid waste.

There were thoughts after the war that the trade might return to the City with the Holford plan published in 1950 which earmarked a large part of Cripplegate and small areas north and south of St. Paul's as suitable for textiles. Like so many of the grand post-war concepts, this, too, came to nothing. The few small wholesalers and agents who did return to buildings that had survived the blitz were soon forced out when redevelopment for new office buildings got under way in the late 1950's.

*

Two small postscripts. Rightly enough John Henderson did not mention the City's most marvellous department store – Nicholsons in St. Paul's Churchyard – its counters filled with all manner of haberdashery and where the money paid by customers would wing its way along overhead wires to the cashier sitting in her glass cubicle.

Another memory from the early 1970's when I was seeking votes in our annual Cripplegate Ward elections was the discovery of just one remaining bit of the once great textile industry. Up a wooden staircase in Russia Row I met a one-man wholesaler selling bedspreads and eiderdowns. C.D.W.

*   *   *

The Wine Trade

The wine trade, how delightful an occupation, what joy to sip its products. Little wonder that two at least of our Historians felt obliged to sing its praises. Others might well have done so but recognised the ground had been well covered. Alan Lamboll was first in June 1952 with "The Wine Trade and the City of London". Then came Tom Jackson's "The City and the Wine Trade: an Early History" in October 1989. Let us draw on both their excellent papers for our own salute to wine.

As with so many other things the Romans introduced not only wine but the vine from which it came and vineyards flourished in England in the Middle Ages. The wine trade is one of the oldest of occupations in this country and, sensibly enough, wine was England's largest single import in medieval times.

London soon became the centre of the trade. Southampton and Bristol were also wine ports but their tonnages could not compare with London whence came the greatest demand. Much of the wine found its way into the royal cellars and those of the nobles who had found palatial residences in the City. The Mayor and Aldermen were not to be outdone, either. Jackson tells us that in the mid-13th century a third at least of the 25 Aldermen were themselves involved in the wine trade.

The wine trade had to be regulated and protected. The Vintners Guild in 1364 obtained their Royal Charter from Edward III (they had been in existence years earlier) and built a livery hall from which to control and direct the trade which they ruled with a rod of iron. Punishment was severe. In November of the year of their Charter John Penrose, convicted of selling unsound wine, was ordered to drink a substantial quantity of the offending substance, had even more poured over his head – and rather more serious – would forswear the calling of Vintner for ever.

Lamboll tells us of one of the most famous of Master Vintners, Henry Picard (a recent Mayor of London), who in 1363 entertained no fewer than four kings at his house in Vintry: Edward III, John of

France (who had been captured by the Black Prince at the Battle of Poitiers and in whose honour the dinner was given), David of Scotland and Pierre de Lusignan of Cyprus.

The wines being imported were those of Gascony, particularly those from the lands around Bordeaux, the whole vast province of Aquitaine being a possession of English kings during much of the Hundred Years War with France. In the 1360's England was taking one half of Bordeaux's entire vintage.

Until the 14th century the wine trade was mainly in the hands of foreign merchants*. Bordeaux shippers who had settled in London formed their own association which eventually was merged into the Vintners Guild. City regulations excluded all but citizens of London from the right to sell wine "by retail".

The second of the wine trade's major imports came from Portugal. In contrast to the 18th century's almost universal taste for spirits, port was the most popular kind of wine drunk by the wealthier classes of society. It started off, says Lamboll, by being cheap and poor in quality but gradually improved – and became more expensive – a favourite drink in aristocratic and political circles. When properly bottled and corked port could be laid down and left for many years offering the possibility of vintage wines.

The industrial revolution created a new aristocracy of wealth and a large increase in the number of buyers of good wine. Even more cellars were laid down. It became, says Lamboll, part of a gentleman's education for him to have a knowledge of wine.

So the wine trade flourished, its small number of dedicated importing and retailing firms enjoying an expanding clientele.

*   *   *

---

* College Hill, that important little street where Whittington lived, was originally called La Riole in recognition that a good many of its inhabitants were shippers of wine from the town of La Riole a few miles east of Bordeaux.

Printers of the City

In 1954 the Court of Common Council had temporarily to vacate Guildhall while it was undergoing the final stages of restoration after its war-time destruction. They were meeting instead in the Victorian splendour of what was then the Guildhall Library and has since become the "Old Library".

So that a Common Councilman who grew bored with the proceedings could look up over the head of the Lord Mayor on the dais and enjoy the images in the stained glass window above him.

For one such Councilman, Lord Ebbisham who was a printer by trade, three of those images were of particular interest: Caxton, Gutenberg, Wynkin de Worde and Pynson, the great forebears of printing (and, of course, exactly the right men to adorn the Guildhall's great collection of books).

The stained glass window was the starting point for Ebbisham's GHA paper of May 1954 on City printers, a paper as amusing as it was learned.

To Gutenberg who lived in Mainz is ascribed the invention of printing in about 1440. Five hundred years later a great festival was planned to take place at Mainz to mark printing's fifth centenary. The War intervened and "As far as I know" wrote Ebbisham, "Elliot Viney of the firm Hazel, Watson & Viney and I were the only British Master-printers to be present in Mainz at that date. But as we were unwilling guests of Hitler and heavily escorted, we were hardly in a position to do much about the festival".

It was Caxton who brought the art of printing to this country from the Continent. When he returned to England from the Low Countries he set up the first English press at Westminster in 1476. Although his books were produced in Westminster he was very much a man of the City, apprenticed in his youth as a mercer and a liveryman of the Mercers' Guild.

When Caxton, father of English printing, died all his printing plant was inherited by his apprentice and assistant, Wynkin de Worde. The business was moved in 1500 to premises in Fleet Street. Ebbisham writes that he showed little vigour or enterprise and was content to issue small popular books rather than the class of book which Caxton had produced.

The fourth of the figures in the window was that of Richard Pynson, another printer working at the same time as Wynkin de Worde but who was a much better craftsman. He, too, moved in the year 1500 from just outside Temple Bar to just inside, from where he produced work for Guildhall.

In time the City authorities came to avail themselves of the new art of printing. John Day was probably the first to hold the official position of City Printer in the mid 1550's. As with others working for the City he was granted accommodation for his office and home above one of the City gates, his being Aldersgate.

The office of City Printer was held for life, subject to good behaviour, but was not all that highly regarded. According to a pamphlet in the British Museum the price of Printer to the City was £200, that of Carpenter £300, Paviour £250. The post was not of great gain. He did not even get all the official printing. As the centuries went by the amount of printed matter greatly increased. The Civil War and the Plague gave cause for much printing as did the rebuilding of the City after the Fire.

Several holders of the office of City Printer have been members of the Court of Common Council and one, John Barber, became Lord Mayor in 1732. He was a prominent Jacobite and a friend of Swift and Pope. He must also have been pretty astute, Ebbisham observes, as he made a fortune out of the South Sea Bubble!

Another Lord Mayor he mentions was Henry Winchester. "Although strictly a stationer rather than a printer, he was related to the family of William Clowes whose family business is now connected with my own (Blades) and last year celebrated their 150th anniversary".

Henry Winchester was, according to Ebbisham quite mad, his hatred for those whose political views differed from his own was so strong that he treated them (in his own words) as the Spanish inquisitors treated heretics. In 1826 he was elected Alderman for Vintry Ward – that, after two ballots, two scrutinies and lengthy legal proceedings. In 1835 he was Lord Mayor presiding over a Court of Common Council composed mainly of his political opponents whom he treated with little respect. As his year went on his conduct became increasingly extraordinary. He published a treatise suggesting that the office of Lord Mayor should become vested by heredity in his own family. He liked to be addressed as Lord Winchester. At the end of his year instead of being given a vote of thanks, the Common Council passed a vote of censure and ordered that it should be published in all the London newspapers.

This period was the very last occasion that political division was tolerated in Common Council.

(Ebbisham could have referred to another printer-Lord Mayor – his own father the first Baron Ebbisham who was in the Mansion House from 1926 – 1927. But that would not have been seemly – and anyway most of the Common Council would have been aware of his illustrious forebear).

When Lord Ebbisham presented his paper in 1954 he was able to say that the printing trade was one of strong family connections with a number of firms in the City whose origins went back 100 years and more. At that time there were no fewer than six printers serving on Common Council and a good many Lord Mayors who were printers – Waterlow, Truscott, Greenaway and Ebbisham. The firms had all started in a small way in one or two rooms as had his grandfather who had set up in Abchurch Lane in 1821; and as James Truscott had done in 1825 when he walked from Truro to start his small printing business in Southwark, later moving to Suffolk Lane in the City where it stayed until it was destroyed in 1941.

Ebbisham tells of the time in 1914 when, for the first time, paper money was to replace gold and the family firm was asked by the Bank of England to help with the numbering of the new £1 and 10s. notes. 'It was a matter of the utmost secrecy and the Bank asked my father what special measures he proposed to take'. After some thought he replied 'Absolutely none'. It was better to treat the job as routine and none of the workpeople had any idea of what they had been handling.

*

Alas, the art of printing using hot metal with all its mysteries and intricacies has long since passed away. So, too, the proof readers who made certain that any errors were corrected, have vanished. It is quicker and possibly cheaper to print today but some of the quality and all the romance have disappeared since Ebbisham's day.

*   *   *

The Romance of Private Banking

While the manufacture and sale of goods and materials was ever part of City activity – as witness its guilds of mercers, clothworkers and drapers – increasingly there was also the closest of involvement in the financial aspects of trade and commerce. It was the goldsmiths who provided a coming together of these two streams of commercial activity.

In his paper to the GHA of December 1951 Alderman Frederick Hoare, himself a member of a private banking family, observed that it was Charles II's inability to repay the million pounds he owed London merchants that prompted them to seek a more reliable haven for their wealth.

Goldsmiths were the answer. At first they were no more than safe deposits, valuables lodged with them for a term and then handed back. By degrees, however, the goldsmith's receipt notes for so many gold and silver coins began to pass from hand to hand. Eventually came the idea of giving receipt notes not only to depositors of gold but to those who came to borrow. So it was that goldsmiths, some of them at least, became bankers.

In London the two oldest of the private banks were Childs and Hoares. In 1694 Sir Francis Child and Sir Richard Hoare, close friends, both Aldermen and both having served as Lord Mayor, opposed the establishment of the Bank of England.

Both houses laid claim to being the oldest bank. Both banks were first goldsmiths and that is why in their elegant bank buildings the front office is called the shop and the back one the Counting House. Hoares was situated at No. 37 Fleet Street immediately opposite the church of St. Dunstan and Childs at No. 1. Both banks have had royal accounts – Childs were bankers to William and Mary and Hoares to Queen Anne.

Customers have come to the rescue at times of crisis, wrote Hoare. In 1689 when Childs ran short of gold Sarah, Duchess of Marlborough, collected a great quantity and took it to No. 1 Fleet

Street. Hogarth made a famous cartoon of the Duchess making the delivery. In 1825 at a time of great financial crisis one of Hoares' customers wrote offering the bank £10,000.

The two banks had something else in common – they each had among their famous clientele a mistress each of Charles II. Childs had the more romantic figure of Nell Gwynn, Hoares the more scholarly Barbara Villiers, Duchess of Cleveland, who could write; Nell could but make her mark. "My father" said Hoare" brought me up to believe that it was our Duchess of Cleveland who appeared as Britannia on every penny for the past 200 years. It was however her rival Frances, Duchess of Richmond who posed as Britannia".

When in 1690 Richard Hoare moved from goldsmith to banking the business was not so very different from modern banking. He received money on current account and on deposit. He paid customers' cheques and collected money owing to them. He advised on investments, the main difficulty then to find much in which to invest. Apart from land, mortgages and government loans there were only two major companies – the East India Company and the Company of Adventurers trading into Hudson Bay.

The first Richard Hoare's grandson – another Richard – became the youngest-ever Lord Mayor. It was in the fateful year of 1745 when the Young Pretender marched on London. Lord Mayor Richard Hoare went out to meet him at the head of London's Train Bands – but Prince Charlie turned back well short of the City.

In 1951 when Alderman Hoare (who would himself become Lord Mayor) concluded his paper with these words: "You may wonder why our bank has been left as the last survivor of the once 721 private banks. I think perhaps it is because we have paid just a little more attention to the old saying – Credit is to a Banker what chastity is to a woman".

*   *   *

A London Chamber of Commerce and Industry

"Chambers of Commerce" with what we would now call their "lobbying" role on behalf of commercial interests, had existed in Europe from the end of the 16th century. In his paper of June 2007 Brian Harris pointed out that London, which might have been expected to be among the first to have such a body, lagged far behind. Indeed, the first Chambers in the English-speaking world were in Jersey and the state of New York (then an English colony) in 1768.

After Jersey, and over the next 25 years, Chambers of Commerce were formed in many of this country's cities and towns, their aim being to urge changes on the government in respect of commercial and industrial interests. Such bodies were not always welcome! Pitt the Younger when Prime Minister saw them as wandering into the paths of legislation and government.

In 1782 there was a first attempt to establish a Chamber in the City and a second try in 1823 when a meeting of merchants and bankers was held at the City of London Tavern but was talked out by aldermen and others as being mischievous. Perhaps some of those attending felt that the City was already strong enough to secure its mercantile position?

At long last, in 1881, it was a meeting at the Mansion House, with Lord Mayor Sir William McArthur in the chair that took the plunge. While there were Chambers in every great commercial centre of the world, London was without one, he told the meeting. He was aware that there were in London large representative bodies connected with every department of trade "but they are not wholly representative of the identity of this great town".

Eight hundred circulars were sent out and with a very favourable response a London Chamber was incorporated in October 1881 with offices in Nicholas Lane. At its first meeting the Lord Mayor and Governor of the Bank of England was elected ex-officio as members of its Council – an arrangement that has continued to the present time.

Although the Chamber's establishment was a City initiative it was agreed from the start that it was "for the Metropolis" being concerned for the business community of London as a whole. (This was a time when the City Corporation was being pressed on all sides to take over the running of all London but feared for loss of its independence should it accede).

A first Annual Dinner was held in 1883, under the presidency of Lord Mayor Sir Henry Knight, at the Cannon Street Hotel. The Chamber could congratulate itself on its progress, 1,400 companies having joined, a Chamber of Commerce journal launched and the first commercial arbitration case settled.

An international victory was gained when the Suez Canal Company under Count Ferdinand de Lesseps agreed to changes in the running of the canal which ensured that all vessels whatever their size or number could pass through it at reasonable prices. Another success was the appointment of the London Chamber to arbitrate with the New York Chamber in a worsening Anglo-American dispute about the Venezuelan-British Guiana boundary line. A peaceful solution was secured and in 1901 a New York delegation was entertained at Windsor Castle by King Edward.

By this time the Chamber had some 40 different areas of trade under its wing ranging from the engineering and allied trades to toys and fancy goods. There were also sections for specific countries – Sir William McArthur chairing the Australian section. The Chamber moved to larger premises, first to Eastcheap then Cannon Street.

A curious offshoot of the London Chamber's work was in commercial education. In its still early days it turned out that 40 per cent or more of staff in City offices were foreigners – the reason being that they were better educated (and prepared to work longer hours for lesser salary) than the English. The Chamber set its own examinations and awarded certificates to successful candidates which were presented by the Lord Mayor at Mansion House ceremonies. Harris tells us in his paper that this education scheme continued to flourish and at the millennium over 500,000 students a year, many from overseas, took the examinations.

The centenary year of 1981 was a time of much celebration including a reception at Guildhall hosted by the Lord Mayor and attended by the Queen and Duke of Edinburgh.

*   *   *

An explosion in Property Development

London, the City, has always been a place that valued property, the City's own portfolio of property holdings, over the centuries, the bedrock of its wealth and power.

Michael Cassidy's paper to the GHA in May 1990 focuses on just one recent ten-year period which was quite as remarkable for new building as was the time London was rebuilt after the Great Fire or the City was recreated after the Blitz. It is a tale which tells how the City, perhaps more than ever before, has been transformed in recent times – and certainly has its place in this part of the GHA history as an important aspect of City enterprise.

Cassidy opens with a very telling comparison: From 1900 to 1939 a fifth of the buildings in the City were redeveloped; in the decade he describes nearly one half of the City's floor space was rebuilt. It was a period coinciding with Margaret Thatcher's premiership and the economic "Big Bang" of 1986; a time of unparalleled opportunity with investment returns averaging 23% a year, the FT30 Share Index rising by over 400%. (A time, too, of Stock Market collapse in 1987!)

After the recessions of the 1970's empty buildings began to be let and in 1980 one million square feet of new office space was being built, the figure doubling in 1981. The banking and financial services sector was mainly responsible for growth, foreign banks among the leading occupants. Some 460 banks were represented in the Square Mile with more American banks here than in New York and more Japanese banks than in Tokyo.

Cassidy writes that in the early 1980's a central location was still crucial to certain key City activities – banking had to be close to the Bank of England, insurance near Lloyds. There came a radical change in the perception of where to locate and where new space could be located – this change being the major theme of his paper.

The publication of a draft Development Plan for the City in 1984 was met, in Cassidy's words, "with howls of outrage" from the building development lobby as being too conservation-oriented, that it would "freeze" the City and inhibit expansion of new office space. In the outcome the Development Plan was much changed before its adoption two years later.

Alongside this change came the Government's decision to break the monopoly position of stockbrokers and jobbers forcing them to join forces with banks to provide the capital needed for a wholly new business climate. This, said Cassidy, had a direct impact on property development. A totally new category of space was required with large open trading areas, with as few columns as possible, generous floor to ceiling height and telecommunications. The historic core of the City could not absorb new buildings of 25,000 square feet and upwards per floor. Developers were obliged to consider peripheral locations. Such new areas were found over railway stations and roads.

"To facilitate this trend" wrote Cassidy,

- plot ratio which controlled average density on each site was increased to 5:1;
- basement areas were excluded from plot ratio control leaving developers free to enlarge space below ground;
- there would be no more "conservation areas" and the City's 450 "listed buildings" would not be added to;
- external decorative features would be encouraged to improve the look of buildings.

Developers welcomed these changes in Guildhall policy and the City planners would see a large increase in the volume of planning applications received and in the amount of space under construction. From some 2 million square feet being built in 1984 the figure rose to 17 million by the end of the decade.

Among notable developments of this period were the Broadgate project over and alongside Liverpool Street Station, schemes for Cannon Street and Fenchurch Street stations and replacement of the Lee House tower block on London Wall – first of a series of new developments along the whole length of London Wall between Moorgate and the Museum of London.

Michael Cassidy as Chairman of the City's Planning Committee had invited the Prince of Wales to speak at the Committee's Dinner in 1987. "Reverberations from this speech are still with us and will no doubt continue into the future as public opinion becomes mobilised on matters of design" wrote Cassidy in 1990.

He mentioned two "casualties" of the decade's fast-moving changes – the newspaper and fur trade industries.

Fleet Street was transformed in four years as a consequence of the exodus of printing works with some 540,000 square feet becoming available for other purposes. At the time of Cassidy's paper he was forecasting that all the previous newspaper sites were likely to be used for banking or other professional purposes – as indeed has happened.

The fur trade historically located in and around Garlick Hill succumbed to attack from the anti-fur lobby and the high cost of locating in an expensive commercial area and took itself off to a more hospitable Finland.

Something of a plus-point was that intense development provided unique opportunities for the exploration of historic remains. The Museum of London, with extra funding from developers, was able to employ a great many archaeologists on sites throughout the City; by the end of the decade 54 sites were being investigated.

Michael Cassidy will, I am sure, forgive me this footnote to his paper. First to commend his modesty in not revealing his own powerful contribution to the City's transformation. I would say that in his position as Chairman of the Planning Committee he was its driving force. Second, I suppose I was his particular adversary (as Chairman of the City Heritage Society) and we were outgunned in our efforts to curb the explosion in development at this time. However, conservation was far from a spent force and the Court of Common Council remained strongly opposed to Peter Palumbo's plans for Poultry and the destruction of Mappin and Webb. – C.D.W.

*   *   *

Changing City

In all its years of recorded history the prosperity of the City has depended almost entirely on its effectiveness as a trading centre and today it remains one of the most influential "open" markets in the world. These words of Historian Peter Revell-Smith in his paper of April 1968 introduced a survey of how the City had so dramatically changed over a 400-year period from its Tudor splendours to modern times.

His story begins with Sir Thomas Gresham's creation of the Royal Exchange in 1566. His building in addition to becoming the home of the emerging insurance and commodity markets signalled the end of the coffee house era. The Merchant Adventurers, Muscovy Company and East India Company were the forerunners of a new age in the City – "an age of collective capitalism".

Theoretically, wrote Revell-Smith, the City renews its physical skin approximately every 120 years. At the time of the Great Fire construction was for the most part in small timber-framed houses with thatched roofs; after the destruction they were of stone or brick although remaining small. Between 1730 and 1830 sites and buildings started to become larger, a process which accelerated in Victoria's reign. Between 1901 and 1939 large steel-framed buildings faced in stone predominated – a pattern which has continued to the present day (i.e. 1968) with the substitution of glass and steel cladding.

Before the Plague and Fire the population of the City and Liberties was about 500,000, 150,000 within the walls. With post-Fire reconstruction virtually complete by the beginning of the 18th century wealthier citizens were moving to the villages of Hackney, Islington and Highgate. By 1831 the City population numbered 125,000. During the reign of Queen Victoria the City had changed from a residential to a commercial area.

Workers, who had regularly walked many miles a day now had railways. In 1836 London Bridge terminus was opened to serve the City and six others were completed by 1874.

After the vast destruction in the City during the Second World War, with a third of its buildings gone, the way was opened for comprehensive redevelopment and to expedite the process the City Corporation bought much of the land that was available so that it owned one-tenth of the City. New policies emerged: the east-west routes across the City; separation of pedestrians and vehicles with upper-level walkways and shops; precincts such as Paternoster Square; and buildings allowed to rise above St. Paul's in height.

(Not all these developments were successful, notably the upper walkway system to link much of the City which, except in the Barbican area, has had to be written off – people prefer to do their shopping at street level but it was an interesting proposal. Then again, in 1968, Revell-Smith could say of the Pool of London that it was still the third biggest port in the world).

The sea change in post-war business activity was that offices took the place of the warehouses that were destroyed by bombs. Behind this structural change in the economics of the City came a wave of increased specialisation in banking, insurance, professional and financial services. By 1980, said Revell-Smith, it was anticipated that over half the City's workforce would be engaged in such specialised areas.

In 1968 he could refer to such new developments as Telstar and Telex as well as Webb Offset and computers. The GPO had six communication centres in the City employing 16,000 people. He noted, even then, the question mark over the future of Fleet Street and the printing industry in the City.

*

Revell-Smith's really quite masterly brief survey of change in the City has been overtaken by events as demonstrated in the previous section on the explosion in commercial property development. Which serves to emphasise how very rapidly indeed change can now affect the City. But let us applaud Peter Revell-Smith's final words: "In short the City will remain as it has been for the last 2,000 years, a unique square mile in the history of Western Civilisation". Indeed, a consummation greatly to be wished!

*   *   *

A Livery Company for the 21st Century

To see just how dramatically the City has changed over the centuries one has only to compare today's almost total involvement in aspects of finance with such earlier activities as the manufacture of silks and porcelain. Even more telling is to see how the oldest of the City's livery companies – the Clothworkers, Skinners and Fishmongers – have been joined in recent years by Actuaries, Environmental Cleaners and Information Technologists. It was GHA President Sir Brian Jenkins who in his paper of June 1998 celebrated the arrival of the Information Technologists as the City's 100th livery company.

On that occasion Brian Jenkins was the current President of the British Computer Society. He told us that the vast IT industry "which underpins the City" barely existed 40 years ago; 50 years ago it was unheard of. What a fascinating new candidate for the 700 year old livery structure.

Britain had always led in computer technology since the time in 1948 when Professor Tim Kilburn switched on the Baby, the first stored program computer in the world. That was at Manchester University. Soon afterwards Maurice Wilkes was leading the team at Cambridge which launched EDSAC, a stored program computer with serious computational ability. John Pinkerton designed and built the world's first business computer for J. Lyons and Company. It was called LEO, short for Lyons Electronic Office.

By 1980 with mainframe computing and remote terminals commonplace and stand-alone micros growing, concern was spreading that the UK industry with its many successes, was being overshadowed by American and Japanese competition. It was Alan Benjamin of ICL who had the idea of making 1982 "Computer Year" in Britain to raise public awareness of Britain's achievements. He chaired the committee of IT82, a member of which was Bernard Harty, soon to become Chamberlain to the City of London. The friendship formed between these two was the catalyst for the IT livery company.

They discussed how the growing information needs of the City might be aligned better with developments in associated technologies – it was important the City stayed ahead with deregulation of the stock market and "Big Bang" impending. Bernard Harty hosted a lunch in the Chamberlain's Court in 1985 where the idea of forming a new livery company was greeted with enthusiasm.

Between 1985 and 1987 the initiators worked hard to prepare for City Company status wrote Jenkins. One hundred founder members from among the leaders of the industry were individually invited to join.

Progress towards full livery company is, inevitably, a lengthy process. There came a half-way point in 1987 when, in acknowledgement of the work already done – not least the funding of a charitable trust – and the close association with its professional body, the British Computer Society, the Court of Aldermen granted company status without livery.

Membership grew rapidly each year to over 300. Now (i.e. 1998) it stands at 563, 58 being women and over 30% under the age of 50. A modern apprenticeship scheme was established. An application for livery was made in 1991 emphasising the very special circumstances of information technology in the City: "Bearing in mind the speed of development of IT around the world your petitioners believe it would be strongly in the interests of the City that their petition be presented earlier rather than later".

The Court of Aldermen – presided over by Brian Jenkins then Lord Mayor – approved the petition in January 1992. There was much attendant publicity in The Times, London Evening Standard and that so greatly valued local weekly The City of London Recorder which headlined the event: "Ton-up as hi-tech gets a new status. Computer-ace Lord Mayor's joy over boost to City links".

The celebratory banquet in Guildhall was attended by 600 liverymen, freemen and guests. There were congratulatory messages from the Prime Minister, Margaret Thatcher.

In all this lengthy journey from a bright idea to the coming into being of the 100th Livery Company there was, said Jenkins, enormous help and encouragement from the Mercers' Company which as No. 1 had felt there to be a special relationship with IT Co. No. 100.

The concluding words of his paper (which he acknowledges as coming from the Company's Founder Master, Barney Gibbens) are something of a gem:

"We don't know where we're going – but we're going there fast".

In 2012 the number of members had risen to the astonishingly high total of 789.

*   *   *

PART SEVEN

A MILITARY INTERLUDE

London and its Militia

It is not surprising that the City of London should have as its own the oldest regiment in the British army, for the efficiency and discipline of its citizens under arms was ever the model for the levies and militia of England's other cities and the counties. With these words John Newson-Smith (son of the founding President of the GHA) began his paper of May 1949 on the long history of London's citizen-soldiers. The regiment to which he referred is the Honourable Artillery Company which incorporates the Pikemen and Musketeers who guard the Lord Mayor on ceremonial occasions but which, in the wider sense, is an important part of the Territorial Army.

The origins of the HAC were in 1537 under a Charter of Henry VIII. But, as Newson-Smith recounted, the foundation of a militia came centuries earlier. London auxiliaries marched with King Alfred to dislodge the Danes from Hertford. In 1066 it was the levies raised in London who (unsuccessfully on that occasion) guarded King Harold's banner at Hastings. There was one other example of the City backing the wrong horse when the citizens of London sided with Simon de Montford against Henry III's troops at the Battle of Lewes.

By the reign of Edward III the City was frequently being called upon to supply the King with men. Although the Charters of 1321 and 1327 made clear that citizens of London were not compelled to serve outside the City, many of the calls were for services far away. In 1334 a hundred horsemen and a hundred men on foot were sent to Scotland; in 1338 forty men of arms and sixty archers were provided for the campaign in France; in 1346 the City raised 400 men for the Navy and 280 for the army.

Nearer home London troops were at the forefront of the fight against Jack Cade's rebellious Kentishmen at London Bridge and sent Falconbridge packing in 1471 when he attempted to storm London in a final blow for the cause of Lancaster against York.

It was the 25 wards of the City that were called on to supply the soldiery, each having to provide so many men. It was the guilds or companies who were responsible for the bowmen. By 1585, with much prodding from Henry VIII, the number supplied by the 26 principal companies amounted to 2,800, the Grocers and Haberdashers mustering 395 each, the Stationers 27 and the Barbers and Surgeons 24.

Proclamations by the Lord Mayor in 1568 reminded citizens that for all boys aged from seven to seventeen a bow and two arrows were to be kept; for able men from seventeen to sixty there had to be a bow and four arrows.

Archery was practised in the Artillery Garden close to Bishopsgate (Artillery Passage still marks the site), a field appointed for this purpose by Henry VIII when he granted charters for both archers and "the Fraternity of Artillery in Great and Small Ordnance" also known as "Gunners of the Tower". Oddly enough it seems that the archers were known as the Artillery Company. It was from these early gatherings that there would come the Honourable Artillery Company of later times.

It was in 1585 that London's "Train Bands" came into being as a result of Queen Elizabeth's call for "two thousand armed pikes and two thousand shot be sorted into bands" for the defence of England against foreign attack. Three years later, with the Armada in the Channel, London was able to provide ten thousand men of the Train Bands to be sent to Tilbury "for the defence of the City and the Queen's person". The bands, held in high regard for their high standards of training and fighting qualities, were acknowledged to be the best in the country.

Other towns and cities followed London's example in establishing train bands of their own but all withered away in time – save the one set up in Boston, Massachusetts which survives to this day as the Ancient and Honourable Artillery Company of Boston, far and away the oldest regiment in America.

The London Train Bands really came into their own during the Civil War when the City (if not its Lord Mayor) swung into total support for Parliament and against the King. A force of eight thousand trained soldiers was placed at the disposal of Parliament in 1642 which, at that time, represented its greatest military resource. A year later the Train Bands and London Auxiliaries were called on to help in raising the Royalist siege of the City of Gloucester and later took part in the battle of Newbury.

With the Restoration in 1660 and for the next 25 years the Artillery Society and Train Bands were for the most part engaged in ceremonial parades and it became the custom for the Gentlemen of the Artillery Garden to attend as a bodyguard to the Lord Mayor on the day of his Pageant through the streets.

In the final years of the 1600's a number of fighting units were founded, the first being the Ordnance Regiment whose job it was to protect the army's guns, chiefly stored at the Tower. They took the title of Regiment of Fusiliers.

In 1690 City troops were called to stand by for possible action when King William was absent in Ireland and a French invasion was feared. The train bands, 9,000 strong, were mustered but the expected landing was not attempted. Two years later Queen Mary reviewed the City forces in Hyde Park, the parade consisting of six regiments of train bands numbering 10,000 men under the command of Lord Mayor Sir John Fleet who was also the President of the Artillery Company.

It was not until 1745 that, the first time in nearly a century City troops were once more mustered for action to defend the City from possible attack from Prince Charles and his Highland levies. But that threat, too, did not materialise. Gradually the train bands came increasingly under the control of Parliament and were finally merged into a national Militia. The close connection between the Corporation and the Artillery Company also came to an end, in 1780.

The final chapter in this story of London's military connections came in 1859 when the City under the leadership of the Lord Mayor formed the London Rifle Brigade, a regiment that in its early days was officered by Aldermen and their friends but a few years later the Brigade saw the value of having professional soldiers in command. Common Council nevertheless granted the Brigade the privilege of drilling in Guildhall on Saturdays.

Still today, wrote Newson-Smith, the Lord Mayor, Aldermen and high officers of the Corporation have honorary membership of a number of regiments – a reminder of the far closer connections of earlier times.

* * *

The City and the Buffs

Who better than Alderman Sir Ronald Gardner-Thorpe to recount the stirring history of the Buffs whose regiment it was. Five years after he had served as Lord Mayor this distinguished soldier and then man of the City began his 1985 paper by reminding us that sailors, soldiers and airmen can proceed in any manner their commanders direct through any part of the Queen's realm – except in the City of London.

The City's unusual position goes back to 1327 when Edward III granted a charter to the Mayor and Commonalty of London which provided that no citizen should be compelled to go to war. It followed that recruiting or impressment could not be conducted by the Crown within the City, a principle repeated in all militia enactments from the time of the Restoration onwards.

In 1769 in assertion of the City's rights to bar anything savouring of military intrusion the then Lord Mayor complained to the Secretary-at-War that a detachment of Guards returning to the Tower after suppressing a riot (outside the walls) had marched through the City. "By whose orders" demanded the Mayor "had this unusual procedure taken place?" The Secretary-at-War gave it as his opinion that no troops should march through the City without previous notice. The officer commanding the offending party would be appropriately dealt with. In 1842 the Law Officers upheld this long-established common law right of the Lord Mayor and citizens to close the City's gates against entry by the Sovereign's troops. To this day whenever a party of the armed forces desires to enter the City, the Lord Mayor's permission must first be obtained.

So, on to the story of the Buffs.

It began in the 16th century when the United Provinces of the Netherlands were struggling to free themselves from the dominion of Spain. England's involvement did not become official (there had been a private move by English soldiers for the relief of Flushing in 1572) until 1585 when Sir Philip Sidney was appointed Governor of Flushing together with a regiment of troops who were the forerunners of the Buffs.

When the Dutch (somewhat ungratefully after all the help they had received in overcoming Spanish domination) went to war with Britain in 1665 the English regiments still in Holland were called on by the Dutch to swear allegiance to them or be dismissed. Half refused and somehow managed to reach England where Charles II formed the survivors into a single unit which he called the Holland Regiment – the second manifestation of the Buffs. They immediately went to war against their former Dutch paymasters – but as sea soldiers with the Royal Navy.

A Royal Warrant was issued in 1668 giving the Colonel of the Holland Regiment permission for his captains to raise recruits "by beating the drum in the City of London on producing the warrant for the Lord Mayor to see". The first such recorded authorisation was in 1670 when a company stationed at Jersey sought to recruit 32 "volunteers" requiring Sergeant John Mowat to show the warrant to "our right trusty and well-beloved Lord Mayor", first.

In those days recruiting parties carried a colour and this is the origin of the privilege enabling the Holland Regiment (and their successors) to march through the City of London with drums beating, bayonets fixed and colours flying.

With William III on the throne the Holland Regiment became the 3rd Regiment of Foot and the King appointed his brother-in-law, Prince George of Denmark, as Honorary Colonel. (Many years later, in 1906, King Frederik of Denmark was appointed Colonel in Chief, a royal connection that was never again broken, wrote Gardner-Thorpe in 1985).

It was not until 1751 that the Regiment became known officially as the "Third Regiment, or the Buffs". The name had evolved from an earlier nickname of "Old Buffs" when new junior regiments appeared wearing the buff-coloured facings and waistcoats that had been worn by the Holland regiment.

The Buffs became frequent visitors to the City, twice to receive new colours from the Lord Mayor, these events taking place at the headquarters of the Honourable Artillery Company. One of these colours is in the church of St. Lawrence Jewry. On 4th May 1974

Queen Margrethe of Denmark came to the City to present colours to all four battalions of what had become the Queens Own Buffs, the Royal Kent Regiment.

A few years earlier, in 1960, King Frederik of Denmark presented the Regiment with new colours bearing a selection of the 121 battle honours that it had been awarded since its foundation. "I had the great honour that day to command the parade as Commanding Officer" wrote Gardner Thorpe. Twenty-one years later "as the first Buff to become Lord Mayor of London" he entertained members of the Queen's Regiment to a luncheon at Guildhall after they had marched from the Tower and through the City with colours flying, drums beating and bayonets fixed.

Other regiments have earned that privilege – the Royal Marines, Grenadier Guards and Royal Fusiliers – and, of course, the Honourable Artillery Company which, in any case, had been marching through the City for the past 250 years! It remains a jealously regarded privilege with only three more additions in the 1950's and 1960's – the Coldstream Guards, Royal Dragoons (the Blues and Royals) and the 600 (City of London) Squadron, Royal Auxiliary Air Force until they were disbanded in 1957.

* * *

London and the Royal Navy

If we had one of its Commanding Officers to recount the history of the Buffs we have a naval Commander, Jack Hayward, who soon after the founding of the GHA delivered this paper in 1950 on London's long connections with the Royal Navy.

England's principal port had from earliest times to protect its mercantile trade and under the Norman and Plantagenet kings they invariably looked to London's mayor and its citizens to provide the ships and men needed for their constant wars in France. During the reign of Edward III, with the beginning of the Hundred Years War, London was pressed to the limits of its purse to supply such resources. For his expedition of 1340 five ships were supplied by the City while the Wards provided the crews to man them. They took part in the Battle of Sluys at the siege of Calais which ended in a great victory for the English, all but 24 of a French fleet of 190 said to have been captured or lost. But the demands for more and more ships continued inexorably over the years. Wealthy as London was in the 14th century the constant calls for money, men and ships was a serious drain on its strength. There was little respite until the end of the Hundred Years War when, observed Hayward, interest turned from the wars in France to the Wars of the Roses.

With the reign of Queen Elizabeth and the threat from Spain London was again called on to supply, in addition to a land force, sixteen large ships with between 60 and 120 men each, and four pinnaces with up to 30 men. The money was raised by a tax of 3s. in the £ with victuals for five months campaigning put on board at the City's expense.

Of the commanders of Elizabeth's fleet at least two of the most famous were from the City – Frobisher who lived in Cripplegate and was buried in the churchyard of St. Giles; and Hawkins who lived in Mincing Lane where once was a monument to him and his wife at St. Dunstan in the East.

During the troubled reign of Charles I London was at the centre of the national outcry against the King's demands for Ship Money.

Hitherto London had always been ready to supply ships and men but now the City claimed exemption from what it considered exorbitant sums of money. The claim was rejected and some £30,000 raised through the Wards to fit out seven ships.

With the coming of the Commonwealth came the beginnings of both a standing army and navy paid for out of Parliamentary taxes to which the City, with its enthusiastic support of Parliament, might have gladly contributed (perhaps!). Certainly it was the Chamber of London at Guildhall who acted as what Hayward called a subsidiary exchequer. This assistance to the State continued into the early years of the Restoration.

His paper tells us of the various Navy ships which were called "London", the first of which was launched in 1656 – just before Charles II's return. She was large, over a thousand tons and 150 feet long. She never saw battle action but is remembered as firing a salute on the death of Cromwell – and then at the Restoration. When preparing for sea at the onset of the Second Dutch War in 1665 she blew up in the Thames with grievous loss of life.

When rumour had it that the City was to raise the money for the replacement Samuel Pepys voiced doubts about the outcome and how right he was. What with the Plague just passed these were hard times for the City and contributions very slow to come in. Somehow, though, a new frigate called "Loyal London" was built and launched in June 1666. Her guns on being tested at the butts in Moorfields all burst. With carpenters still at work on board she joined the fleet at the Nore. The following year the Dutch fleet sailed up the river to Chatham and there in June 1667 poor Loyal London was set on fire. Her inglorious life ended a year after her launch as a burned-out wreck at the bottom of the Medway. At vast expense she was salvaged and rebuilt at Deptford. Her new name, said King Charles, should simply be "London". (The cost, more than £18,000, was not finally repaid until eight years later).

The new frigate did see action – against the Dutch in 1672 with Prince Rupert in command and then against the French in 1695. Soon after she passed into the hands of the ship breakers.

This was the time that poor Admiral Byng was court-martialled for having lost the naval base of Minorca. Prime Minister Pitt pleaded (quite rightly) for his pardon but the City (usually tolerant in such matters) sought a scapegoat it would appear and Byng was shot on his quarterdeck at Portsmouth.

The end of the third "London" marked the withdrawal of the City's hitherto intense interest in the Navy. There was no longer raising of money for ships and men. One final project for the building of a "City of London" in 1782 was quietly dropped because of the lack of enthusiasm in Common Council.

What the City continued, handsomely, to do was to honour the great sailors – Keppel, Rodney, Jervis, Howe and, above all Nelson – with the Honorary Freedom of the City. The City took more practical interest in the welfare of the seamen by providing relief for the wounded and the widows of sailors killed in action.

In the 18th century the Seven Years War, the American War and the French Revolutionary Wars all helped encourage enlistment in the Navy by offering bounties, the money either paid to the men themselves or their families. The City was active, too, in discouraging the widespread use of impressment since so many of the sailors thus forced into service on His Majesty's ships were seized from the merchantmen on which the City relied for its trade.

At last, in 1898, a new "London", a first-class battleship, was built being launched the following year – the first iron-clad of that name. It performed useful service in the Dardanelles and elsewhere in the First World War.

Lord Mayor Sir Horatio Davies entertained representatives of the Navy at a banquet at Mansion House in 1898 and in 1916 Mayor Sir Charles Wakefield visited the Grand Fleet at Scapa Flow in the Orkneys. Admirals Jellicoe and Beatty were received as Honorary Freemen of the City – as were Cunningham and Lord Mountbatten after the last war.

It is surely appropriate that the greatest of England's naval heroes – Nelson, Collingwood and Northesk, Jellicoe and Beatty have their last resting place in the crypt of St. Paul's Cathedral.

*

A year before Hayward read his paper there occurred yet another Navy exploit which he was able to add as an up-to-date post-script. A new "London" launched by the Mayoress Lady Blades some years earlier went to the assistance of HMS Amethyst which had been trapped by Communist Chinese forces on the Yangtze in 1949. On their return to England the officers and men of both ships were entertained at a great luncheon celebration in Guildhall.

*   *   *

Nelson

Alderman David Wootton (Lord Mayor 2011 – 2012) makes some telling points in his paper on England's greatest of naval heroes, read in February 2006.

One was Nelson's unequivocal acceptance of the City's key role in furthering naval achievements; another was his recognition that the demands of trade had dictated the need for Britain to rule the seas – his victories ensured protection of the nation's trade routes and contributed mightily to the fortunes of the City; a third – and less happy feature – was Nelson's never-forgotten pique at the City's neglect after his victory at Copenhagen.

There were four naval battles in which Nelson played a leading part: Cape St. Vincent against the Spanish, the Nile against the French, Copenhagen against the Danes and Trafalgar against both French and Spanish.

The battle of Cape St. Vincent took place in 1797 when a squadron of Royal Navy ships under the command of Sir John Jervis defeated a numerically superior Spanish fleet. In recognition of Nelson's role the Court of Common Council unanimously resolved to award him the Honorary Freedom of the City together with a gold box. These he was presented with at a ceremony in the Chamberlain's Court at Guildhall where the address on behalf of the Lord Mayor was given by Chamberlain John Wilkes beginning with the words "I give you joy".

The Nile was even more significant militarily because it resulted in the destruction of the transports carrying Napoleon's invasion force intended to seize control of Egypt and cut Britain's overland route to India. A week after the victory Nelson wrote to the Lord Mayor presenting the sword surrendered by the French admiral. Common Council passed a congratulatory resolution of thanks for this second of Nelson's victories and agreed that he should be presented with another sword of honour suitably inscribed. Adding to the City's celebration of Nelson's achievement Lloyds raised £38,000 to help the wounded and bereaved and the Drapers livery bestowed on Nelson the Freedom of the Company.

Admiral Lord Nelson was much fêted in the City when he was at the height of his popularity. The sculptor Anne Damer modelled a bust on behalf of the Corporation and Sir William Beechey painted his portrait, both of which form part of the Guildhall Art Gallery collection. The great statue in Guildhall came later to commemorate Trafalgar.

Nelson took part in the pageant of Lord Mayor Sir William Staines in November 1800 when the crowd took the horses from his carriage and hauled him all the way to Guildhall shouting huzza after huzza.

But then came the Battle of Copenhagen in 1801 with the City failing on this occasion to mark his victory in the same way as it had for Cape St. Vincent and the Nile. Indeed, the Stock Exchange marked shares down while Common Council did not choose to record a vote of thanks.

The problem was that the target in Copenhagen was not the French but the Danes, traditionally a friendly people (and engaged in trade with the City). Even the Government were rather cool about the whole affair although Nelson was raised to become the first Viscount. Nelson saw the City's lack of acknowledgement as a slight. Three months later he wrote to a friend saying that if the victory was real, those who fought and won it were, from custom, entitled to the thanks of the City of London. He still hoped for the City's recognition.

"I remember, a few years back" he wrote, "on my observing to a Lord Mayor, that if the City continued its generosity we should ruin them by their gifts, his Lordship put his hand on my shoulder and said – do you find Victories and we find rewards. I have since that time found Victories, I have kept my word, and shall I have the power of saying that the City of London, which exists by Victories at Sea, has not kept its promise".

No doubt about it the City made an ill-advised judgement after Copenhagen, particularly since Nelson had hoped that "the Freedom in a gold box" would be not for himself, as he already had them, but for his next in command. The sadness is that Nelson never wavered in his attitude to the City about Copenhagen (and perhaps this rigidly unforgiving stance indicated some flaw in an otherwise heroic personality?).

Nelson's funeral procession on 9th January 1806 formed up in Hyde Park and escorted the body from the Admiralty to St. Paul's, being joined by the Lord Mayor, Aldermen, Sheriffs and Common Councilmen as it entered at Temple Bar. The doors of St. Paul's were opened at 7 o'clock in the morning although the important guests in the procession did not arrive until 2.00, the coffin at 4.00 and the funeral service did not finish until 6.00 in the evening. It culminated with the lowering of Nelson's body into the crypt below the magnificent sarcophagus made originally for Cardinal Wolsey in the 1520's and left empty since then.

The following year the City honoured Nelson with a monument in Guildhall but it was not until 1810 that the monument was finally unveiled. The inscription with words by the playwright Sheridan reads: "The Lord Mayor, Aldermen and Common Council of the City of London, have caused this monument to be erected, not in the presumptuous hope of aiding the departed hero's glory, but to manifest their estimation of the man and the admiration of his deeds. This testimony of their gratitude they trust will remain as long as their own renowned City shall exist. The period of Nelson's fame can only be the end of time".

*   *   *

The Royal Marines and the City

It is not generally known that the rare privilege enjoyed by the Royal Marines of being able to march through the City streets, drums beating, colours flying and bayonets fixed, stems from the fact that the regiment was originally created from among the men of London's famed train bands.

With war imminent against the Dutch, Charles II and his Council saw an urgent need in October 1664 for some 1,200 "land soldiers" to be raised for service on His Majesty's ships. Inevitably they looked to London's standing militia to provide such a force – almost the only immediate source of trained fighting men. Two hundred and fifty were despatched to sea at once, the remainder quartered at various seaports.

Pepys, writing a year or two later, was by no means impressed when he saw a detachment of the Maritime Regiment tumbling down an alley to the Thames where boats were waiting to take them to a waiting man-of-war. Whatever their merits as soldiers he feared they had received little training for their new role at sea – most of them would never have even seen the sea and the ability to remain upright on a sloping deck let alone the horrors of sea-sickness were still to come.

Nevertheless they certainly took part in some early battles at sea and altogether distinguished themselves on shore in 1666 in the defence of Harwich where the Dutch Admiral Reuter, having sunk a good many English ships in the Medway, attempted a land invasion. The 2,000 troops he landed were hurled back into the sea by the Marines.

Historian John Yates (himself a Marine) in his paper of September 1981 described their uniform of these early days: a yellow coat with red breeches and stockings; hats bound with gold braid. Yellow, it appears, was the favourite colour of the Duke of York who became the Marines' Colonel in Chief.

It was not until 1802 that King George III directed that these soldiers of the Navy should be styled "The Royal Marines". He was guided to this decision by Admiral of the Fleet the Earl of St. Vincent who said of the Marines at the famous battle of Cape St. Vincent: "I but inefficiently did my duty, I never knew an appeal made to them for Honour, Courage or Loyalty that did not more than recognise my expectations; if ever the hour of real danger should come to England, they will be found the Country's sheet anchor".

In recent times new links were established between Marines and the City with the establishment of the Royal Marine Reserve (City of London), the first recruits attested on the HAC ground in November 1948. Another link was with the Stationers Company a year later, the old colours of 45 Commando RM being laid up there in 1969 – the only regimental colours laid up in a City livery hall, it is believed.

On the occasion of the tercentenary of the Corps' foundation the City Corporation gave a reception for 700 officers and men of the Royal Marines in Guildhall. They had marched there, as was their immemorial right, through the streets of the City with "drums beating, colours flying and bayonets fixed" to be inspected in Guildhall Yard by Lord Mayor Sir James Harman.

And a final connection has been with the church of St. Lawrence Jewry by Guildhall. At one time the Royal Marine Association's church had been St. Martin-in-the-Fields but marching there from Wellington Barracks the parade often found itself caught up in the demonstrations that occurred on a Sunday in Trafalgar Square.

Additionally, in 1974, came the first threat of the closure of the Marine barracks at Deal. Happily the Corps found themselves the highly appropriate church of St. Lawrence Jewry where Basil Watson, the Rector (himself I believe a former Navy chaplain) welcomed them. His church was just the right size and adjoining Guildhall Yard which would serve as a very fine parade ground.

*   *   *

The City of London Imperial Volunteers

Such an interesting paper about the Boer War of 1899 to 1902 and the particular part played in it by the City's own volunteer force.

In fact, Historian John Holland reminded us in his presentation to the GHA in November 1999, of the Boer War twenty years earlier in which the Afrikaners had regained control over the Transvaal and acquired self-government under the British Crown.

However in 1899, after a Boer ultimatum calling for the withdrawal of British troops, Afrikaners of the South African Republic and the Orange Free State invaded British territory and over the next three months British troops suffered one defeat after another. Their commanders may have been re-working the Crimean campaign, they were certainly out-manoeuvred by the guerrilla tactics of the Boers.

Britain was amazed and dismayed and in December the Government appointed Field Marshal Lord Roberts as Commander-in-Chief and General Lord Kitchener as Chief of Staff over a force of 47,000 men.

Meanwhile a ground-swell of opinion in the City warmed quickly to sending a volunteer force and on 13th December Colonel Charles Boxall placed a proposal before Lord Mayor Alfred Newton for the City Corporation to take financial and organisational responsibility for raising a force. Two days later at a meeting in the War Office the Lord Mayor was told that such an offer would be welcomed. At a meeting on 19th December in the Mansion House, Livery Companies, merchants and bankers pledged support.

Progress was astonishingly rapid as shown by these announcements by the Lord Mayor to Common Council:

20 December 1899 "The authorities would be willing to consider suggestions from the City of London to provide a regiment of 1,000 men…"

11 January 1900 "Since the meeting on 20 December when the sum of £25,000 was voted towards the cost of raising 'The City of

London Imperial Volunteers' the movement has made rapid progress... the total sum of £100,000 originally asked for has already been subscribed... the scheme has now developed into one of larger proportions, the force will consist of 1,400 men of whom some 350 will be mounted... the Honourable Artillery Company have contributed a substantial quota of men who will be in charge of a battery 12½ - pounder quick-firing guns... the first contingent of 17 officers and 500 men will sail from Southampton on 13 January... The Freedom of the City will be conferred on these first 500 men and officers tomorrow (12 January)".

25 January 1900 "The first 500 men and 17 officers duly embarked on 13 January and a further contingent of 27 officers and 800 men sailed on 20 January. A third contingent of 140 men and four officers will depart for South Africa next Saturday and the battery of guns will be ready for embarkation".

8 February 1900 "The total numbers despatched are 1,559 men and 50 officers, upwards of 350 mounted infantry... Field transport with tent and camp equipment have also been provided. Military experts have expressed their admiration at the physique and bearing of the men... Helmets for the entire Corps are being forwarded".

The speed of the operation was indeed impressive. Colonel Boxall, the man in charge, organised the arrangements from two rooms at the Mansion House, with the Lord Mayor's son, Harry Newton, providing administrative support. The Lord Mayor himself cabled his agent in Cape Town with instructions to purchase 400 mounts for the soldiers and 100 transport horses. The Earl of Albemarle commanding the infantry wrote "I do not think any regiment left England better equipped, in better spirits and with kinder send-off than the City Imperials". The Commandant of the Regiment, Colonel Mackinnon, confided to his diary that the only parts of the outfit found to be defective were their rifles – the only thing the War Office supplied.

Plus ça change!

When Colonel Hamilton stormed the Boer lines at Doornkop in May during the British advance on Johannesburg, he gave the City Imperial Volunteers place of honour at the front of the battle line. It

334

was later recorded that the volunteers suffered fewer casualties than regular units having "little of the Balaclava mentality to unlearn. They had made their charge in short rushes and took care to offer as little of a target as possible".

There was a great deal of ground to be covered in South Africa and at one period the regiment marched 523 miles in 40 days. In addition to skirmishing, convoys and garrison duty the Battalion served with distinction at the Battle of Diamond Hill in June 1900.

The volunteers returned to London in October that year. They were welcomed back with an enthusiasm that was unprecedented, wrote John Holland. They were received by the Lord Mayor and Corporation at Guildhall on 29th October, an event commemorated in a painting by J.H.F. Bacon in the Guildhall Art Gallery Collection.

*   *   *

PART EIGHT

GRAND FINALE OF SILVER, STAMPS AND CIRCLE LINE, OF BANQUETING AND KINGS

So, at the end of dealing with around a hundred and twenty of the GHA's fascinating papers, all of them tidily packaged into seven distinct groups, the exhausted editor/commentator finds himself left with a good many that defy any further gathering into groups. A rich and varied collection they are but to treat many more in this review is a task too much for the compiler let alone to put before readers of this history.

I have however picked an entertaining twenty of them in this mixed bag that Lewis Carroll might have seen through his looking glass. My apologies to all the authors of papers left out – including both of mine!! And the full list of all the GHA papers published to date can be viewed on the internet:

www.guildhallhistoricalassociation.org.uk

When the Strangers came to London: The Huguenot influence

Disenchanted with Rome and in tune with such reformers of the 16th century as Calvin, Knox and Luther, these French Protestants comprised a million people, one-third of the French population.

The established Catholic Church felt threatened by these Protestant heretics leading to a protracted series of reprisals – torture and massacres – leading to the first departures from France.

Emigrating in two distinct waves, the first in 1536, the Huguenots sought refuge in England, Ireland, the German states, Switzerland, Sweden, Denmark, Russia and South Africa (there were Dutch as well as French emigrants). Those remaining in France were forced publicly to recant their Huguenot faith, continuing their true beliefs in secret.

By the end of the 17th century, following Louis XIV's revocation of the Edict of Nantes (which had bestowed religious liberty), 164,000 Huguenots had left France and Holland and of that number 45,000 had come to England. These were the opening paragraphs of the paper given to the GHA in September 1996 by Alderman Michael Savory.

The first mention of French and Dutch congregations in London was as early as 1548 when Edward VI granted these "strangers" the use of St. Anthony's Chapel in Threadneedle Street to the French and St. Augustine's in Austin Friars to the Dutch. The strangers then, and increasingly so as persecution drove the Huguenots from France and Flanders, were mainly skilled craftsmen who brought with them their skills as furniture designers, printers, engineers and bankers and particularly as weavers of silks and linens.

The Huguenots came to England as married couples, some with children and with other children born here. Integration with their neighbours and with English society in general was absolute and a key feature of Huguenot evolution in England, wrote Savory. They had the intelligence that accompanies the easy use of two languages, he added. The church continued to play a central role in their lives and the

Strangers' Church was one of the first to be rebuilt after the Fire of 1666. Their devotion did not diminish as their weather increased.

The community of silk-makers and weavers stretched from the Old Artillery Ground near Bishopsgate, and across Spitalfields to Bethnal Green. Their houses, some of which still stand today in Spitalfields – in Fournier Street particularly – are easily identified with their elegant Georgian fronts of five storeys and large windows designed to let in maximum daylight for weaving.

Huguenots' skills went far beyond weaving, however, and this first influx of new talent galvanised the City guilds and livery companies into protection of their interests. The Goldsmiths created an effective closed shop with tight control over all alien goldsmiths within the City and two miles beyond.

The end of the 17th century saw the dawning of a new age for commerce. Seven of the twenty-two founding fathers of the new Bank of England and its first Governor, Sir John Houblon, were of Huguenot descent; in 1724 Henri Portal signed an agreement with the Bank to supply paper for the printing of its notes. Huguenots made writing paper and newsprint too. It became a popular saying that a drop of Huguenot blood in your veins was worth £1,000 a year!

They were innovators of all kinds, one was said to have invented the corkscrew and another, Robert Thiery, was given the Freedom of the City as being the first to weave silk from silkworms nourished in England. John Pelletier introduced Louis XIV-style baroque furniture to England while Paul de Lamerie was perhaps the country's finest gold and silversmith.

Huguenots have long been associated with both the City financial and the City Corporation. In 1891 it was Lord Mayor Sir Joseph Savory who laid the foundation stone of a new Huguenot church when it had to move from St. Martin's Le Grand to Soho. The writer of this paper, Sir Michael Savory himself Lord Mayor in 2004, is Sir Joseph Savory's distinguished Huguenot descendant.

*   *   *

When England ran out of change and the City came up with the answer

Between 1760 and 1800 there were only three years when George III shillings were issued – the Northumberland shilling of 1763 (today valued at around £300), the 1787 shilling (now worth £50) and the Dorrien-Magens shilling (worth about £4,000). Why is that 1798 shilling so valuable, asked Historian Tom Wilmot in the sparkling paper he read at the Mansion House in January 2000. It was, he said, a tale of "Whitehall Bumbledom" stifling City enterprise.

The year 1798 was a rotten one for England: war with France, threat of invasion, high taxation, high prices and shortage of food. And there was an acute shortage of silver coinage. The problem was that silver coins were worth more when melted down as bullion. A solution would have been to reduce the amount of silver in the coinage but the Government could not quite grasp this and, indeed, allowed the Bank of England to suspend cash payments.

Wilmot digresses to tell us that it was thus the Bank acquired the title "The Old Lady of Threadneedle Street" after Gilbray's cartoon showing a skinny old harridan seated on her padlocked treasure chest. Prime Minister Pitt removes her glittering coinage and leaves her dressed in one-pound notes screaming "Rape, Ravishment, Ruin!!!"

Meanwhile with no silver for trade or to pay wages barter became commonplace. To ease the situation the City sent silver bullion to the Mint for turning into shillings. A first instalment of £30,000 was raised in 1798 by ten merchants led by a prominent City banker, Magens Dorrien Magens (a distant ancestor of Historian Wilmot) who had been elected as a Member of Parliament two years earlier.

His constituency of Ludgershall had been described as "of all the rotten boroughs, the rottenest". From time immemorial, said Wilmot, in another of his splendid digressions, it had the privilege of returning two members to Parliament, but as there were only two electors and corruption was rife the Whigs and Tories agreed that each party should return one MP – saving the electors the trouble of voting and the parties the cost of bribing them.

Under a law of Queen Elizabeth anyone was entitled to send silver bullion to the Mint to be turned into coins of the realm. The supply of new Dorrien Magens shillings was due on 16 May 1798 but on 8 May William Pitt rushed a Bill through Parliament enabling the Privy Council to stop their distribution. Westminster believed that it alone had the responsibility for solving the coinage problem, resenting the City having produced a solution. Indeed, Parliament had been looking at the problem for the past eleven years having set up a powerful committee comprising the whole of the Cabinet, four judges and three MP's. In eleven years all they had achieved was the production of a voluminous series of minutes of their meetings – of action, nothing at all.

Pitt ordered that the Dorrien Magens shillings should be melted back into ingots. Only a very few of the shillings escaped this fate and hence their great rarity value today. For the City merchants the venture proved a great waste of their time and they had to wait eighteen months to receive any financial compensation.

The silver coin shortages lasted until 1816 when Prime Minister Lord Liverpool solved the problem by replacing silver with gold as the standard of exchange, circulating a new coin, the gold sovereign. Adequate supplies of small change were also at last available.

*   *   *

343

Precious plate for wining and dining

The first Lord Mayor to live in the new Mansion House was Sir Crisp Gascoyne. He was driven there in a coach and six on the evening of 9 November 1752 after his Banquet at Guildhall.

Before Crisp Gascoyne's time Lord Mayors lived in their own houses and being merchants or others of great wealth they owned or leased houses of sufficient size and grandeur to accommodate the mayoral household and entertain with a dignity and splendour befitting the civic head.

Until the City's gold and silver plate had a permanent home in the Mansion House it was transferred each November from Guildhall to the house of each new Lord Mayor, a careful inventory drawn up by the City Chamberlain and the Mayor.

Hardly anything is known of the plate the City may have possessed in medieval times – the earliest records are from 1567. At that time the collection was small: two flagons, some smaller pots and cups, two basins and ewers, a dozen spoons and six dozen trenchers, all of silver gilt. Lord Mayors would have had to draw upon their own personal possessions of plate for large banquets, or borrowed from his livery company. Over the last two hundred years, wrote Historian and retailer of gold and silver ware Norman Harding, the collection had been enormously enlarged by purchases, by gifts from distinguished visitors and by the tradition that each Lord Mayor should donate a piece of plate in commemoration of his mayoralty.

Harding told us that the great inventory of plate included two items that were not plate at all: the Lord Mayor's golden "double S" chain of office and the great jewel suspended from it. The beautiful collar with its gold esses interspersed with Tudor roses and knots was acquired in 1545 under the will of Sir John Aleyn who had served twice as Mayor and bequeathed it "to be used always and worn by the Lord Mayor of the City for the time being". In 1558 another Lord Mayor, Goldsmith Sir Martin Bowes gave a cross of gold set with rich stones and pearls to hang from the collar. The jewel seen in the present regalia was made in 1802. At its centre is an onyx cameo carved with the City arms, the encircling wreath of diamonds was added in 1867.

Harding added that although only one piece of the City's collection of plate, the "Firecup" dated 1662, survived the Great Fire most of the collection was indeed saved from Lord Mayor Bludworth's home in Gracechurch Street but was refashioned into new objects. It was the fashion in any case in those days for any pieces that were battered or bruised to be melted down and restyled, often into quite different objects. Nearly all the early 18th century plate in the Mansion House can be shown to have an ancestry going back to the late 16th or 17th centuries.

* * *

A look back at life in the year 1900

Not so very long ago but what profound changes there have been. Historian Ralph Hedderwick's paper of March 1981 presented just some of those changes.

With traffic horse-drawn the crossing sweepers were the vital means of keeping the streets reasonably clean. A cause for concern though were the leakages from fish carts. In addition to the streets being flushed twice a day with water, creosote was used to mask the smells from horse-droppings, fish, cats and other decomposing matter" (unspecified).

Fire engines were drawn by pairs of splendid horses, the firemen with gleaming brass helmets and an equally highly-polished brass boiler at the rear of the engine – the boiler it was that provided pressure for the water hoses.

On a somewhat higher level the newspapers reported in 1900 that Count Zeppelin had flown his first airship 35 miles from Friedrickshafen to Immenstadt.

Here in the City the National Telephone Company opened a new exchange on the top floor of an old warehouse in Lime Street. On the roof was a huge circle of iron poles carrying 1,418 miles of wires serving some 4,000 subscribers.

In the summer families would take their week's holiday at Margate or Southend and on a Saturday a fleet of steamers left London Bridge to take the wealthier of City workers to join their wives and children for the weekend. For the really prosperous there were 14-day excursions to Paris.

The boys of Cripplegate Ward School saved a penny a week towards the cost of their annual camp when, in August, they would march through the City with bad playing and colours flying.

The Corporation made history in 1900 when the Lord Mayor announced the allocation of £25,000 to send the City of London Volunteers to fight in the Boer War (see also Page 333). On their return the force (60 fewer than when they set out but a Victoria Cross

346

among them) marched from Paddington to St. Paul's. The crowds lining the streets to welcome them home were so dense that the soldiers could only march up Fleet Street in single file.

The Corporation approved the design for a new Sessions House in Old Bailey and the consequent demolition of Newgate Prison.

Foreign travel, which takes up so much of a Lord Mayor's year today, was unknown in 1900 but that year Lord Mayor Alfred Newton visited Scarborough to open the Nicholas Gardens, accompanied by the mayors of 14 Yorkshire cities and towns. A highly colourful occasion in a truly eventful year as described by Ralph Hedderwick.

* * *

The Wining and Dining City

"A Mansion House Dinner" was known in the 19th century as the epitome of splendid eating and drinking but Alderman Robert Bellinger, Lord Mayor 1966, in his paper of May six years earlier, went back to Plantagenet times and an enactment of Edward III that warned his noble subjects of the evils arising from excessive and over-many sorts of meats consumed in England. He ruled that the number of dishes and extravagance of sauces be strictly limited. His Act was not effective for long. Indeed, his grandson and successor, Richard II, was described as "the Royalist vyvander of all Christian kings". The City's generosity, hospitality and social inclinations to gather and linger around a well-laden board were, suggested Bellinger, the very excusable factors which moved Londoners to ignore attempted restraints on their own social pleasures.

A glance at the early account books of the City Guilds would certainly have given the impression that one of their major activities was feasting. One of the earliest ordinances of the Grocers was that on St. Anthony's Day all should assemble and dine together as a duty to honour the patron saint and to foster the Christian spirit of neighbourliness.

A typical menu – this from the Brewers in 1419 – listed three courses only – but what courses they were. For the first course there was brawn with mustard, cabbage and soup, swan, roasted capons and large custards (a kind of Yorkshire pudding). For the second course there was venison in broth with almonds and rice, cony, partridges, roasted cocks, spiced pork and small pastries (pasties, perhaps). Finally, for the third course came pears in syrup, pigeons and small birds, fritters, fancy breads and cold baked meat. In 1425 the Brewers did themselves a little better at their election feast adding several types of fish – salt, fresh and shell – as well as geese, woodcock, plovers and larks.

Like earlier Guild or Aldermanic dinners so the Mayors' feasts took place in his own house or at an inn, not at the Guildhall. The first to hold his feast there was Mayor John Shaa in 1501.

The increasing lavishness of City entertaining led in the 16th century to shortages of provisions, particularly around St. Thomas's Day when all twenty-five of the Aldermen were preparing sumptuous dinners in celebration of the annual Ward Motes and elections to Common Council. So in 1534 such feasts were forbidden. Mayors' feasts for the Aldermen and other City dignitaries were similarly to be discontinued on the Monday after Epiphany. Finally, the Lord Mayor was asked by Queen Elizabeth to require the Guilds strictly to limit the extravagance of their feast at the time of their annual election of wardens.

Bellinger writes that ways round these restrictions were always found – indeed, it was impossible to stop the City feasting; to try to do so was flying in the face of long-established custom.

In other parts of this history there have been accounts of the City's entertainment of its own kings and of eminent visitors from other countries. Bellinger tells us of Charles II's first dinner of 1662 at Clothworkers' Hall when he was a guest of the Lord Mayor. In 1671 Charles with the Queen, the Duke of York "and a great court" dined at the Guildhall on Lord Mayor's Day. Clearly he enjoyed the experience for he came again on the next six Lord Mayor's Days. Each of the courses at such repasts wrote Bellinger, would now be viewed as a full-scale banquet in itself – guests must have acquired much discretion in choosing from the poultry, fish, meats and sweetmeats offered as part of any one course.

The tradition of the monarch attending the dinner on Lord Mayor's Day was followed by James II, William and Mary, Anne, the first, second and third of the Georges and Queen Victoria who all attended the first Lord Mayor's Banquet of their reign. Edward VII attended a Coronation Banquet in Guildhall in 1902 and succeeding monarchs have followed this precedent.

In more recent times the guest list grew more varied with Heads of State welcomed to the City's table – the Czar of all the Russias, the Shah of Persia, Kings and Presidents the World over.

*　　*　　*

Gog and Magog

The City Giants, the great wooden figures that look down belligerently upon those meeting or dining in the Guildhall, are rooted in the mists of ancient folklore. Their history, as Winston Churchill remarked when speaking at a Lord Mayor's Banquet, is very confused. Historian Philip Jones attempted in his paper of November 1953 to shed some light on the subject.

The giants' early names were Corineus and Gogmagog. Myth has it that Corineus was one of the followers of Brutus when he fled from Troy and landed in England around 1,000 BC to overcome the ancient inhabitants led by another giant – Gogmagog. It is suggested that the name of Corineus was forgotten and that the name of the other giant was split by the ancient Britons to create Gog and Magog.

Whatever the giants' mythical or even biblical* origins they became associated in the minds of Londoners as founders of their city, and as champions ready to protect the King and the City from all foreign enemies.

Their earliest recorded history is that one giant effigy at least was provided on London Bridge to greet Henry V in 1413 on the way to his coronation. Two years later there were probably two giant figures on the bridge to welcome the King back to London after his triumph at Agincourt and two giants "of immense stature" bowed to Henry V as he brought his Queen, Katherine, to London in 1421 after their marriage in Paris. Mayor Robert Chichele, mace in hand, conducted the Queen, the two of them riding immediately behind Henry, ahead of the Lord Constable and Earl Marshal.

Gog and Magog had been well and truly adopted into London's history and pageantry, their effigies standing in Guildhall probably from the time of Henry V, and paraded through the streets at the Mayor's annual pageant – as indeed they still are. (City records were loath to assign names to the giants, always referring to them simply as

---

* Their reputation in the Bible was not good. For the prophet Ezekiel they were enemies of the God of Israel; for St. John the Divine they were creatures of Satan. C.D.W.

the Giants or the Guildhall Giants. Popularly they became known as Gog and Magog – but no-one really knows which is which!)

The giants of the Lord Mayor's Show of 1605 continued to make an appearance from time to time. They disappeared in the flames of the Great Fire of 1666 probably being stored in Guildhall – if not actually set on pedestals within the Hall itself. They were replaced in 1672 with all due pomp and ceremony.

The giants created by Richard Saunders in 1709 were destroyed with so much else of Guildhall in the fire-bombing of December 1940. Totally new figures, the work of David Evans, were unveiled in June 1953. They stand 9 feet 3 inches high as compared with 14 feet 6 inches of the previous giants. The main bodies are constructed of limewood planks, the heads, arms and weapons (spear for one, mace and spiked ball for the other) glued to the bodies with mortice and tenon joints. Each giant weighs twelve hundredweights.

Jones's concluding words were: Gog and Magog have so endeared themselves to the citizens that from props of pageant masters they have become revered symbols of civic pride.

*   *   *

The Common Hunt and the Doghouse

It is generally known that the Swordbearer and the Common Cryer and Serjeant at Arms (who carries the mace) are Esquires who attend upon the Lord Mayor. A third is the City Marshal. Once upon a time there were no fewer than twenty-four such attendants. They took part in processions and also, in accordance with a weekly rota took their share of duties at the Mayor's house. Some had special additional duties – one was Yeoman of the Waterside on the wharves of Billingsgate, another was Waterbailiff for the Thames. "The Common Hunt" had particular responsibilities arising from the City's age-old hunting privileges.

Harry Oram's paper of October 1978 reminded the Historians that Henry I confirmed in his Charter to the citizens the hunting rights which their ancestors had enjoyed in the Chilterns, Middlesex and Surrey. It is curious, said Oram, that neither Henry's charter nor later ones made any mention of the great royal forest of Essex which lay so conveniently near to the City on its eastern side. And although one is tempted to think it was kept by kings as a royal preserve there is little doubt that the citizens claimed and exercised hunting rights in Essex. When in 1460 John Danyell, a tenant of the Abbot of Stratford, attempted to prevent the Common Hunt from entering the Abbot's lands he was swiftly informed of his error. The Mayor, Aldermen and Sheriffs accompanied by the Common Hunt (and a sufficient number of men), rode out to exercise their rights. The Abbot and his tenant were brought before the Court of Aldermen to make due apology and submission.

The first man we know by name to have held the office of Common Hunt was John Charney who was appointed in 1379. The word "Common" in his title, like that in Common Council or Common Serjeant, implies that it, or they, is of the commonality or citizens in general. Charney and his immediate successors were granted a serjeant's livery and annual fee of £10.

One of their chief duties was the keeping of the City hounds and in 1460 Common Hunt William Sudbery was granted 20s a year to hire a house for his dogs and horses. It was probably in Moorfields as soon afterwards there is reference to "the kennel in the moor". There were complaints from passers-by about the stench from Common Hunt's use of bones and horns to boil meat for the hounds. Mayor and Aldermen forbade the practice, paying Common Hunt 26s 8p a year with which to buy food. In 1512 a more distant part of Moorfields was found for what had become known as Common Hunt's Doghouse. On 16th century maps of this area a building is marked as the "Dogge Hows". It was situated a little north of the present Finsbury Circus.

The new Doghouse was soon in trouble again when deliveries of meat from the Butchers' Company ("diseased pork or brawn") were made in a closed cart as food for the hounds. The Court of Aldermen were petitioned for its removal. The Aldermen suggested that people having gardens near the Doghouse – and most affected by the stench – should each contribute the equivalent of one year's rent of their garden towards the building of a new and more distant Doghouse. It took ten years but eventually a site was found near the brick kilns of Finsbury Fields – few residents there and any that were, unlikely to complain.

A side-line for the Common Hunt's subordinates was to dispose of the vast number of stray dogs (as well as cats "and other carrion") running wild in the City streets. They were believed to spread the plague. After several warning orders the Common Hunt was instructed to arrange for the killing of all dogs found in the streets and lanes – with the exception of hunting animals – greyhounds, spaniels and hounds. John Smith, Common Hunt's man earned a fee of 2d for each animal he killed. Between Michaelmas 1584 and Michaelmas 1585 it is recorded that 995 dogs were killed and the following year 1055. They were buried near the windmills outside Cripplegate.

There are all too few descriptions in the City records of hunting expeditions. One such event took place in September 1562 when Lord Mayor William Harpur and the Aldermen rode to where Tyburn Brook crossed Oxford Street and "afore dinner hunted the hare and after dinner at the Mayor's banqueting house there, went to the hunting of the fox. There was a goodly cry for a mile and after the kill, at St. Giles in the Fields, they all rode through London to his house in Lombard Street".

What of the Doghouse? In 1788 it was discovered by the City Lands Committee that the site had become an estate of a large dwelling house and gardens, another house and cow-yard, a warehouse, four small tenements and an ice-house – no hounds at all. Charles Cotterell, the Common Hunt, received an annual income of £200 from the lettings of these properties. City Lands appropriated the rents but tolerantly enough compensated Cotterell with £160 p.m. for his interest in the estate.

When he died in 1807 it was decided that since the Common Hunt's duties were by now wholly ceremonial the office was abolished. Wrote Harry Oran: Thus ended in 1807 one of the most colourful of the City's ancient offices after a history of more than four hundred years.

* * *

Jubilee Celebrations in the City

When Historian Betty Masters read her paper in March 1977 we were about to celebrate the Queen's Silver Jubilee. Now, as I write these words thirty-five years later, the celebrations are about to take place for her Diamond Jubilee – a truly great event, achieved only once before, in 1897, with Queen Victoria's sixty years on the throne.

Betty Masters' paper was, however, concerned with far earlier jubilees which, she told her fellow historians, had begun as religion maintained a jubilee year once every fifty years in accordance with Leviticus Chapter 25: "And ye shall hallow the fiftieth year and proclaim liberty throughout the land unto all the inhabitants; it shall be a jubilee unto you; it shall be holy unto you". In the Roman Catholic Church a jubilee was originally a year of remission from the consequences of sin when indulgence might be obtained by a pilgrimage to Rome.

It was much later that the word jubilee came to be associated with secular events, particularly those celebrating the reign of monarchs. The first of these was to mark the fiftieth anniversary of the accession of George III in October 1809. The Times made much of the word "jubilee" and could even be said as having popularised its use at that time. The City Corporation continued to refer in its own records to the anniversary of the King's accession.

This more restrained approach revealed the City's opposition to so many of George III's policies (including freedom of the press and the grievances of the American colonists). Three Lord Mayors – William Beckford, Brass Crosby and John Wilkes earned the King's considerable displeasure.

There was much disagreement in Common Council as to the scale of City involvement in the jubilee celebrations. There was a loyal address but other suggestions were whittled down until all that was left was a grant of £1,000 for the relief of small debtors – not much of a jubilee celebration. Members of Common Council even gave up a proposal that they should dine together on the day of the jubilee.

George III's sons, George IV and William IV, reigned for only ten and seven years respectively and the question of a royal jubilee would not arise again until the fiftieth anniversary of Queen Victoria's accession in June 1887. How vastly different were the circumstances then from those of 1809.

When Reginald Hanson became Lord Mayor in November 1886 it was immediately resolved to commemorate the next year's Golden Jubilee and a Committee of the whole Court of Common Council was appointed to oversee the arrangements. Its two major proposals were that a loyal and dutiful address be presented to Her Majesty and that a Reception and Ball be held in Guildhall to which the Queen, members of the Royal Family and foreign sovereigns in London at that time be invited. In the event the Queen, who had expressed a wish to visit the Mansion House in May did not feel able to visit again on her Jubilee only five weeks later but that the Prince and Princess of Wales would head the royal party at Guildhall.

Meanwhile the Queen's Mansion House visit was itself a splendid occasion. She was accompanied by ten members of the royal family and the Crown Prince of Denmark. Four days after the event a baronetcy was conferred upon the Lord Mayor and knighthoods on the two Sheriffs.

At the Jubilee Service at Westminster Abbey on 21 June the City deputation consisted of the Lord Mayor and Lady Mayoress, the Sheriffs and a hundred Aldermen and Common Councilmen who travelled from Guildhall to the Abbey "in state".

The great reception at Guildhall followed a week later with the astonishing number of 4,646 people somehow crowded into the Great Hall and every available corner. There was an unprecedented gathering of royalty including the King of Denmark, King and Queen of the Belgians, the King of Saxony and King of the Hellenes, as well as a bevy of Crown Princes and Princesses, Grand Dukes and Duchesses and Princes and Princesses from all the European Courts – so many of whom were of course, related to Victoria. There also were present Princes of Japan, Siam and Persia and Maharajas of the Indian states. Among the delights on offer were dancing, the singing of glees, a "museum of antiquities" and six refreshment and supper rooms.

(Having with my wife tasted similar – if slightly less grand – entertainments at Guildhall during the 1970's to 1990's I can well imagine the jockeying for position on the part of Aldermen and Councilmen to be as near as possible to the royals. C.D.W.)

Ten years later the country was celebrating the Queen's Diamond Jubilee, the culmination of sixty glorious years. On 22 June there was a procession through the City, Lord Mayor George Faudel-Phillips tendering the City Sword to the Queen at Temple Bar and then riding bare-headed and carrying the sword before Her Majesty in front of the Sovereign's Escort of Household Cavalry. There were halts at St. Paul's and the Mansion House, Victoria there being presented with a bouquet by the Lady Mayoress.

At night the Dome of St. Paul's, Mansion House, London Bridge and other City buildings were illuminated by searchlights.

On 5 July there followed a Reception and Ball at the Guildhall. It was not quite the glittering occasion of 1887, the great array of foreign royalty being absent and the Royal Family represented only by the Duke of Cambridge. Nevertheless, the 3,800 people attending included every one of the Ambassadors to the Court of St. James's, Government Ministers and members of both Houses of Parliament and dignitaries galore. Four bands played and music in the Council Chamber ranged from "I'll sing thee songs of Araby" to "Rule Britannia".

Betty Masters' paper of 1977 had only one other jubilee to record – that of Victoria's grandson, George V a Silver Jubilee this time to commemorate the 25th year of his reign.

On 6 May, the actual anniversary of his accession, King George and Queen Mary attended a service at St. Paul's with all the attendant ceremonies of a state visit by the sovereign to the City. The streets were splendidly decorated and special provision made for school children to view the procession. The Monument remained open until midnight so that people could view the City's floodlit buildings.

Two weeks later there was a Reception and Ball at Guildhall for 1,750 guests. The King and Queen arrived at 10.00 p.m. and were conducted by Lord Mayor Sir Stephen Killik to the dais in Great Hall where a royal canopy had been erected. Their Majesties spent an hour progressing through the various parts of the building, receiving a presentation of an antique Tompion clock, and watching the dancing in the Great Hall.

Earlier the Corporation had made a gift of £25,000 to the King George Jubilee Trust.

Since in March 1977 when Historian Masters read her paper the Queen's Silver Jubilee was still to come, there was only a brief reference to the coming ceremonies at Temple Bar and St. Paul's – but also the innovation by the Queen and Prince Philip of a "walkabout" from St. Paul's along Cheapside to the celebratory Luncheon at Guildhall.

*   *   *

Riot, Revolution and Retribution

The Gordon Riots have been described as the greatest outburst of civil disorder in modern British history and while religious differences were at their core, they were seized upon by the London mob as an opportunity to create mayhem, to run wild, loot and destroy.

It began peacefully enough with a great gathering of men in St. George's Fields south of the River. They had been summoned there on Friday 2nd June 1780 by advertisements inserted in the newspapers by the Protestant Association. Led by the virulently anti-Catholic Lord George Gordon, they were to march across London Bridge and through the City to deliver a great petition to Westminster. It called on Members of Parliament to reject Government proposals aimed at easing the extraordinarily severe penalties borne by Catholics in the practice of their religion.

Historian Allan Davis in his paper of July 1984 described the marchers as "quiet sober-looking men clutching hymn-books". They were however joined in the City streets by others less reputable. The mob had already attached itself and even as the petitioners arrived at Westminster the wilder element were attacking Lords and Commoners attempting to enter their respective chambers.

Eventually the petition was considered and after six hours of tumult in the House of Commons Lord George Gordon's motion to reject the Catholic relief measures was overwhelmingly defeated by 192 votes to six.

In the early hours of Saturday 3rd June a group of half-drunk venomous-looking men armed with crowbars and pickaxes broke into the chapel adjoining the residences of the Sardinian ambassador and smashed everything within it; pews, vestments and altar ornaments were set alight. Later that morning the mob turned their attention on Cripplegate with its colony of Irish labourers who lived and worked in the area.

The next night, Sunday, the rioters returned to Cripplegate, finding a new target in a small Catholic chapel in Ropemakers' Alley and houses adjoining it of those who worshipped there. The chapel, its contents and the houses were looted and burned.

From Cripplegate the rioting spread to engulf the whole of the City and further afield as so graphically described by Dickens in "Barnaby Rudge".

On 6th June Newgate Prison was attacked and set on fire, its prisoners released. Other prisons, too, were targets – the King's Bench, the Fleet, the Clink across the River and Surrey Bridewell, the Poultry Comptor, all their inmates gone. An attack on the Bank of England at last brought sufficient troops into the City for the authorities to regain control.

After seven days of turmoil calm was finally restored on Saturday 7th June – apart from the remaining presence of soldiers everywhere.

That Parliament had every reason to ease the disabilities suffered by Catholics was made clear, wrote Alderman Allan Davis, in the words of the Attorney-General at Lord George Gordon's trial. Those disabilities stemmed from an Act of Parliament of 1700 which decreed:

"Every popish priest exercising any part of his function in the United Kingdom was liable to perpetual imprisonment, every person of the popish religion keeping a school or taking on himself the education of youth was liable to the same punishment. Roman Catholics were rendered incapable of inheriting any estates from their parents or others".

It is hard to say whether or not Lord Mayor Brackley Kennett, the Sheriffs, Aldermen and Councilmen did all they should have done to control the rioters. Allan Davis says that numerous meetings of the Court of Aldermen and Common Council were held, that the Lord Mayor and a few Aldermen went to scenes of disorder and attempted by their presence to calm the troublemakers. They ordered out the City marshals and constables and sent to the Tower for military aid. But London as a whole was ill-prepared to deal with violence on the scale of the Gordon Riots.

Christopher Hibbert in his book "King Mob" wrote of grossly inadequate preventative measures. But the events of June 1780 were beyond the control of a civilian authority and were only eventually overcome by deployment of troops in large numbers.

*

Disturbances of a very different kind, but also involving religious differences, were recounted in a paper he read to the GHA in June 2011 by Historian Bill Fraser.

With the ringing title of **Highland Chiefs at the Tower in 1745** it told of the trials and tribulations of those Highlanders who were at the heart of the 1745 Jacobite rising. After the Battle of Culloden many were tried for treason and executed in Carlisle, York, Manchester and on Kennington Common – and at the Tower of London.

Three Scottish noblemen, the Earls of Cromarty and Kilmarnock and Lord Balmarino were each arrested, imprisoned in the Tower and then taken to Westminster to be tried for treason by their peers.

The two earls pleaded guilty in the hope of a light sentence but Lord Balmerino pleaded Not Guilty as he declared he was not present when the crimes of which he stood accused took place. The earls made heartrending pleas for mercy but all three were found guilty and sentenced to be hung, drawn and quartered, that ghastly fate avoided with the sentence changed to beheading because of their noble rank. The Earl of Cromarty was saved by the pleadings of his pregnant wife. The other two were executed on the scaffold at Tower Hill.

Fraser devoted much of his paper however to his forebear (however remote) Lord Lovat, Simon Fraser, whom he truly describes as a remarkable man in many ways.

The Frasers were originally of French descent but the French influence had long been overwhelmed by Highland customs and traditions. Early in life Simon had an ambition to be not only Chief of Clan Fraser but to be the greatest Chief of all the Highland Clans.

When his father died and he became Chief of the Frasers his first step in this direction was to win a decisive military victory over the Murrays of Atholl.

Then came a setback when the young Lord Lovat was found to have been talking to the exiled Court of the Stuarts at St. Germain en Laye in France and he was obliged to flee Scotland and to spend the next ten years of his life in France during which time he became a Catholic and gained the confidence of Louis XIV.

On his return to Scotland he veered somewhat wildly in his political allegiances – pro-Jacobite, pro-Hanoverians and then again in 1745 supporting the rebellion with men and money. After Culloden he was arrested, brought to the Tower and charged with treason. He was sentenced to death, aged 80. Such was the excitement at his execution that the scaffolding erected on Tower Hill for spectators collapsed killing 20 of them.

Historian Bill Fraser assured his GHA audience that the vanity and hypocrisy shown by the eleventh Earl were by no means typical characteristics of the Frasers. He instanced the more recent fifteenth Lord Lovat who led one of Britain's commando units from 1939 to 1945. On D-Day 1944 he led his men at the Normandy landings, wading ashore with an old Winchester rifle and a rolled-up umbrella, his personal piper at his side.

*   *   *

Reform of the Post Office and the coming of the penny post

The story told by Historian Anthony Eskenzi in June 2000 related how the Post Office was dragged kicking and screaming into the 19th century. It was, he said, a revolution and one, as might be expected, strongly promoted by the City of London.

The Duke of Wellington, speaking in the House of Lords during a debate on the 1839 Postage Bill – which would lead to the introduction, eventually, of uniform penny postage and the "penny red stamp" – observed "that from the very institution of the Post Office no important improvement has had its origin in that establishment". Reformers such as John Palmer with his network of high-speed mail coaches were opposed by the Post Office.

Rowland Hill and some Members of Parliament led by Robert Wallace had put forward a programme of reforms in 1837 including proposals that postage should be uniform across the country, should cost 1d per half-ounce and that pre-payment of letters should be facilitated by the use of a "stamp", the back of which was covered with a "glutinous wash". While, a year later, Hill's proposals were favoured in Parliament, they were bitterly opposed by the Postmaster-General and in particular by Colonel Maberly, Secretary to the Post Office. After another year of struggle the Government brought forward its Postage Bill of 1839.

In the City the Egyptian Hall of the Mansion House was used for a meeting of merchants, bankers and traders, Lord Mayor Samuel Wilson in the Chair, to urge acceptance of Rowland Hill's proposal for a penny-post. The following day Common Council petitioned the House of Commons not to delay so important a national measure. The Postage Bill passed into law in August 1839.

It was far from plain sailing even then, for while Hill was overseeing the change from penny black to penny red stamps, he and Maberly were placed together in a kind of partnership that was never going to succeed. Eventually Maberly was moved to another post and Hill took over full responsibility but not until 1854.

* * *

The eminent Walpole, much supported by the Aldermen but heartily disliked by the rest of the City

Few of England's statesmen have figured in these pages but one who does justify a place, not only on account of his political eminence, but equally because of his uneasy association with the City, is Robert Walpole. The story was told by Dr. James Cope in March 2004.

There was a most auspicious beginning when, in 1700, aged twenty-four, Walpole married the grand-daughter of Sir John Shorter (who had been Lord Mayor in 1687) and a year later, having inherited the family estate in Norfolk, Walpole was elected to Parliament in the Whig interest for Castle Rising, a family-owned pocket borough. The election which followed the accession of Queen Anne returned a Tory government but Walpole was again elected, this time for Lynn, another family-owned borough, which he would continue to represent throughout his Parliamentary career.

Walpole's was something of a lone voice in Parliament in opposing the South Sea Act in 1720 when the Government opened the floodgates to a frenzy of wild speculation and the subsequent ruin of thousands who had gambled their all. His integrity was rewarded in appointment as Chief Minister.

Although Walpole succeeded in restoring public credit and enjoyed support from most of the City's Aldermen he was far from popular with the army of 234 Common Councilmen. Proposals for construction of a bridge at Westminster in 1721 were vehemently opposed by the City as a whole as an attack on the almost sacred position of London Bridge and highly destructive of the City's trade. The Bill was dropped, killed off for at least the next fifteen years.

With King George I spending much of his time in Hanover, Walpole was able to establish government by the House of Commons and the Cabinet, thereby becoming Prime Minister in the modern sense – and the first to live at 10 Downing Street.

After the Jacobite rising of 1715 and then a Parliament lasting seven years, Walpole and the Whigs were returned in 1722 with a large majority. It was a time of increasing antagonism in Guildhall between the Aldermen, major players in the City (and Whig supporters of Walpole) and the more humble Councilmen whose interests were quite different.

In 1725 the Aldermen sought to put the Commoners once and for all in their place. No longer would Common Council be able to enact its own legislation as was its historic right, but any such Act would now have first to be approved by the Court of Aldermen. Thus the votes of 224 Councilmen could be overridden by those of the 26 Aldermen. Since this change resulted from a Bill in Parliament, Councilmen and citizens laid the blame on Walpole.

It was, however, wealthy City merchants (not least Aldermen) who would protest most strongly against Walpole's Excise Bill of 1733 as an assault on their trade. His proposal was that tobacco and wine should be imported free of tax, stored in bonded warehouses, tax would be collected only when the products were released to the domestic market (the system still in operation today). It was a change from customs duty on entry to excise tax on release from bond.

The City Corporation lobbied its members in Parliament while City residents and liverymen were drummed up by the Wards and the Companies to demonstrate their anger at the House of Commons. On 14 March 1733 a petition against Walpole's Bill was carried by the Sheriffs to Westminster in a procession of over 200 coaches. The Bill was abandoned.

Walpole still managed to gain a majority in the general election of 1734. By 1738, however, he had lost much of his aldermanic support. Indeed, Aldermen and Councilmen were coming to realise just how much their interests were in common.

There was a final chapter in the City-v-Walpole saga. It was over the regulation of English ships trading with Spain's South American colonies and their frequent clashes with Spanish coastguard vessels. Walpole (and Spain) sought a peaceful settlement but his proposed convention satisfied neither City traders nor the Parliamentary Tory opposition. In Parliament only three Aldermen were now supportive. Another of them said, somewhat emotively: "Our countrymen in chains and slaves to the Spaniards. And shall we sit here debating about forms of words whilst the suffering of our countrymen calls for redress". William Pitt, as opposition leader, was fiercely critical.

War against Spain was declared in October 1739 to great public delight – not least in Guildhall and among the citizens. Walpole resigned office soon after.

Dr. Cope ends his paper with these words: "… this war which had its origin in the demands of City traders became merged into the Europe-wide struggle of the War of the Austrian Succession". He could have added that it brought about the closure of Walpole's battles with the City of London.

*   *   *

The Remembrancer takes a trip to Russia

On 19 December 1586 Lord Mayor Sir George Barne received a somewhat strange letter from Queen Elizabeth in which she requested the appointment of Dr. Giles Fletcher to the office of City Remembrancer – a position clearly not held in the highest regard by Mayor and Aldermen since it had been left vacant after the death of its first holder, Thomas Norton, two years earlier.

Still, the City loved the Queen and her word was to be obeyed. And Dr. Fletcher was a man of learning, integrity and other good qualities, she wrote, and he might serve also "for some other purposes which we esteeme verie expedient both for us and you".

The "other purposes" were not specified but would become clearer the following year. The letter made clear that a civic refusal was not contemplated. So began a strange tale in City history.

Who was this Dr. Fletcher? Historian James Sewell, author of this paper (October 1997), tells us he was the son of the Vicar of Bishop's Stortford and educated at Eton and Cambridge. He became an M.P. for Winchelsea. His brother became Bishop of London. His nephew John Fletcher would become the noted dramatist.

In January 1587 at a meeting of the Court of Aldermen Giles Fletcher was sworn into office at a salary of £50 per annum. His duties were described as acting as secretary to the Lord Mayor, but lasted only a few months. Those "other purposes" were appearing. In June he was in Hamburg with the Governor of the City's Merchant Adventurers negotiating with the Hanseatic League concerning customs duties on English imports.

The following year Fletcher (still City Remembrancer and Lord Mayor's Secretary) was elevated as ambassador to Russia. It was a long, arduous and dangerous journey which took him and his entourage three months to get from Germany to Archangel and then to Moscow.

How and why was it that the Queen contrived to send Fletcher to Russia?

Trade between the two nations had begun 35 years earlier following an English expedition to discover a north-east passage to the Indies. Only one of the three ships reached Russia, its Captain, Richard Chancellor, making his way to Moscow at the invitation of Tsar Ivan IV – more commonly known as Ivan the Terrible. He secured very favourable commercial privileges for the London merchants who had financed the expedition. Queen Elizabeth was much pleased with the expansion of trade (as was Tsar Ivan) and she granted the merchants a charter establishing the Muscovy Company. England exported cloth, guns, pewter, sugar and wine while Russian sold oil, tallow, wax, flax and furs.

The Tsar looked for a formal military alliance but while Elizabeth was happy to provide armaments she feared that any closer ties would antagonise the Baltic states, source of grain and supplies for her navy. Relations between Russia and England deteriorated and grew worse after Ivan's death and the succession of his son Fedor, a man it was said, of limited intelligence who relied on his advisers, chief of whom was Boris Goudunov.

Fletcher was dispatched to restore the situation.

Alas, poor Fletcher's welcome in Moscow was far from warm. He wrote: "I was placed in an house very unhandsoom, unholsoom, of purpose to doe me disgrace and to hurt my health, whear I was kept a prisoner, not as an ambassador". The rather mean gifts sent with him to the Russian court were "very contemptuouslie cast down" before him.

Goudunov objected to letters to him from London coming from the Privy Council and not the Queen. Fletcher caused offence by not addressing the Tsar with the full list of his numerous titles. To make matters worse the Russians were also negotiating with Elizabeth's greatest enemy, Philip of Spain, concerning joint action against the Turks.

Then the clouds lifted with the news reaching Moscow of the annihilation of the Spanish Armada in 1588. Fletcher was able to re-establish England's trading privileges with some additional benefits. The Queen was later to send a strong letter of complaint about his earlier treatment.

A relieved Fletcher arrived back in London in the summer of 1589 bearing letters to the Queen from the Tsar and Goudunov. He told a friend: "The poets cannot fansie Ulysses more glad to come out of the den of Polyphemus than he was to be out of the power of such a barbarous Prince".

His greatest achievement, wrote James Sewell, was the publication in 1591 of his book Of the Russe Common Wealth – "one of the most important works of Elizabethan travel literature".

The book deals with every aspect of Russian life. He did not pull his punches, reporting the story of the murder of Ivan the Terrible's son by his father, the inability of Tsar Fedor and his wife to beget children and the somewhat unpleasant pursuits of Fedor's brother aged seven. The merchants of the Muscovy Company took fright at the effect it would have on their trade with Russia and the book was quickly suppressed. Happily some copies survived and when Milton composed his Brief History of Muscovia in the 1630's he drew extensively on Fletcher. The Great Soviet Encyclopaedia describes Fletcher as "one of the most important historians of Russia in the second half of the sixteenth century".

And what of Fletcher the Rememberancer? He came back to the City in 1597 (at the Queen's wish) as Treasurer of St. Paul's Cathedral and remained in his civic office – which had somehow reverted to the appointment of Remembrancer until 1605.

Historian Sewell points out that his absences first in Hamburg and then Moscow left a large gap in the civic records and "that his tenure of the post of Secretary to the Lord Mayor can hardly be considered an unqualified success". Sewell tells us that earlier in 1997 (when he wrote his paper) he had been in Moscow and had the privilege of visiting the Old English Court there. It had been given to the Muscovy Company by Ivan the Terrible. "It was a sobering thought to consider that Giles Fletcher had sat in that court room four hundred years previously".

*　　*　　*

The World's first underground railway

On January 10th 1863 the first underground railway in the world was opened to the public. It ran from Paddington to Farringdon Street. It was the realisation of a personal dream after eight years of unremitting effort on the part of Charles Pearson, the City of London Solicitor and was celebrated in grand style with a banquet at Farringdon Street Station and an inaugural trip the day before the public opening. Alas Charles Pearson was not there to be feted for he had died four months earlier.

Pearson was a great man of many parts. He was a Common Councilman before becoming City Solicitor and he was elected to the House of Commons. He was an enthusiastic campaigner for good causes: against the bar on the admission of Jews to the Freedom of the City; for the removal of the lines in St. Paul's attributing the Great Fire to Catholics; and as Chairman of the City Board of Health dealing with a severe outbreak of cholera.

He would dearly have loved to have created a single Grand Central Railway Terminus in Farringdon to serve all the railways coming into London. That he could not achieve but he found something else to satisfy his thrusting enterprise – a ring of underground railway stations linking all existing main line termini – the Inner Circle, of which the first stretch was that from Paddington to Farringdon.

Here, in this 3¾ mile track with its steam-driven locomotives, was the starting point of the Circle Line with its twenty-seven stations – and, indeed, the whole vast network of the Underground.

When Historian Keith Calder read this paper in October 1963 he observed that they had just started digging the Victoria line – a development calculated to warm the heart of Charles Pearson. And, of course, there have been many further additions in the years since then.

*   *   *

A Charity that never asks for money

The City of London has ever been engaged in the pursuit of good works but there is one charity that is particularly its own, hardly known outside the City and of a quite special kind.

Its name is Morden College (College in the old sense of the word, a place where people of similar interests are gathered together).

A Wren building set in twelve acres of parkland on the heights of Blackheath, close to Greenwich Park, its roots go back far into the past. It was founded in 1695 by John Morden, a wealthy 17th century merchant, who commissioned Sir Christopher Wren to build a home which would give peace and security to fellow merchants who had lost estates, businesses and homes through illness or misfortune, causing them in old age to be in needy circumstances – by no means an unusual occurrence in those days of mercantile adventure. (The College clearly has similarities to the London Charterhouse and even to the Royal Hospital at Chelsea).

At Blackheath there were, and still are, 42 apartments for resident members who must be widowers or bachelors and, primarily, whose working lives have been concerned with trade. The main building is designed as a quadrangle around which the members' apartments are situated. Each member has his own sitting room and bedroom. Domestic and nursing care are provided together with the main meals.

It was actually in the year 1700 that the first of the many residents who have since followed were admitted by the founder who, in the last eight years of his life, administered his College as Treasurer – the office held by former Lord Mayor Sir Cullum Welch, as Chairman of the College's Trustees, when he presented this paper to the GHA in March 1971.

It is quite a romantic story. John Morden was the son of a City Goldsmith but orphaned at an early age. Not much is known about his childhood or young adult life but in middle age he prospered as a merchant doing business with the Middle East. When three of his windjammers laden with valuable cargoes were lost at sea he faced financial ruin. He made a vow that if by divine providence his fortunes were restored he would build a home for others suffering from misfortune.

His ships, scattered by great storms, eventually all reached home, their cargoes intact and John Morden lost no time in fulfilling his vow.

He was a member of the Turkey Company and after he and his wife died it was the Turkey Company which continued to administer the College until 1826. In accordance with Sir John Morden's will, administration then devolved to trustees chosen from the Honourable the East India Company and, when that undertaking ceased to exist, trustees had to be chosen from the Court of Aldermen of the City of London. The Aldermen continue to fulfil that function today. They have continued the policy of investing in land and property and the wealth of the Morden College Trust has grown.

Since 1945, in addition to maintaining 42 elderly gentlemen, the College has been extended to include married quarters, flatlets for widows and daughters – the charity now accommodates 180 elderly people drawn, in addition to former merchants, from among doctors, barristers, solicitors and others who through illness, accident or misfortune in retirement are in needy circumstances.

This, then, is the story of a charity that never has to ask for money and has brought security and peace to so many over the past three hundred years.

* * *

The mystery of the missing Magna Cartas

It is, perhaps, late in the telling of this history of the Guildhall Historical Association to arrive at Magna Carta – but there it is, at last we come to this most famous of documents, but only to find that it scarcely exists.

When King John originally conceded the Magna Carta in June 1215 a copy would have been sent to the Sheriff of each English county, to high ecclesiastics and other great pillars of the State. Since FitzAilwin the newly created Mayor of London was at Runnymede and one of those appointed to enforce Magna Carta's provisions, the Sheriffs of London (or at least one of the two) would also have been sent a copy.

Yet no copy has survived in the City although, strangely enough, the London Charter granted by King John five weeks before Magna Carta has been safely secured in the City archives for close on 800 years.

Historian Douglas Hill, who presented his paper in June 1958, records the fact that of the many copies produced by the scribes after Runnymede only four have survived, one each in the Cathedrals of Salisbury and Lincoln and two, one of which is badly damaged, that were at the British Museum, now in the British Library.

There is no evidence that a single Magna Carta was "written up and sealed" when King John met the barons in 1215, as popular belief would have it. According to the British Library, once the terms of Magna Carta had been agreed, they were retrospectively written up into a "grant" by scribes working in the royal chancery. Many copies of this grant – which later became known as Magna Carta – were sent out to the bishops, sheriffs and other officials throughout the country.

Magna Carta was far from being a once-and-for-all declaration of legal principle – it was frequently updated by England's kings: for Henry III in 1216 and 1217, both times with some amendments; it was reissued again in 1225; it was "confirmed" three times by Henry III, three times by Edward I, fourteen times by Edward III, six times by

Henry IV and once each by Henry V and Henry VI. Of all these confirmations, copies of which would also have been issued to the sheriffs of every county and bishops of every see, very few have survived. Most are to be found in cathedral muniments. The City of London with two examples of a confirmation copy must be counted rich.

The earliest of the City copies is dated 12 October 1297. This would have been the "eighth issue" of Magna Carta; that of Edward I. There is no trace or record of the seven earlier editions that it almost certainly would have received. This 1297 "inspeximus" is in excellent condition complete with seal and the writ addressed to the Sheriffs of London.

The City's second inspeximus of Magna Carta is dated 28 March 1300, also in the reign of Edward I. The earls and bishops had not been satisfied with the reliability of the 1297 edition and pursued the King to Ghent where he was persuaded to inspect and confirm Magna Carta anew.

This second of the City's two confirmation copies of the Magna Carta had somehow strayed from the Guildhall archives around the 1830's finishing up at the Public Records office. It was returned into the Lord Mayor's hands on St. George's Day 1958 by Lord Evershed, Master of the Rolls (and responsible then for the Public Records) at the annual banquet of the Royal Society of St. George.

Lord Mayor Sir Denis Truscott said in his speech of thanks "There is nowhere quite like home".

*   *   *

The "Houndsditch Murders" and a miscarriage of justice that led to mass murder

In December 1910 three unarmed City of London policemen were shot by a gang of armed terrorists; two other officers were wounded. The policemen had disturbed the gang trying to rob a jewellery shop in Houndsditch.

This bloody carnage, declared Historian Bob Duffield in his paper of October 2010, had led a few days later to an even more notorious outrage, the Siege of Sidney Street. The criminals in Houndsditch and Sidney Street were all revolutionaries who had found refuge in London from repression in Russia, Latvia and other parts of eastern Europe.

At this time the East End was full of immigrants, mostly Jews fleeing the pogroms instituted by the Tsarish regime in Russia. In the thirty years leading to 1914 some 120,000 settled in the small area between Aldgate and Spitalfields.

Among this great wave of people seeking succour in London some were revolutionaries and anarchists having suffered imprisonment and torture; included in their number were highly politicised men whose objective was the overthrow of Tsarist Russia. There were also spies and agents working for the Russian secret police. It was they who had recruited four youths and a girl in a plot (happily aborted) to throw a bomb at the Lord Mayor's Show in November 1909.

The terrorist groups needed money for their revolutionary activities and it was this that led the Houndsditch gang under the leadership of George Gardstein – a man of many identities and with a long record of staging armed robberies across Europe – to attempt a break-in at a Houndsditch jewellers.

Their plan was to gain entry to the shop from an adjacent building. Their noise of hammering alerted a passing police officer who, with five others, took up positions around the buildings. When the police sought entry they were fired upon by Gardstein and another of the gunmen. Twenty-two rounds were fired at unarmed police officers that night.

The trial of three of the criminals (not Gardstein who had been accidentally shot by one of his confederates) took place at the Old Bailey in May 1911 before Mr. Justice Grantham but early in the proceedings the judge declared there was no case for a verdict of guilty of murder against those in the dock. Duffield wrote that this was a bungled prosecution.

As a result Jacob Peters who was later identified as the killer of the three police officers escaped the hangman's noose. He went on to become a leading Bolshevik revolutionary and one of the masterminds of the October Revolution. He was appointed by Lenin as head of the Cheka which in 1918 unleashed "mass Red Terror". Peters became known as "The Executioner" signing thousands of death warrants.

A commentator writing in the Daily Express in September 1918 said: The most awful figure of the Russian Red Terror, the man with the most murder in his soul, is a dapper little Lett named Peters who lived in England so long that he speaks Russian with an English accent". Justice of a sort did catch up with him, and he perished in 1938 in Stalin's Great Purge.

*   *   *

The Baronetcy – a new honour for Lord Mayors

It had long been a practice for the Lord Mayor of London to be honoured with the accolade of knighthood. Then, in 1611, James I introduced the new "dignitie" of Baronetcy – a knighthood that was, in addition, hereditary.

The development was described by Historian Robin Gillett in the paper he read in June 1992. He was the second Baronet and Lord Mayor of the family, inheriting the title from his father, Harold, who had also served as Lord Mayor.

Of King James's creation of the baronetcy, Sir Robin observed that while not strictly comparable with Lloyd George's sale of honours it did have "a strong fund-raising element, typical of the House of Stuart". The early baronets were "fined" on creation often after much pressure had been brought to bear. However, at the Restoration it became a true reward for service with no strings attached.

The first Baronet to become a Lord Mayor was Sir Robert Ducye in 1629. The first Lord Mayor to be created Baronet while in office was the admirable Sir Richard Gurney, awarded the accolade by Charles I in 1641. He was later confined in the Tower by a hostile Parliament. The first Lord Mayor to inherit a baronetcy (from his brother in 1701) was Sir Samuel Garrard.

Around the year 1900 it had become customary to give Lord Mayors a baronetcy at the end of their year of office, a practice that continued until the mayoralty of Sir Ralph Perring in 1962.

That year saw the end of Baronet Mayors. For the next thirty years the contribution made by Lord Mayors of London to the well-being of the City – and the country as a whole – was recognised by their award of the GBE, the Knight Grand Cross of the Most Excellent Order of the British Empire. It was given on the day the Sovereign approved the election of the new Lord Mayor so that he went into Office with a "K", clearly of advantage in the arduous year ahead of him.

That remained the practice until 1994 when Prime Minister John Major decided that in future all automatic honours would cease. So from that date honours for Lord Mayors are dealt with in the same way as all others.

Returning to the baronetcy it is pleasing that Sir David Howard (now the Senior Alderman) was the third member of his family (father and grandfather before him) to be a Lord Mayor and Baronet.

* * *

The drinking habits at Greek and Roman banquets

So, what better way to end this (mostly) serious and learned history of the Guildhall Historical Association than with something which, while still on the learned side, has nothing whatsoever to do with the City of London and touches on the merely frivolous and effete?

In 1960 we'd heard an Alderman giving praise to eating and drinking habits at City banquets. Historian John Rutherford, wine-merchant in his day job, was probably present that day and maybe was then inspired to tell us five years later, November 1965, how Greeks and Romans approached this so important part of their lives.

Rutherford reminds us that the Greeks have been reproached for their love of wine and their "parties of pleasure" stigmatised as drinking competitions. And yet, he writes, they were studious to preserve a degree of decorum at their feasts, seldom giving into such gross debauches as disgraced the Romans under the emperors. When they drank freely their wine was much diluted. In one respect there was a major difference between the customs of the two nations: the Romans allowed their women to mix in their festive gatherings but forbade them wine; the Greeks allowed them to drink wine but they were excluded from all entertainments other than family occasions.

In Homer's day the fare at banquets was solid and plain, roast beef the norm. But with the passage of time the entertainments of the Greeks became noted for the multiplicity of dishes and the refinement in their preparation, together with greater choice in the wines to accompany them.

Rutherford thinks it likely that the horns of animals served as the first drinking vessels. For the most wealthy there were cups of silver and gold. It was from the banks of the Nile that the Romans were supplied with their wine-glasses, the Egyptians long celebrated for their glass-making skills.

At the banquets of Greece's heroic times larger cups and purer wine were presented to the principal guests and it was a mark of respect to keep their cups always replenished. Wealthy Athenians had their butlers whose business it was to see that all the guests were properly supplied. For the dinner the wine was served diluted. At its conclusion pure wine was handed round but before it was drunk a portion was poured on the ground as an oblation to Jupiter and all the gods. The wine would be of the sweet red kind, rich and strong. The Italian appellation of vino santo, given to their most luscious growths, continues the tradition.

The custom of making offerings to the gods was further elaborated at Grecian festivals: the first cup of pure wine sacred to Bacchus, the second to Jupiter, the third, diluted, was designated the cup of Health (when the company washed their hands), the fourth was the cup of Mercury as patron of the night and dispenser of sleep and pleasant dreams. The Roman gods were similarly honoured.

During the course of the dinner guests were given chaplets of leaves or flowers to place on their foreheads. Perfumes were offered to those who chose to anoint their face and hands. Such adornments, borrowed from the Asiatic nations became, in time, an essential accompaniment of the feast. Myrrh in particular was said to counteract the noxious effects of wine and to have both a cooling and exhilarating influence on the mind. To appear in a disordered chaplet was taken as a sign of inebriety.

Drinking to the health of distinguished guests and absent friends was another common practice which has come down to us in modern times but we appear to have drawn the line at toasting the mistresses of guests. It would seem that the regard of the proposer for his chosen guest could only be shown by the number of cups. A favourite system was to drink as many cups as there were letters in the name of the man toasted. Caesar was celebrated with six glasses; Germanicus with ten. (It is reminiscent of those stories about English visitors to the Soviet Kremlin who had themselves to respond to Russian toasts with innumerable shots of vodka).

The best of the Greek wines – usually drunk with the dessert - were from Thace and Lesbos; those of the Romans, the Cecuban, Albanian and Falernian. The loving cup may have had its origin when, in the middle of a banquet a female attendant would go round the table with a rich silver vessel from which each guest would drink in turn.

My own unbounded admiration is reserved for the practice introduced by both Greeks and Romans of reclining on couches during their meals, the couches of great magnificence with frames of ivory and tortoiseshell or precious metals, the coverings of purple cloth enriched with embroidery. What luxury and, indigestion somehow controlled, one could nod off during the speeches. But I expect that beforehand, a battle or two with warring neighbours would have helped to build up one's constitution to cope with such delights!

*   *   *